First World War
and Army of Occupation
War Diary
France, Belgium and Germany

15 DIVISION
Headquarters, Branches and Services
General Staff
1 September 1915 - 30 September 1915

WO95/1911/5

The Naval & Military Press Ltd
www.nmarchive.com
Published in association with The National Archives

Published by

The Naval & Military Press Ltd

Unit 10 Ridgewood Industrial Park,

Uckfield, East Sussex,

TN22 5QE England

Tel: +44 (0) 1825 749494

www.naval-military-press.com

www.nmarchive.com

This diary has been reprinted in facsimile from the original. Any imperfections are inevitably reproduced and the quality may fall short of modern type and cartographic standards.

Contents

Document type	Place/Title	Date From	Date To
Heading	WO95/1910-4 15 Div HQ Gen Staff & Depts Sep 1915 to apps		
Heading	War Diary General Staff 15th Division September 1915		
Heading	Report On The Operations From September 21st to September 30th, Inclusive.		
Miscellaneous	4th Corps Report On The Operation From September 21st to September 30th, Inclusive.	05/10/1915	05/10/1915
Miscellaneous	Casualties Sufferred by The 15th Division for The Period 25th, 26th & 27th September.		
Heading	War Diary. IA		
War Diary	Vaudricourt	08/09/1915	12/09/1915
War Diary	Drouvin	01/09/1915	02/09/1915
War Diary	Vaudricourt (E.28.d.0.6)	03/09/1915	07/09/1915
War Diary	Vaudricourt	13/09/1915	23/09/1915
War Diary	Mazingarbe	24/09/1915	27/09/1915
War Diary	Drouvin	28/09/1915	28/09/1915
War Diary	Labuissiere	29/09/1915	30/09/1915
Heading	Appendices 1 to XVI		
Operation(al) Order(s)	15th Division Operation Order No. 7.	04/09/1915	04/09/1915
Miscellaneous	A Form. Messages And Signals.		
Miscellaneous	IVth Corps H.R.S. No. 510 App II 15th Division	05/09/1915	05/09/1915
Miscellaneous	IVth Corps No. H.R.S. 506/1 Appendix III	07/09/1915	07/09/1915
Miscellaneous	15th Division G. 715. Appendix IV	07/09/1915	07/09/1915
Operation(al) Order(s)	15th Division Preliminary Operation Order No. 8.	07/09/1915	07/09/1915
Miscellaneous			
Miscellaneous	A Form. Messages And Signals.		
Map			
Miscellaneous	15th Division Preliminary Operation Order No. 8.	07/09/1915	07/09/1915
Miscellaneous	A Form. Messages And Signals.		
Map	46th Bde. 91st Fd. Coy. R.E. 1 Coy 9th Gordons. Map 3		
Diagram etc	Sketch of Country Between Vermelles & Grenay.		
Miscellaneous	Billets, 15th Division, 8th Sept. 1915 App V		
Miscellaneous	Transport & Wagon Lines, 15th Division, Sept. 8th.		
Miscellaneous	15th Division 41/G. Appendix VII	11/09/1915	11/09/1915
Miscellaneous	15th Division No 12. Fourth Corps. Reference Your H.R. I/S 12 App VIII	10/09/1915	10/09/1915
Miscellaneous	15th Division Reference IV Corps N	12/09/1915	12/09/1915
Miscellaneous	15th Division 41/7/G. App. VIII	11/09/1915	11/09/1915
Miscellaneous	Prisoners of War.	08/09/1916	08/09/1916
Miscellaneous	15th Division 41/7/G	12/09/1915	12/09/1915
Miscellaneous	15th Division G/806 App IX	13/09/1915	13/09/1915
Miscellaneous	15th Division G/832 App X	14/09/1915	14/09/1915
Miscellaneous	15th Division G/831. 1st Group H.A.R.	14/09/1915	14/09/1915
Miscellaneous	15th Division	13/09/1915	13/09/1915
Miscellaneous	Brigade Commanders, H.A.R. Instructions	13/09/1915	13/09/1915
Miscellaneous	Administrative Instructions. App XI	14/09/1915	14/09/1915
Miscellaneous	Administrative Instructions.	14/09/1915	14/09/1915
Miscellaneous	With Reference to Administrative Instructions	17/09/1915	17/09/1915
Operation(al) Order(s)	15th Division Operation Order No. 9. App. XII	17/09/1915	17/09/1915

Miscellaneous			
Miscellaneous	15th Division G/915. App 2		
Map	Sketch Appendix. I.H.R.S. 512 15th Div. O.O. No. 9 Dt. 17-9-15		
Map	Sketch of Country Between Vermelles & Grenay. App.II.		
Miscellaneous	A Form. Messages And Signals.		
Miscellaneous	15th Div. No. G 952. Dt. 20-9-15		
Miscellaneous	A Form. Messages And Signals.		
Miscellaneous	Messages And Signals.		
Miscellaneous	A Form. Messages And Signals.		
Miscellaneous	Medical Arrangement On Day of Assault. App. (iii).		
Miscellaneous	A Form Messages And Signals.		
Miscellaneous	15th Division G/908.	19/09/1915	19/09/1915
Miscellaneous	IVth Corps No. H.R.S. 517	18/09/1915	18/09/1915
Operation(al) Order(s)	15th Division Operation Order No. 10.	21/09/1915	21/09/1915
Operation(al) Order(s)	15th Division Operation Order No. 11.	27/09/1915	27/09/1915
Miscellaneous			
Miscellaneous	Special Divisional Order. App XVI 15th Division G/167	27/09/1915	27/09/1915
Miscellaneous	15th Division.	27/09/1915	27/09/1915
Miscellaneous	15th Division G/989.	22/09/1915	22/09/1915
Miscellaneous	Special Order Of The Day. A	27/09/1915	27/09/1915
Miscellaneous	G. 755.		
Miscellaneous	A Form. Messages And Signals.		
Miscellaneous	15th Division C. 977. 187 Coy. R.E.	21/09/1915	21/09/1915
Miscellaneous	Bays.		
Miscellaneous			
Heading	General Instructions & Papers Re Attack On 21st September.		
Miscellaneous	IVth Corps No. H.R.S. 506/3 App 321 15th Division.	02/09/1915	02/09/1915
Miscellaneous	IVth Corps No. H.R.S. 506/5 App 32 15th Division.	03/09/1915	03/09/1915
Miscellaneous	IVth Corps No. H.R.S. 506/11 15th Division.	03/09/1915	03/09/1915
Miscellaneous	IVth Corps No. H.R.S. 508/7 15th Division.	03/09/1915	03/09/1915
Miscellaneous	H.R.S. 506/4 15th Division. App 327	03/09/1915	03/09/1915
Miscellaneous	IVth Corps No. H.R.S. 399 (a). 15th Division.	04/09/1915	04/09/1915
Miscellaneous	46.1.B.	06/09/1915	06/09/1915
Miscellaneous	46th Infantry Brigade Detail of Working parties For Special Duty First Night		
Miscellaneous	46th Infantry Brigade Detail of Working Parties For Special Duty Second Night.		
Miscellaneous	46th Infantry Brigade Detail of Working Parties For Special Duty Second Night. (para 2)		
Miscellaneous	46 Infantry Brigade Detail of Working Parties For Special Duty Third Night.		
Miscellaneous	IVth Corps. No. H.R.S. 510/1 15th Division.	08/09/1915	08/09/1915
Miscellaneous	IVth Corps No. H.R.S. 508/4 App	09/09/1915	09/09/1915
Miscellaneous	1st Army No. 206 (IM) 4th Corps.	05/09/1915	05/09/1915
Miscellaneous	IVth Corps No. H.R.S. 507 General Principles For The Attack	09/09/1915	09/09/1915
Miscellaneous	15th Division.	11/09/1915	11/09/1915
Miscellaneous	IVth Corps No. H.R.S. 508/2 15th Division.	13/09/1915	13/09/1915
Miscellaneous	IVth Corps No. H.R.S. 511/3 15th Division.	15/09/1915	16/09/1915
Miscellaneous	1st Division 509 (G) IVth Corps.	10/09/1915	10/09/1915
Miscellaneous	H.R.S. 519. 1st Division.	16/09/1915	16/09/1915
Miscellaneous	IVth Corps H.R.S. No. 518/2. 15th Division.	15/09/1915	16/09/1915

Miscellaneous	A Form Messages And Signals.		
Miscellaneous	15th Division G/916. Secret Memorandum	19/09/1915	19/09/1915
Miscellaneous	IVth Corps No. H.R.S. 524 15th Division.	18/09/1915	18/09/1915
Miscellaneous	Result of experiments carried out in the Vermelles sector of line, hold by Dismounted Division.	29/01/1916	29/01/1916
Miscellaneous	Emergency Circuits Dismounted Division	29/01/1916	29/01/1916
Heading	Draft Instructions For Attack On 21st September.		
Miscellaneous	G. 600 G.O.C. 44th I. Bde. Headquarters. 12th September, 1915 No. S. 25 44th Infantry Brigade.	30/08/1915	30/08/1915
Miscellaneous	Draft Instructions For Attack.	30/08/1915	30/08/1915
Heading	Notes Re Conferences.		
Miscellaneous	IVth Corps. H.R.S. 398 1st Army. G.S. 164/2 (a) Memorandum.	02/09/1915	02/09/1915
Miscellaneous	H.R.S. 525/1 15th Division.	21/09/1915	21/09/1915
Heading	Artillery Instructions. 6		
Miscellaneous	IVth Corps No. H.R. 506/2 15th Division. App 322	02/09/1915	02/09/1915
Miscellaneous	IVth Corps No. H.R.S. 15th Division.	10/09/1915	10/09/1915
Miscellaneous	IVth Corps No. H.R.S. 509 Head-qrs	10/09/1915	10/09/1915
Miscellaneous	15th Division S/38	15/09/1915	15/09/1915
Miscellaneous	Instruction re-preliminary Bombardment.		
Miscellaneous	Table A		
Miscellaneous	Enfilade and Oblique Fire. App 4		
Miscellaneous	Battery Commanders in The Trenches		
Miscellaneous	Officers With Infantry App 8		
Miscellaneous	IVth Corps No. H.R.S. 517 C.A. 64 Headquarters, IVth Corps.	17/09/1915	17/09/1915
Diagram etc	Identification Trace For Use With Artillery Maps.		
Miscellaneous	15th Division G. 976. Fourth Corps.	21/09/1916	21/09/1916
Miscellaneous	A Form Messages And Signals.		
Heading	Letters And Instructions Re Gas.		
Miscellaneous	IVth Corps No. H.R.S. 506 App 308 15th Division.	31/08/1915	31/08/1915
Miscellaneous	Plan A Not Drawn to Scale. Partition-25 Yards.		
Miscellaneous	Notes to Explain Plan "A"		
Miscellaneous	Dimensions of Cylinders.		
Miscellaneous	A Form. Messages And Signals.		
Miscellaneous	15th Division. App 311	01/09/1915	01/09/1915
Miscellaneous	IVth Corps No. H.R.S. 506/9 15th Division.	03/09/1915	03/09/1915
Miscellaneous	Plan "A"		
Miscellaneous	Notes to explain Plan "A"		
Miscellaneous	IVth Corps No. H.R.S. 508/2 15th Division	07/09/1915	07/09/1915
Miscellaneous	Plan "A"	07/09/1915	07/09/1915
Miscellaneous	IVth Corps No. H.R.S. Notes to Explain "Plan "A".		
Miscellaneous	IVth Corps No. H.R.S. 508 15th Division	13/09/1915	13/09/1915
Miscellaneous	A Secret.-(Not to be carried forward in the Assault). Time Table Of Gas. Attacks South Of The LA Bassee Canal.		
Miscellaneous	IVth Corps No. H.R.S. 518 15th Division.	16/09/1915	16/09/1915
Miscellaneous	A Form Messages And Signals.		
Miscellaneous	1st Army No. Q. 432 (G). IVth Corps No. H.R.S. 518. IVth Corps.	18/09/1915	18/09/1915
Miscellaneous	IVth Corps No. H.R.S. 518/1 15th Division.	18/09/1915	18/09/1915
Miscellaneous	46th Infantry Brigade. Instructions for candlemen.	19/09/1915	19/09/1915
Miscellaneous	IVth Corps. No. H.R.S. 528 15th Division.	22/09/1915	23/09/1915
Miscellaneous			
Miscellaneous	First Army No. G.S. 177/5 (a) Notes In Connection With The Employment Of Gas In The Attack	22/09/1915	22/09/1915

Miscellaneous	Instructions Re Stores.		
Miscellaneous			
Miscellaneous	Extracts from Summary Carrying of Stores on nights A.B. & C. Sept 1915		
Miscellaneous	Issued for instructional purposes only. Carrying of stores on Nights A.B. and C. September 1915.		
Miscellaneous	Carrying of Stores on Nights A.B. &. C. September 1915.	14/09/1915	14/09/1915
Miscellaneous			
Heading	Fighting Strengths.		
Miscellaneous	Fighting Strength Return of The 15th Division at Midnight, Friday, 3rd September, 1915	04/09/1915	04/09/1915
Miscellaneous	Fighting Strength Return At the 15th Division At Midnight, Friday, 10 September 1915.	11/09/1915	11/09/1915
Miscellaneous	Fighting Strength Return Of The 15th Division At Midnight, Friday, 17 September, 1915.	18/09/1915	18/09/1915
Miscellaneous	Fighting Strength Return Of The 15th Division At Midnight, Friday, 24th September, 1915.	24/09/1915	24/09/1915
Miscellaneous	Fighting Strength Of 15th Division On 30th September, 1915.	30/12/1915	30/12/1915
Miscellaneous	7th Bn K.O. Sco. Bord. Table. 1.		
Miscellaneous	8th Bn. K.O. Sco. Bord. Table 1		
Miscellaneous	10th Bn Sco. Rif. Table 1		
Miscellaneous	12th Bn High. L.I. Table 1.		
Miscellaneous	Casualties.		
Miscellaneous	15th Division 3/A. A.A.G. 1st Army. Fourth Corps.	01/10/1915	01/10/1915
Miscellaneous			
Miscellaneous	Messages And Signals.		
Miscellaneous			
Miscellaneous	Messages And Signals.		
Heading	Instructions For Attack On 26th September.		
Miscellaneous	IVth Corps No. H.R.S 525 15th Division	21/09/1915	21/09/1915
Miscellaneous	IVth Corps No. H.R.S. 518 15th Division.	21/09/1915	21/09/1915
Miscellaneous	Demonstrate on 44th Bde Front. Five open by 46th Bde		
Miscellaneous	IVth Corps. No. H.R.S. 530/1	24/09/1915	24/09/1915
Miscellaneous	IVth Corps. No. H.R.S. 530	25/09/1915	25/09/1915
Miscellaneous	IVth Corps. No. H.R.S. 530/2	25/09/1915	25/09/1915
Miscellaneous	IVth Corps. No. H.R.S. 530/1	26/09/1915	26/09/1915
Miscellaneous	C Form (Duplicate). Messages And Signals.		
Heading	Maps And Tracings.		
Map	To cutting made under the Railway		
Map			
Diagram etc	Sketch Of Country Between Vermelles & Grenay. App II.		
Miscellaneous	Sketch of Country Between Vermelles And Grenay Showing Preparatory Arrangements.		
Map			
Miscellaneous	XV Division	21/09/1915	21/09/1915
Map	Dispositions 46th I.B. Night 24/25		
Miscellaneous			
Miscellaneous	A Form Messages And Signals.		
Map			
Miscellaneous			
Map	Sketch of Country between Vermelles of Grenay		
Map	Auchy Lens 1st Edition June 11th 1915		
Map			

Map	Identification Trace For Use With Artillery Maps.
Map	France Provisional Edition
Miscellaneous	
Map	France Provisional Edition
Miscellaneous	
Miscellaneous	27th Division

WO95/1910 - 4

15 Div HQ Gen Staff & Depts

Sep 1915 + Apps

WAR
DIARY

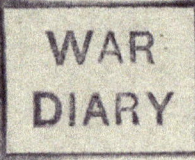

G E N E R A L   S T A F F

1 5 t h   D I V I S I O N

S E P T E M B E R

1 9 1 5

Attached:

1. Report on Operations 21st/30th September.
1A. War Diary.
1B. Appendices I to XVI.
2. G. Papers.
3. General Instructions re attack 21.9.15.
4. Draft Instructions re attack 21.9.15.
5. Notes re Conferences.
6. Artillery Instructions.
7. Gas.
8. Stores.
9. Fighting Strengths.
10. Casualties.
11. Instructions re attack 26.9.15.
12. Maps.

1

REPORT ON THE OPERATIONS FROM SEPTEMBER 21st to SEPTEMBER 30th, INCLUSIVE.

(Note: Appendices 2, 3, 4, 5, 6, 7, 8, 9, 10 & 11 referred to in the attached Report will be found in the War Diaries of the respective Brigades and Units)

4th Corps   15th Div / G.275/1

REPORT ON THE OPERATIONS FROM SEPTEMBER 21st to SEPTEMBER 30th, INCLUSIVE.

1. Copies of Operation Orders (the last of which were issued on September 21st) were sent to the Fourth Corps at the time of issue. None of these are therefore attached to this report.

2. Preparations for the attack were completed by the night of September 20th; these included:-

(a) The digging of about 8 miles of new communicating and reserve trenches, the latter provided at intervals with spinter proof cover.

(b) The construction of deep dugouts for Advanced Divisional, Divisional Artillery, 3 Brigades and Divisional R.E. Headquarters.

(c) The provision and stocking of 7 grenade stores, 4 S.A.A. Stores and 2 R.E. stores in the forward trenches, and of a central R.E. store and S.A.A. Depot in QUALITY STREET.

(d) The placing of 10 water tanks and a large number of barrels and petrol tins in the support trenches, and the improvisation of a large regular water supply at FOSSE 7.

(e) Construction of 28 bridges for the passage of guns and transport through the system of trenches.

(f) The multiplication and safe laying of telephone wires and the provision of visual signal stations.

(g) The construction of Advanced and Divisional dressing and collecting stations at FOSSE 7, QUALITY STREET, LE PHILOSOPHE and MAZINGARBE; and of regimental aid posts and a central evacuation trench.

(h) The laying of a tramway from MAZINGARBE to LE PHILOSOPHE, FOSSE 7 and QUALITY STREET for the conveyance of stores and the evacuation of wounded; and the construction of trucks.

2

(i) The construction of recesses in the front parapet for the gas cylinders, and the conveyance of 996 cylinders into the trenches.

(j) The laying out of a special Divisional Road from VAUDRICOURT to MAZINGARBE for passage of troops.

(k) The exact mapping and labelling of all trenches in the area.

(l) The construction of three Russian Saps towards the enemy's front line.

(m) The placing of one day's iron ration for the Division in the CORONS DE FOSSE 7.

The above work, together with other minor preparations, was carried out with unremitting energy by the Divisional R.E. working with the 9th Gordon Highlanders (Pioneers). The labour demanded from the Infantry was great, and was cheerfully and effectively given.

3. The bombardment commenced on September 21st and continued up to the hour of assault on September 25th; during this period the front trenches were lightly held.

The enemy's reply was weak, increasing slightly on the third and fourth days.

The wire on the enemy's front and support trenches was difficult to observe, but was examined nightly by patrols and proved to be well cut. A demonstration by the Divisional Artillery at 4 p.m. on September 23rd drew weak hostile rifle and machine gun fire.

Our own wire on the front of our assault was cut in diagonal strips on the night of September 23rd/24th.

The preliminary moves of the Division were completed by the evening of September 23rd; and at 4 p.m. on the 24th Advanced Divisional Headquarters moved to MAZINGARBE (next door to Divisional Artillery Headquarters), the 2nd échelon moving to NOEUX-les-MINES.

At 8:5 p.m. on the 24th the message to "carry on" was received from Advanced Fourth Corps and Brigades began moving into their forming up places.

At 11 p.m. information was reeeived that Fourth Corps Operation order No 35 for the attack held good.

4. The troops of the Division were in their forming up places by 2 a.m. on the 25th. The whole of the Infantry and R.E. of the Division were thus formed up underground on a front of 2000 yards and a depth of 3000 yards.

At 3:35 a.m. instructions were received that the hour of ZERO = 5:50 a.m., and all concerned were informed.

5. At 5:50 a.m. the discharge of gas and smoke commenced; the morning was dull, with slight rain; the wind light and varying from S.S.W. to W. The weather conditions were thus not very favourable for an attack by gas.

At 6:30 a.m. precisely the ~~attack~~ assault was launched.

6. The casualties from shrapnel and machine gun fire were heavy on leaving our front trenches, but the assault was not checked. The effect of the gas on the enemy's front line was disappointing; the smoke candles provided an effective curtain for covering the assault.

At 6:50 a.m. our Infantry were reported to be through the enemy's support trench; and ten minutes later the third lines of the assaulting columns were reported as crossing the German front trench. The reserve (45th) Bde had begun to move forward without difficulty. The smoke was still very thick, making observation difficult.

By 7:40 a.m. the whole of the assaulting columns of both leading Brigades had left our trenches, and the Brigade reserves were in our front line preparing to follow. The leading troops of the 44th Brigade had reported at 7:5 a.m. that they were approaching LOOS.

The 180th (Tunnelling) Company R.E., less two sections already forward, was now ordered up to LE SAULCHOY FME from VERQUIN.

7. At 9 a.m. the probability of our left being attracted against PUITS 14 Bis owing to the delay of the 1st Division became apparent; a message was therefore sent to Advanced Fourth Corps suggesting that the H.A.R. should bombard the strong points in H.25 and H.31 previously indicated to them. This was done.

At 9:25 a.m. a report was received from 73rd Brigade R.F.A. that they had seen our Infantry advancing through G.36.b and G.30.d at 9:10 a.m.

8. At 9:30 a.m. orders were issued through the C.R.E. to prepare crossing places for the cavalry and artillery over our own and the German front line trenches. This task was allotted to the 74th Field Company assisted by the 180th Company. A portion of the later Company had already been placed at the disposal of the Divisional Bombing Officer for the transport of grenades to the assaulting Brigades.

At the same time the C.R.A. was instructed to move up two batteries to positions of readiness at FOSSE 7.

Our Infantry were now reported to be in PUITS 14 Bis and advancing up HILL 70.

9. At 9:50 a.m. the greater part of the leading Brigades were through or past LOOS; and the 45th (reserve) Brigade was in our front line trenches, less one Battalion which had moved on in support of the 44th Brigade.

As the advance had gone so fast, the C.R.A. was now instructed to arrange to group the 70th Bde R.F.A. with the 44th Infantry Brigade and the 71st Bde R.F.A. with the 46th Infantry Brigade, and Brigades were so informed.

This grouping was canclled again in the evening.

10. At 10:20 a.m. the First Division reported that their 2nd Brigade was hung up in front of the German front trench by the wire, and asked that a Battalion from the 45th Bde be detached to work northwards to assist. The great extent

of ground now covered by our own troops did not admit of ~~a~~ the detachment of a Battalion for this purpose. The grenadiers of the 6th Camerons were, however, ordered to bomb northwards and rendered great assistance in relieving the situation.

The 46th Infantry Brigade reported HILL 70 taken at 10:10 a.m. and estimated the casualties of the Brigade at 10 per cent.

11. The 45th Infantry Brigade were now ordered to push forward their leading Battalions on the right and left into the German front line trenches; but no further.

As a matter of fact the right Battalion had already gone forward unknown to the Brigadier.

At the same time the 11th M.M.G. Battery was ordered to QUALITY STREET to come under the G.O.C. 44th Infantry Brigade and to be pushed forward to LOOS at his discretion.

Later on orders were sent for this Battery to report to 46th Infantry Brigade. The Battery commander was unable to do this, but went right forward on his own initiative, and rendered valuable service in assisting to hold the line on HILL 70.

12. At 11 a.m. G.O.C. 46th Infantry Brigade reported his left in PUITS 14 Bis and his right pushing on to CITÉ ST AUGUSTE; he reported his left quite exposed and his No 5 Column (half Battalion 12th H.L.I., which connected with the 2nd Brigade) checked in the German front trenches and suffering heavily.

A Battalion of the 45th Infantry Brigade (6th Camerons) were immediately ordered forward to his support, directed with their right on PUITS 14 Bis.

At 11:15 a.m. the C.R.A. was instructed to arrange with the H.A.R. to lift their barrages previously arranged to N.1.d, N.2.c, N.2.d, and 1000 yards E of the German trenches on the west of ST AUGUSTE, and H.26.d.3.6. to North and East.

General Mc Cracken explained the situation by telephone to the Corps Commander, and earnestly pressed for the forward movement of the Army reserves.

At 11:30 a.m. the Divisional Squadron was moved up to join the Cyclist Company at MAZINGARBE, and the Fourth Corps were informed that only two Battalions now remained in hand as Divisional reserve.

13. At noon there were no signs of the approach of other troops to reinforce the Division. The 44th and 46th Infantry Brigades were reported to be holding HILL 70, but unable to progress against CITE ST AUGUSTE; the losses amongst the troops who had pushed on over the HILL were heavy; and the left flank was exposed owing to the failure of the First Division to advance. The 45th Infantry Brigade (less the Battalions already detached) was therefore ordered to push on to LOOS and hold it, and release the troops of the 44th and 46th Infantry Brigades to go forward. The H.A.R. were requested to bombard for a complete period of half an hour the trenches and CITE of ST: AUGUSTE; and at 12-40 p.m. the two Companies 9th Gordons (Pioneers) in reserve were ordered up to LOOS to put it in a state of defence.

14. At 1-40 p.m. the G.O.C. 21st Division and G.O.C. 62nd Brigade arrived at Divisional Headquarters. The former did not remain to discuss the situation but wrote some message and immediately left again. At 2 p.m. a message was received from Advanced Fourth Corps ordering 21st Division to advance on LOOS via FOSSE 7 and to place the leading Brigade at the disposal of 15th Division.

Hooker 11 Walker

Soon after 2 p.m. G.O.C. 62nd Brigade returned and the situation was explained to him by General Mc Cracken. Verbal orders were given him to move his Brigade by QUALITY STREET to LOOS; to get into touch with G.Os C 44th and 45th Infantry Brigades; if HILL 70 was lost to retake it; if held, to relieve our troops on it; if situation favoured a further advance on CITE ST AUGUSTE, to act accordingly in cooperation with 44th and 45th Infantry Brigades. He then left. These orders were then confirmed in writing, and sent after him. He was also provided with some trench maps, which he did not appear to possess. He said nothing about the state of his Brigade.

The subsequent movements of this Brigade are difficult to follow. The leading Battalion was reported as reaching QUALITY STREET at 3:30 p.m. but it seems probable that at least one other Battalion went more to the South and arrived at LOOS Cemetery. The Brigadier on his return on the 27th reported that he never got touch with his Battalions, though he himself met the G.Os C 44th, 45th and 46th Infantry Brigades. Traces of the doings of his Battalions are recorded in the reports of the Brigadiers of this Division, which are attached.

Brigade Major 62nd Brigade appeared at Divisional Headquarters at about 7:30 p.m.; received an account of the situation as far as it was known, and the orders given below in para 16, was provided with maps, and went off again to find his Brigadier.

15. At 2:30 p.m. 44th Infantry Brigade reported mixed bodies of our troops entrenching on the reverse slope of HILL 70 from H.31.b.6.6. to H.31.a.7.2., and at 3:15 p.m. 44th Infantry Brigade Headquarters moved forward to LOOS.

At 4 p.m. First Division reported the capture of the Germans who were holding up the 2nd Brigade; at 4:40 p.m. the 2nd Brigade was reported ~~as~~ moving forward, and the anxiety as to our left flank was lessened.

16. At 6 p.m. orders were issued to Brigades to consolidate their positions from HILL 70 to PUITS 14 Bis connecting up with 47th Division on the right and 2nd Brigade on the left; 45th Infantry Brigade to relieve 44th Infantry Brigade on slopes of HILL 70, the latter to withdraw behind LOOS into Divisional reserve; 62nd Brigade to place one Battalion at

disposal of 46th Infantry Brigade and to hold remainder in support of ~~44th~~ 45th and 46th Infantry Brigades about PUITS No 15. These orders were duly acknowledged by all Brigades, but apparently the 62nd Brigade were unable to ~~reply~~ comply.

17. The situation at the close of the 25th was a follows:- the crest of HILL 70 and the work on top of it were in German hands. A mixture of the troops of the 44th, 45th and 46th Infantry Brigades were digging themselves in below the crest; the line extended to PUITS 14 Bis, which was still held by us. Major Wace, G.S. went down to LOOS in the afternoon and ~~their~~ there met all Brigadiers in the course of the evening. He was able to explain the situation and materially assist them. During the night the 44th Infantry Brigade were withdrawn to our own trenches.

The general tendancy of the advance had been to the South East towards the CITE ST LAURENT, rather than due E. This can only be accounted for by the attraction of the natural features, and by the heavy fire which came from the neighbourhood of the DYNAMITIERE. In many of the reports sent in the CITE ST AUGUSTE was mentioned in mistake for the CITE ST LAURENT. This tendancy to drift South East was very marked all through the operations.

18. At 9:7 p.m. orders were received from Advanced Fourth Corps that the Division was to be prepared to resume the offensive on the 26th and the 2nd Brigade was placed under our orders. This latter provision was revoked two hours later, and the 2nd Brigade ordered to rejoin its own Division West of BOIS CARRÉE.

X General Mc Cracken explained to the Corps Commander on the telephone the state of the Division and his doubts as to its fitness to resume the offensive.

19. At 11:30 p.m. a telephone message was received from Advanced Fourth Corps that the Division assisted by the 62nd

Brigade would attack HILL 70 at 9 a.m. on the 26th after one hours intense bombardment.

At 1:45 a.m. on the 26th an order was received confirming this message, and orders were issued for the attack to be carried out by the 45th and 62nd Brigades.

20. At 12:30 a.m. the enemy delivered a counter attack on the right Battalion of the 45th Infantry Brigade which was repulsed by machine gun fire.

At about 5:30 a.m. the enemy delivered another and heavy counter attack from the Southeast which was repulsed.

At 8 a.m. the bombardment of HILL 70 commenced and was very accurate. At 9.a.m. the assault was delivered and came under heavy machine gun fire from the S.E. corner of the DOUBLE CRASSIER, and under the fire of our own artillery.

The assault failed; was renewed, and failed again. The 62nd Brigade in support, it iss stated, did not come on. Had they done so, the G.O.C. 45th Infantry Brigade considers that the attack would have suceeded, as the enemy were reported to be evacuating the REDOUBT.

A request was sent at 8:35 a.m. to 47th Division to be ready to assist with one Battalion. A Battalion was told off by the 47th Division for this purpose, but the 141st Brigade failing to get into touch with the 45th Infantry Brigade, this assistance was not forthcoming.

21. At about 10 a.m. the situation began to be critical. The retirement of other troops effected the men of the Division, who being mostly without officers, began to retire. The G.O.C. 46th Infantry Brigade, some of whose men were on the HILL greatly distinguished himself by rallying men and taking them back, and in this work he was ably assisted by Capt SAYER, R.E. and other officers. The men of the 15th Division responded at once, and the original line was retained; the men of the 62nd Brigade could not be rallied.

22. The situation remained much the same till noon, when an attack delivered by another Brigade on our left (presumably of 21st Division) against the CITE ST AUGUSTE broke in disorder under shell fire and retired from the field. This increased the difficulty of holding the line on HILL 70, which began to break; and apparently it was about this time that PUITS 14 Bis was lost. The men, however, responded to every effort to reform them and with the assistance of some 100 volunteers of his own and the 45th Brigade sent forward by G.O.C. 46th Infantry Brigade, the line was reinforced about 5 p.m. and maintained.

23. At 2:35 p.m., the 6th Cavalry Brigade (less one Regt) was placed at the disposal of the Division and pushed forward into LOOS to hold it at all costs with the remaining troops of the Division still there. The remainder of the 46th and 44th Infantry Brigades with the Divisional Squadron and a platoon of cyclists were ordered to hold the old line of German front trenches between the LENS ROAD REDOUBT and the LOOS ROAD REDOUBT, both inclusive.

At 3:30 p.m. the G.O.C. 6th Cavalry Brigade arrived a in LOOS and was placed in command of the troops there. The wireless set and pigeons were handed over to him and 45th Infantry Brigade Headquarters withdrew to QUALITY STREET. All available officers were sent to LE PHILOSOPHE to collect stragglers, and take them forward to our old front trenches. Several hundreds of men of the 21st Division were collected in this way.

At 6:30 p.m. owing to reports received chiefly from the 46th Infantry Brigade, that our troops were still holding on to the line on HILL 70, orders were sent to G.O.C. 6th Cavalry Brigade to get into touch with them and reinforce them. Arrangements were made at the same time for the establishment of a barrage of artillery fire to cover them. This barrage was very effective.

24. At 10:30 p.m. orders were received from Advanced Fourth Corps for the 62nd Brigade to rejoin its Division. The remnants of it were therefore collected and sent away.

At 12:25 a.m. on the 27th orders were issued, in accordance with instructions from advanced Fourth Corps, for the withdrawal of the Division (less Artillery) to MAZINGARBE. This was carried out without incident.

At 3:45 p.m. orders were issued for the move of the Division on the 28th to DROUVIN - HOUCHIN - HAILLICOURT.

At 11:30 p.m. the Mounted Troops were warned to be ready to move at an hours notice - apparently forward - nothing happened and the order was subsequently cancelled.

On the 28th the Division moved to the area allotted - one third of the Infantry bivouacked in the open - Headquarters moved to DROUVIN.

On the 29th Headquarters moved to LABUISSIERE.

On the 30th one Brigade at HAILLICOURT was ordered to move out to make room for the French; it marched to LABUISSIERE and BRUAY.

25. Reports of my Infantry Brigadiers, C.R.E., O.C. Signal Coy, O.C. 9th Gordons (Pioneers), Divisional Squadron, Cyclist Company, and M.M.G.Battery commanders and A.D.M.S. are attached. I consider these reports too valuable to be omitted and they are too detailed for inclusion in my own report.

The Divisional Artillery worked throughout under the orders of the Fourth Corps, and will doubtless render their report direct. Brigadier General Alexander worked in the closest cooperation with me throughout the operations, and rendered valuable service.

The work done by the Artillery in cutting the wire during the preliminary bombardment, in supporting the attacks, and in placing barrages of fire where required was conspicuously good. The First Group H.A.R. also rendered prompt and effective assistance whenever called upon.

26. I consider that none of my elaborate preliminary preparations were wasted. The Division was launched to the attack under the most favourable conditions, the casualties up to the time of the actual assault were negligible, the supply of grenades, ammunition and tools was well maintained, and the large numbers of wounded were attended to and evacuated with despatch.

27. Communications throughout were very good. Except for very short intervals, communication between Division and Brigade Headquarters was maintained by telegraph and telephone during the whole period under report. The wireless and pigeon service proved very valuable in keeping up communication with LOOS. The work of the Divisional Signal Company was excellent; it was owing to their efforts, and to the frequent reports sent in by Artillery observers, and by the officers actually engaged, that I was kept in close and constant touch with the situation.

28. Between 14,000 and 15,000 grenades were taken into action on the men. These proved very useful and materially assisted the advance. The grenadiers of all Battalions showed conspicuous courage and resource.

29. The Lewis machine gun proved a serviceable weapon. The machine gun detachments greatly distinguished themselves and their losses were heavy. The 11th M.M.G. Battery also rendered most valuable service.

30. I am of opinion that the arrangements for discharging the gas require more organisation and study. A number of cylinders remained undischarged, and a good deal of gas found its way into our own trenches.

I suggest that the cylinders should be connected up in batteries, and manipulated from well under cover; also the discharge pipes should be buried in the parapet to prevent their being blown back into the trench by shells.

The smoke candles were very effective. But a holder on a long stick is required for them, so that the candlemen can keep well under cover.

The discharge of gas drew a heavy artillery fire on our front trenches.

31. I have no hesitation in saying that had fresh troops of good quality been held in readiness to follow closely on the heels of my Division, the German line would have been pierced. My Division carried out its orders to the letter, at great speed, and exhausted itself in the effort. The Division sent to support me came too late, and was not in a fit condition to enter such a fight. Its commander and staff appeared quite unfamiliar with the ground or the situation and made no effort to get into close touch with me or my staff. No member of the staff of the Guards Division or of the 11th Corps came near my Headquarters, though the G.O.C. 3rd Cavalry Division kept in constant touch with me.

It is beyond my province to suggest that the task allotted to the Divisions or Corps destined to support my attack required as careful preparation and previous study as did the task of my own Division. But I must beg permission to point out that these precautions were apparently lacking, and to deplore the result.

My orders to push on to the full extent of the power of the Division were clear and definite and were carried out to the full in the confident assurance that the promised flow of reinforcements behind me would be maintained. In the event, I consider that nothing but the high soldierly qualities displayed by officers and men of my Division averted a disastrous retreat from the positions won.

32. I cannot close this report without paying a tribute to the discipline, bravery and resource shown by all ranks under my command.

The spirit of officers and men remains high in spite of the heavy losses sustained, and the fighting value of the Division will be completely restored as soon as reinforcements of personnel and material are received.

The following appendices are attached:-

App: 1.		Total Casualties.
" 2.	Report	- G.O.C. 44th Bde.
" 3.	"	" 45th Bde.
" 4th	"	" 46th Bde.
" 5.	"	of C.R.E.
" 6.	"	of O.C. 9th Gordons.
" 7.	"	of O.C. Divl. Squadron.
" 8.	"	of O.C. Cyclist Coy.
" 9.	"	of M.M.G. Battery.
" 10.	"	of O.C. Signal Coy.
" 11.	"	of A.D.M.S.

F. W. N. McCracken

Major General,

5th October, 1915. Commanding 15th (Scottish) Division.

CASUALTIES SUFFERRED BY THE 15th DIVISION FOR THE PERIOD

25th, 26th & 27th SEPTEMBER.

UNITS.	OFFICERS					OTHER RANKS.				
	KILLED.	WOUNDED.	MISSing.	GASSED.	TOTAL.	KILLED.	WOUNDED.	MISSING.	GASSED.	TOTAL.
Hd.Qrs.44th Bde.	-	-	1	-	1	-	-	-	-	-
9th Black Watch.	8	11	1	-	20	68	314	292	5	679
8th Seaforth Hrs.	5	10	4	-	19	44	362	294	-	700
10th Gordon Hrs.	-	5	2	-	7	23	221	130	-	374
7th Cameron Hrs.	4	6	4	-	14	64	255	215	-	534
13th Royal Scots.	6	9	1	-	16	37	224	105	4	370
7th R. S. Fusrs.	6	11	1	-	18	63	240	83	-	386
11th A & S Hrs.	7	4	1	-	12	36	214	64	-	314
6th Cameron Hrs.	8	8	-	1	17	30	270	70	-	370
7th K.O.S.Bs.	9	7	3	-	19	12	221	404	-	645
8th K.O.S.Bs.	3	7	4	-	14	23	124	228	4	379
10th Sco.Rifles.	12	5	4	-	21	68	318	239	-	625
12th H. L. I.	7	11	-	-	18	59	184	315	-	558
9th Gordon Hrs. (Pioneers).	5	4	-	-	9	21	179	64	4	268
70th Bde.R.F.A.	-	2	-	-	2	1	12	-	-	13
71st ,, ,,	-	-	-	-	-	1	14	2	2	19
72nd ,, ,,	-	1	-	-	1	-	1	-	-	1
73rd ,, ,,	-	-	-	-	-	2	8	-	-	10
11th M.M.G.Batty.	-	2	-	-	2	-	3	-	-	3
15th Divl.Cyclists	-	-	-	-	-	1	6	-	-	7
73rd FLD.Coy.R.E.	2	2	1	-	5	10	14	29	-	53
74th Fld.Coy.R.E.	-	-	-	-	-	3	3	1	10	17
91st Fld.Coy.R.E.	-	-	1	-	1	9	32	11	-	52
45th Fld.Amb.R.A.M.C.	-	-	-	-	-	-	4	-	-	4
46th Fld.Amb.R.A.M.C.	-	1	-	-	1	-	1	-	4	5
47th Fld.Amb.R.A.M.C.	-	-	-	-	-	-	3	-	-	3
TOTALS.	82	106	28	1	217	575	3227	2546	41	6389
ATTACHED UNITS										
180 Coy. R.E.	~~1~~	~~22~~	~~2~~	~~-~~	~~25~~	1	22	2	-	25
187 Coy. R.E.	-	-	-	-	-	-	1	-	4	5

G

1A

W A R   D I A R Y .

Instructions regarding War Diaries and Intelligence Summaries are contained in F. S. Regs., Part II. and the Staff Manual respectively. Title Pages will be prepared in manuscript.

WAR DIARY
or
INTELLIGENCE SUMMARY
(Erase heading not required.)

Army Form C. 2118

Place	Date	Hour	Summary of Events and Information	Remarks and references to Appendices
VAUDRICOURT	8/9/15		No change – Weather fine – wind NE	
"	9/9/15		GOC held conference at Divl HQ, attended by CRA, Inf Bde Commanders, CRE, ADMS, & staff.	
			Situation normal. Weather fine. wind NE.	
"	10/9/15		Situation normal. Weather fine. wind NE.	
			– Owing to postponement of operation, orders issued for 2 Bns of 45th Inf Bde to be lent to 44th + 46th Inf Bdes to relieve a Bn each in front line from 12th to 17th. Latter to come back to vacated billets.	G.755
"	11/9/15		– Copies of instructions for preliminary bombardment drawn up by CRA issued to Inf. Bdes.	App.
			– Map showing work in construction of reserve and communication trenches by the Division attached.	App. IV a
			– Instructions issued (a) as to steps to be taken in event of troops entering town vacated by enemy.	App. VII
			(b) re Corps and Divisional Collecting stations for prisoners.	App. VIII
			~~(c) re grenadier squads.~~	~~App. IX~~
			– Situation normal – Weather fine. wind N.E.	
	12/9/15		– Question of attack of Southern Sap raised by GOC 46th Inf. Bde. G.O.C 15 Div. decided that no sap should be run out from our front but that original order must stand. A direct attack on the head of the sap must be made simultaneously with the main assaults to N. and S. of it. Artillery will pay particular attention to this sap & to wire in front of it. 46th Inf Bde informed.	
			– Instructions issued amending previous instructions re collecting station for prisoners.	App. VIII
			– Relief of 8th K.O.S.B., 46th I.B., by 11th A + S. Highlrs., 45th I.B., and of 7th Cameron Highlrs., 44th I.B., by 13th R. Scots, 45th IB, complete.	
			– Situation normal. Weather fine. wind E.	

1875 Wt. W593/826 1,000,000 4/15 J.B.C. & A. A.D.S.S./Forms/C. 2118.

Instructions regarding War Diaries and Intelligence Summaries are contained in F. S. Regs., Part II. and the Staff Manual respectively. Title Pages will be prepared in manuscript.

15th Div WAR DIARY or ~~INTELLIGENCE SUMMARY~~ September 1915.

(Erase heading not required.)

Army Form C. 2118

Place	Date	Hour	Summary of Events and Information	Remarks and references to Appendices
DROUVIN	1/9/15.		No change. One Bn. 46th Inf Bde ordered to move on 2nd to bivouac NW of MAZINGARBE to provide working party of 300 each day & night for 3 ds under CRE	G 641
"	2/9/15		No change	
VAUDRICOURT (E. 28.d 0.6)	3/9/15		No change. Message to Div. Art. saying that CRA will assume control of the artillery for the defence of the 47th Divl. front from 10 am 4/9/15.	G 674
"	4/9/15		No change. Major E G WACE RE arrived from GHQ as GSO. 2nd grade vice Maj E.G. HENDERSON RE. Operation Order No.7 issued for relief of 45th by 44th and ~~46th~~ Inf Bdes. Weather wet.	App I
"	5/9/15		No change. Weather improves. Orders received regarding taking over Y0 & Y1.	App II
"	6/9/15		Troops of 2nd Inf Bde on left of 15th Div, & under 15th Div. for defence, ordered to extend to their right as far as Boyau 19 inclusive.	
			G.O.C., CRA and GSO 1st Grade attended conference at Adv. First Army HQ, HINGES.	
			No 63 Trench Battery (1½") ordered to QUALITY ST.	G 707
			No change in situation & very quiet. Weather fine, but wind changed to the East.	
"	7/9/15		Y0 and Y1 taken over by 3rd Inf. Bde. under 15th Div for defence. Relief of 45th by 44th & 46th Inf Bdes reported complete at 11.25 pm	App. III
			Preliminary Operation Order No. 8 issued – ~~[illegible]~~ IV Corps No HRS 508/1 received, announcing postponement of proposed operations – Issued G 715 accordingly – Two Bns of 45th Inf. Bde moved to LABOEUVRIERE from NOEUX-LES-MINES, and replaced by 1 Bn each of 44th & 46th Inf Bdes.	G. 715 App IV
			No change. Weather fine, wind easterly. Statement of billets of Div attached	App. V
			Message issued, with map, amending areas allotted to Bdes.	App. VI

1875 Wt. W593/826 1,000,000 4/15 J.B.C. & A. A.D.S.S./Forms/C. 2118.

Instructions regarding War Diaries and Intelligence Summaries are contained in F. S. Regs., Part II. and the Staff Manual respectively. Title Pages will be prepared in manuscript.

WAR DIARY
or
~~INTELLIGENCE SUMMARY~~
(Erase heading not required.)

Army Form C. 2118

Place	Date	Hour	Summary of Events and Information	Remarks and references to Appendices
VAUDRICOURT	13.9.15		Instructions issued re Grenadier squads –	App. IX
			Situation unchanged. Weather fine; wind changed to S.W.	
"	14.9.15		Copy of instructions of No.1 Group H.A.R. issued to Inf. Bdes.	App. X
			Administrative instructions issued by AA+QMG.	App. XI
			No change. Rain at first, then fine; wind S.W.	
"	15.9.15		Special instructions by Divl. Art. for bombardment, prior to, during, and after assault issued to Inf. Bdes.	App.
			~~4.7 H.B.~~ No change. Fine. Wind S.W.	
"	16.9.15		Large fire broke out about CITE ST PIERRE in evening. Nothing else happened of importance.	
"	17.9.15		Operation Order No.9 and G.874 issued.	App. XII
			Amendments issued by AA+QMG to administrative instructions (App. XI)	App.
			No change. Weather fine – hot. Wind S.W.	
"	18.9.15		Conference at Divl. HQ at 9.0am when Gen BUDWORTH, IV Corps Artillery, explained the tasks of the artillery and the periodical "lifts" of fire. These lifts to be strictly adhered to, whatever the situation, as communication renders any change very difficult to effect. At end of 2nd + 3rd lifts the bombardment will be intense for 5 min to indicate to infantry the time for their further advance.	
			German prisoner taken in afternoon opposite the end of Boyau 19 (G.28.a.9.6); deserter of 157 Rgt. Passed to Corps to examine.	
			Gas cylinders started going in to trenches this night (18/19); 7 cylinders per bay put in. Detail of arrangements followed is attached.	App.
			No change in situation. Weather fine.	
"	19.9.15		Wind turned in night 18/19 to NE. No change in situation. Big explosion apparently just E of HILL 70 Redoubt (G.33	
			Instructions issued (1) re "lifts" of artillery fire and special bombardments (2) in amendment of gas programme on day of assault	(1) G.908 (2) G.915 App. XIV
			Placing of gas cylinders in front trenches completed to 12 per bay.	App. XIII

1875 Wt. W593/826 1,000,000 4/15 J.B.C. & A. A.D.S.S./Forms/C. 2118.

Instructions regarding War Diaries and Intelligence Summaries are contained in F. S. Regs., Part II. and the Staff Manual respectively. Title Pages will be prepared in manuscript.

WAR DIARY
or
INTELLIGENCE SUMMARY
(Erase heading not required.)

Army Form C. 2118

Place	Date	Hour	Summary of Events and Information	Remarks and references to Appendices
VAUDRICOURT	20/9/15	–	Corps Operation Order 35 received, detailing orders for 21st to 25th and after. No change – Fine. E. Wind.	
"	21/9/15	–	Bombardment began in morning. Weather misty rendering observation for H.A.R. difficult, so their participation was postponed. Reports in evening of effect of field artillery on enemy's wire were satisfactory. Very little response by enemy. Operation Order No. 10 issued, also G.977 for move of ~~gas~~ men to front line trenches on 24th.	App. XV G 977.
"	22/9/15	–	Bombardment continued. Weather clearer. Satisfactory reports from R.A. re wire cutting. Enemy very quiet. Wind S.E. Reports on wire cutting by gunners satisfactory; very little reply by enemy.	
"	23/9/15	–	Bombardment continued, results satisfactory as far as can be seen. Enemy shelled our trenches more heavily today. A trench mortar from the direction of the LENS ROAD REDOUBT did considerable damage to bay 48. Demonstration at 4 pm today drew weak hostile rifle fire. Orders issued for move of remainder of Advanced Dressing Stations to QUALITY ST and FOSSE 7 on 24th. 1st Army instruction re gas communicated to Bdes. These require gas helmets to be lowered by men in front trenches when gas is turned on. F Trench Battery ordered to accompany 11th M.M.G. Batty to latter's forming-up place on 24th. Nos 3 & 63 Trench Batts (4" + 1½" resp.) moved back to Divl. Ammn Col. The former has no ammunition and the latter has only bad fuzes resulting in majority of rounds being blind. HQ 45 Inf Bde established at NOEUX LES MINES 1st Div took over defence of sections Y0 and Y1.	

Army Form C. 2118

Instructions regarding War Diaries and Intelligence Summaries are contained in F. S. Regs., Part II. and the Staff Manual respectively. Title Pages will be prepared in manuscript.

WAR DIARY
or
~~INTELLIGENCE SUMMARY~~
(Erase heading not required.)

Place	Date	Hour	Summary of Events and Information	Remarks and references to Appendices
MAZINGARBE	24/9/15.		HQ moved from VAUDRICOURT at 5.0 pm, established at Adv. HQ at 5.30 pm	
			GSO.1. attended conference at Adv. IV AC., obtained information of Corps Commanders intentions regarding possible alternatives to the operations for which orders have been issued - Message issued to Bdes.	G 28
			Bombardment continued. Results apparently satisfactory, but wire cutting difficult to examine.	G 33
			Move to forming-up places of 45 + 46 Inf. Bdes. delayed till 8.5 pm. when telephone message was received from Adv. IV AC to "carry on". 45 + 46 Inf. Bdes. instructed accordingly.	
			Following accompanied GOC to Adv. H.Q. :- All GSO's, DAA + QMG (Capt SNOW), 1 ADC (Lt Sir J. Tichborne) and Liaison Officers.	
		11.0 pm.	Telephone message received from IV AC to say that IV AC Operation Order No 35 stands, hour of zero will be communicated later. Divl Art informed verbally, Inf Bdes by wire.	G. 38
	25/9/15	1.0 am	IV Corps HRS 530/1 received at 0.50 am. confirming telephone message.	
		3.0 am	Watches of 44, 45 and 46 Inf. Bdes. checked by 'phone with Divl HQ time, which was checked with Corps time.	
		3.35 am	Received instructions by telephone from Adv. IV AC that the hour "zero" is 5.50 am. (from Maj STEWART. GSO II) Information passed accordingly to all concerned.	G 40 + 41
			Gas attack commenced. Weather dull, light rain, wind very light apparently.	
		5.50 am	Observer reports infantry are through to enemy's support trench with little opposition.	G 46
		6.50 am	- ditto - our third line crossing enemy's first line trenches, observation further forward is difficult.	G. 47
		7.0 am	45th Inf Bde moving slowly up without difficulty.	

1875 Wt. W593/826 1,000,000 4/15 J.B.C. & A. A.D.S.S./Forms/C. 2118.

Instructions regarding War Diaries and Intelligence Summaries are contained in F. S. Regs., Part II. and the Staff Manual respectively. Title Pages will be prepared in manuscript.

WAR DIARY
or
~~INTELLIGENCE SUMMARY~~
(Erase heading not required.)

Army Form C. 2118

Place	Date	Hour	Summary of Events and Information	Remarks and references to Appendices
MAZINGARBE	25/9	7.25 am	Message sent at 7.10 from 46 Inf Bde states that infantry still advancing, all three columns over to enemy's trenches – smoke still very thick –	
"	"	7.40 am	44 Inf. Bde. reports whole of the 2 assaulting columns are into the German trenches, reserve battalion in our front line preparing to proceed –	
"	"	7.50 am	Seaforths reported at 7.5 that they were close to LOOS. (telephone from GOC 44 Inf Bde) LOOS visible through smoke from R. column.	
"	"	8.10 am	CRE asked to bring up the 180th (Tunnelling Co) RE. less 2 sections, from VERQUIN to LE SAULCHOY; this will enable them to get up in front of Corps reserves.	
"	"	9.0 am	After consulting with CRA. regarding probability of our left being drawn into attacking PUITS 14 BIS (H 25 c) through difficulties experienced by advance of 1st Div, a message was sent to 4th Corps suggesting HAR should bombard strong points in H 25 + H 31	G 54
"	"	9.25 am	73rd Bde RFA report they have seen our infantry pushing forward at 9.10 am. through G 36 D and G 30 D. (from CRA)	
"	"	9.30 am	CRE told to fill in cavalry crossings over our + German front line trenches. CRA. to move up 2 batteries to positions of readiness by FOSSE 7.	
		9.35 am	Observing Officer 72 Bde RFA reports our infantry in PUITS 14 BIS and at 9.15 am. infantry are advancing on hill 70. (from CRA)	
"	"	9.40 am	CRA instructed verbally to arrange to group artillery now with leading Inf. Bdes., as their advance has progressed so satisfactorily; 70th Bde RFA with 44th, 71st with 46th Inf Bde.	
"	"	9.50	Situation report sent out. Leading Bdes through LOOS. Reserve Bde in our front line.	G 55.

1875 Wt. W593/826 1,000,000 4/15 J.B.C. & A. A.D.S.S./Forms/C. 2118.

Instructions regarding War Diaries and Intelligence Summaries are contained in F. S. Regs., Part II. and the Staff Manual respectively. Title Pages will be prepared in manuscript.

WAR DIARY
or
INTELLIGENCE SUMMARY
(Erase heading not required.)

Army Form C. 2118

Place	Date	Hour	Summary of Events and Information	Remarks and references to Appendices
MAZINGARBE	25/9	10.20 am	2nd Inf. Bde. reports delayed in front of German wire between Northern Sap and Lone Tree – Grenadiers of 6th Cam. Hghrs ordered to bomb up northwards to assist.	
		–	46th I.B. report 10.10 a.m. that Hill 70 has been taken with no opposition. At same time the Bde Major reports that he estimates the total casualties of 46 I.B. at 10 %.	
		10.15	45. I.B. ordered to push forward leading Bn on right to German Third line trenches, ~~to~~ and leading Bn on left into German front line trenches. No further without orders.	G 57.
		10 ~~35~~ 10 am	11th M. M. G. Batty ordered to QUALITY ST to come under 44 I.B., & be moved up to N. outskirts of LOOS at discretion of G.O.C. 44 I.B.	G. 56
		11.0 am	G.O.C. 46th Inf. Bde. reports his left on PUITS 14 BIS and he is pushing on towards CITE ST AUGUSTE, his left is exposed and No. 5 Column (HLI) is hung up through difficulties of 2nd Inf. Bde. & suffering heavily. One Bn 45 I.B. ordered up in support.	G.62.
		11.15 am	CRA asked to arrange with H.A.R. to lift the barrage previously arranged to N.1.a, N 2 C, N 2 D, and 1000 yards E. of German trenches W. of ST AUGUSTE, and H 26 a 3.6 to N and E –	
		11 25 am	Situation explained to Corps, & suggestion made to move up Corps reserve in readiness.	G. 63
		11 30 am	Squadron moved up to join cyclists at MAZINGARBE.	
		–	Corps informed that only 2 Bns remain in reserve.	G 66

1875 Wt. W593/826 1,000,000 4/15 J.B.C. & A. A.D.S.S./Forms/C. 2118.

Army Form C. 2118

WAR DIARY
or
INTELLIGENCE SUMMARY
(Erase heading not required.)

Instructions regarding War Diaries and Intelligence Summaries are contained in F. S. Regs., Part II. and the Staff Manual respectively. Title Pages will be prepared in manuscript.

Place	Date	Hour	Summary of Events and Information	Remarks and references to Appendices
MAZINGARBE	25/9	12.15 pm	45th Bde less 6th Camerons to LOOS to hold it and release troops of 44 & 46th IB. Heavy artillery will shell german trenches in front of CITE ST AUGUSTE for a complete period of half an hour. Situation about this time 44 & 46 IB holding on to hill 70 unable to make progress against CITE ST AUGUSTE.	G 68
		12 20 pm	11th Mtn. Batty placed under orders of 46 Inf. Bde.	G. 69.
		12.30 pm	HAR to bombard CITE ST AUGUSTE trenches for half an hour. 44 & 46 IB informed.	G 71
		12.40 pm	2 Co 9th Gordons ordered to LOOS to put it in a state of defence	G 72
		12.50 pm	GOC 45th IB reported he has only 2 Bns left, as 6th Camerons have gone to 46th IB and R Scots to 44 IB. (on phone)	
		1.40 pm	GOC 21st Div with Commander of 62nd Inf Bde arrived and discussed 4th AC "orders" re move of 21st Div.	*unnumbered message received at 2.0 pm at 21st HQ
		2.25 pm.	62nd Bde ordered to march via Quality Street on LOOS. If Hill 70 is abandoned the 62nd Bde will retake it. If situation admits of it the Bde to ~~attack~~ CITE ST AUGUSTE in cooperation with 44th & 46th Bdes.	G 77
		2.30 pm	44th Bde reports mixed parties entrenching east of LOOS from H31B66 to H31A72.	
		3.15 pm	44th Bde Hd Qrs reported moving to LOOS	
		4 pm.	1st Div reported capture of Germans who were holding up first line.	cf. B 526
		4.40 pm.	1st Div reports that it is moving on the german trenches from H26D36 to H27A55	
		6 pm.	Orders issued to brigades to consolidate position gained from Hill 70 to PUITS 14 Bis	G 82

1875 Wt. W593/826 1,000,000 4/15 J.B.C. & A. A.D.S.S./Forms/C. 2118.

Instructions regarding War Diaries and Intelligence Summaries are contained in F. S. Regs., Part II. and the Staff Manual respectively. Title Pages will be prepared in manuscript.

WAR DIARY
or
INTELLIGENCE SUMMARY
(Erase heading not required.)

Army Form C. 2118

Place	Date	Hour	Summary of Events and Information	Remarks and references to Appendices
MAZINGARBE	25th Sept	6pm	Orders issued to bdes to consolidate their positions on Hill 70 to Pits 14 Bis	
	25th	9.7pm	Instructions received from 4th Corps that Div will be prepared to resume offensive on 26th and placing 2nd bde 1st Div at disposal of G.O.C. 15th Div for operations	IV AC G.132
	25th	11.30pm	Telephone message from 4th Corps that Div will attack Hill 70 at 9 a.m. tomorrow after one hours intense bombardment, & stating 2nd Bde was to rejoin its division.	
	25th Sept	11.45am in night	Instructions issued to 2nd Bde to rejoin the 1st div at 9 a m west of the Bois Carree Sent up Capt Lord Dudley Gordon with bombs to 44, 46 IBis, and Lt ELLIOT with F (Stokes) Trench Batty to 46th I.B. adv. HQ at G 29 b. 2.4.	
	26th	12.25am	Grouping of artillery with Inf Bdes cancelled	
		1.45am	Orders received from 4th Corps that 15th Div with 62nd Bde attached will attack Hill 70 at 9 am after 1 hours intense bombardment.	
		2.30am	Orders issued for attack of Hill 70.	G.95
		5.55am	45th I.B report counterattack developing against Hill 70 from E and SE.	
		8.35am	47th Div asked to hold one Battalion in readiness to prolong their left in event of attack of 45th I.B being all drawn to Hill 70.	G 99
		9.0am	45th I.B. report on telephone that the assault has started.	
		9.45am	Report from 44th I.B that enemy are using asphyxiating shell on our old front line trenches.	
		10.0am	Attack on Hill 70 failed 45th Inf. Bde calling for reinforcements.	
		10.30am	45th Inf. Bde. report their position apparently Right holding about H.31 c. 1.5 Left being reinforced and working forward. 8th E. Yorks and 10th Yorks of 62nd Inf. Bde apparently in front line (Right ?) of Hill 70, 12th and 13th Northumberland 62nd Inf Bde chiefly retiring in disorder along LENS road, which is congested with transport and dead animals.	

Instructions regarding War Diaries and Intelligence Summaries are contained in F. S. Regs., Part II. and the Staff Manual respectively. Title Pages will be prepared in manuscript.

WAR DIARY
or
INTELLIGENCE SUMMARY
(Erase heading not required.)

Army Form C. 2118

Place	Date	Hour	Summary of Events and Information	Remarks and references to Appendices
MAZINGARBE	26/9/15.	11am	45th Inf. Bde. reports at 10.30 a.m. their right holding about H.31. c.1.5, left being reinforced and working forward.	
			Bns of 62nd Inf. Bde. retiring in disorder through our lines (44th + 46th Inf Bdes.) in rear of LOOS; efforts to rally proved useless. 15 Div troops standing firm.	
		1.30 pm	G.156. from Adv. IV A.C. received informing us that we can call on one Bde of 3rd Cav Div for defensive purposes.	
		2.35 pm	45 Inf Bde HQ back at QUALITY ST., but LOOS + western slopes of Hill 70 still held.	
			6th Cav Bde (less 1 Regt) about this time was pushed forward into LOOS to hold the place at all costs with remaining troops of 15th Div. still there. Remainder of Div. (i.e. 44th + 46th Inf Bdes), squadron + reserve platoon cyclists sent forward to hold old German 1st line system of trenches between LENS Road redoubt and LOOS Road redoubt, both inclusive.	G. 122.
		3.30 pm	Gen CAMPBELL, 6th Cav Bde, placed in command of troops in LOOS. Arrangements made by telephone with 45th Inf Bde to hand over the short range wireless set and pigeons to 6th Cav. Bde.	
		4.15 pm	C.R.E. instructed to send all available officers + men to collect stragglers off the A.P.M. and to take them forward to the front line on the ridge. Capt Cooke, Cyclist Co, ordered to do the same.	
		6.30 pm	Owing to reports received, chiefly from 46th Inf Bde, that our troops were still holding on to Hill 70 a message was sent to Gen CAMPBELL to get touch + reinforce, while arrangements were made with CRA for an artillery barrage in support.	G. 131

1875 Wt. W593/826 1,000,000 4/15 J.B.C. & A. A.D.S.S./Forms/C. 2118.

Instructions regarding War Diaries and Intelligence Summaries are contained in F. S. Regs., Part II. and the Staff Manual respectively. Title Pages will be prepared in manuscript.

WAR DIARY
or
INTELLIGENCE SUMMARY
(Erase heading not required.)

Army Form C. 2118

Place	Date	Hour	Summary of Events and Information	Remarks and references to Appendices
MAZINGARBE	26/9/15	10.30 pm	62nd Inf Bde ordered by 4th AC to rejoin its Division.	
"	27/9/15	12.25 am	In accordance with IV AC HRS 530/1 of 26th, orders issued for withdrawal of the Div, less artillery, to MAZINGARBE. This was carried out without incidents of any kind. The remaining troops of 15th Div that continued to hold LOOS and Hill 70 in conjunction with the Cavalry were collected by degrees and moved back to their units.	G 143
"		3.45 pm	Orders issued for move of Div, less artillery, on 28th to DROUVIN, HOUCHIN, HAILLICOURT.	App
"		11.30 pm	In accordance with instructions received by telephone from IV A.C., the mounted troops were warned to be ready to move at one hour's notice. Apparently some wireless message has been received which indicated the possibility of the germans breaking, and of all available mounted troops being required to hold & widen the gap. Nothing happened.	
			Reports of fighting strength before and after these operations, and messages re casualties are attached.	
			Special Divisional Order issued	App XVI

1875 Wt. W593/826 1,000,000 4/15 J.B.C. & A. A.D.S.S./Forms/C. 2118.

Instructions regarding War Diaries and Intelligence Summaries are contained in F. S. Regs., Part II. and the Staff Manual respectively. Title Pages will be prepared in manuscript.

WAR DIARY
or
~~INTELLIGENCE SUMMARY~~
(Erase heading not required.)

Army Form C. 2118

Place	Date	Hour	Summary of Events and Information	Remarks and references to Appendices
DROUVIN	28/9/15		Hd Qrs moved to chateau at DROUVIN at noon. Weather fine, but ground very wet. All the troops were not able to obtain cover in the billets allotted to them and some had to bivouac.	
			The Division was warned by telephone about 1.0 pm to prepare to march to reserve area further West the next day; this was subsequently cancelled.	
LABUISSIERE	29/9/15		Hd Qrs moved to LABUISSIERE in forenoon. Weather showery, ground very wet. ~~44th Inf Bde moved to LABUISSIERE~~, ~~and 9th Gordons to DROUVIN~~.	
"	30/9/15		45th Inf Bde moved out of ~~HOUCHIN~~ HAILLICOURT in morning to make room for ~~[illegible]~~ french troops; after interview with the french Corps to south arrangements were made for 3 Bns to billet in BRUAY, remainder of Bde. being established in LABUISSIERE. 9th Gordons moved to DROUVIN.	
			"F" Trench Btty (Stokes mortars) transferred to 12th Div., sent by motor to 12th D.A.C. at LABOURSE, less its C.O. Lt ELLIOTT, A+S. Highlrs.	

[illegible] Lt Col. G.S.
for GOC 15th Div.

1875 Wt. W593/826 1,000,000 4/15 J.B.C. & A. A.D.S.S./Forms/C. 2118.

1B

A P P E N D I C E S

I to XVI

(<u>Note:</u> Appendices VI & XIII <u>are missing.</u>)

App I.

S E C R E T.

Copy No. 24

15th Division Operation Order No. 7.

4th Sep. 1915.

1. On the night of September 7th/8th the 44th and 46th Infantry Brigades will take over the line from Sap 18 to the junction of trenches 26 and 12 (inclusive). The 45th Infantry Brigade on relief will go into Divisional Reserve in NOEUX-LES-MINES and VERQUIN, leaving one battalion to hold the line from the junction of trenches 26 and 12 to A.1 (exclusive).

This battalion will come under the command of the G.O.C. 46th Infantry Brigade.

The relief will be carried out under arrangements to be made between Brigades.

2. The exact areas which the 44th and 46th Infantry Brigades will take over respectively, are shown on the attached map. West of this map the boundaries will be as follows:-

46th Infantry Brigade. Northern Boundary - the line L.18.a.0.8. - L.17.a.0.8. - L.10.d.3.2. - L.9.a.8.0. - L.8.b.1.8. Southern Boundary - a straight line from MAZINGARBE CHURCH to the Railway junction at L.14.a.5.5.

44th Infantry Brigade. Northern Boundary - a straight line from MAZINGARBE CHURCH to the railway junction at L.14.a.5.5.

Southern Boundary - a line from L.22.d.3.0. to the railway at L.20.a.3.9.

The Western boundary for both Brigades will be the railway line L.8.b to L.20.a.

3. Headquarters 44th Infantry Brigade will be at MAZINGARBE CHATEAU, Headquarters 45th Infantry Brigade

at the/

at the WHITE HOUSE, NOEUX-LES-MINES, and Headquarters 46th Infantry Brigade will be at the house in MAZINGARBE, which has been prepared as a Divisional Headquarters.

4. The two and a half battalions of the 1st Division in occupation of Y.1. will be grouped under the senior commander and come under the command (for tactical purposes only) of the G.O.C. 46th Infantry Brigade.

5. The 73rd and 91st Field Companies R.E., each with one Company of 9th Gordons (Pioneers) attached, will be allotted to the two sectors, but will continue to work under the C.R.E.

6. The machine guns of the 9th Gordons will be at the disposal of the G.O.C. 44th Infantry Brigade.

J.T.BURNETT-STUART.
Lieut Colonel,
General Staff.

Issued at 10.10 pm
through Signals.

Distribution as in Divl.
War Standing Orders and
to:-
IVth Corps.
1st Division.
47th Division.
9th Division.
No 1 Group H.A.R.

Note. Plan sent to Inf Bdes only

"A" Form. Army Form C. 2121.

MESSAGES AND SIGNALS. No. of Message

Prefix Code m. | Words | Charge

Office of Origin and Service Instructions

PRIORITY

Sent
At m.
To
By

This message is on a/c of: Service.

(Signature of "Franking Officer.")

Recd. at m.
Date
From
By

TO		
46th Bde		Div ART.
45th Bde		4th Corps
46th Bde		1st DIV:

* Sender's Number	Day of Month	In reply to Number	AAA
G.692	5th		

Operation order No 7 of yesterday is amended as follows AAA. Front to be taken over by 46th Bde will be extended Northwards to BOYAU 19 exclusive AAA. 45th Bde will not leave one Battn in the trenches but will be relieved complete AAA. First Division Troops will take over front down to BOYAU 19 inclusive from 45th Bde tomorrow AAA. Battns of 1st DIV in Y.1. will be replaced by a complete Bde on 7th inst. This ~~Bde~~ Bde will come directly under 15th DIV from that date and will have its HD Qrs in MAZINGARBE AAA. Trenches 16 and 16a. as far as dotted road in G 21 b. are allotted to 1st DIV from tomorrow AAA addressed all Bdes repeated Div Arty Fourth Corps and 1st DIV AAA acknowledge

From 15th DIV
Place
Time 6.5 am.

The above may be forwarded as now corrected. (Z) [illegible signature]

Censor — Signature of Addressor or person authorised to telegraph in his name.

* This line should be erased if not required.

(15491) S. & Co. Ltd. W 14142/641. 90,000. 4/15. Forms C 2121/10.

App II

SECRET

IVth Corps H.R.S. No. 510

HEADQUARTERS 4th CORPS
5 SEP 1915
GENERAL STAFF

~~1st Division.~~

15th Division.

~~47th Division.~~

On the morning of September 7th, the $2\frac{1}{2}$ battalions of the 2nd Infantry Brigade now in Y.0. and Y.1., will be relieved by $2\frac{1}{2}$ battalions of the 3rd Infantry Brigade. On completion of this relief, the 3rd Infantry Brigade will come under the orders of the G.O.C. 15th Division, who will arrange Brigade Headquarters for this brigade and for communication between it and 15th Divisional Headquarters.

A. A. Montgomery

H.Q. IVth Corps.
5th Sept., 1915.

Brigadier-General,
General Staff, IVth Corps.

II

SECRET

IVth Corps No. H.R.S. 506/1

~~1st Division.~~
15th Division.
~~47th Division.~~
~~187 Special Co. R.E.~~
~~G.O.C. IVth Corps Artillery.~~
~~G.O.C. No. 1 Group, H.A.R.~~

1. Under instructions received, the date of the attack has been postponed from 15th September.

2. The exact length of the postponement is not yet definitely known, but probably for at least four days.

3. As soon as the definite date is known it will be communicated to you, meanwhile all preparations will be continued on the lines already laid down.

4. The number of days to be occupied in the preliminary bombardment and the general programme remains the same, and the gas will be taken up on the three nights preceding the preliminary bombardment.

Boles notified verbally – BBS

A A Montgomery

Brigadier-General,
General Staff, IVth Corps.

H.Q. IVth Corps.
7th September, 1915.

IV

15th Division G.715.

S E C R E T . Copy No 1

7th Sept, 1915.

1. Reference 15th Division Preliminary Operation Order No 8 issued today, instructions have just been received from the 4th Corps that the date of attack has been postponed from the 15th September. The exact extent of the postponement is not yet definitely known, but it will probably be for at least four days. It will be communicated as soon as known.

2. The dates in the above mentioned Operation Order are therefore relative only, not actual. The sequence of events, however, remains the same.

The gas cylinders will not be put in until three days before the bombardment is timed to commence.

3. It is too late to stop the relief now taking place; but in consequence of this alteration in the plans, billetting accommodation for one Battalion each of the 44th and 46th Infantry Brigades will be allotted in NOEUX-les-MINES from tomorrow inclusive, and the 45th Infantry Brigade moved into billets further back. Definite instructions as to this will be sent out this evening. Order issued by "A". (13/A of 7-9-15)

J Burnett Stuart

Lieut Colonel.

General Staff.

Issued at 4 pm
through Signals. by Lt. Lace

To 44th Infantry Brigade.
45th Infantry Brigade.
46th Infantry Brigade.
15th Divl. Artillery.
4th Corps.
1st Division.
47th Division.
One for G. Office.
one for War Diary.

distribution As for op order No. 8.

[illegible] to "A"

Note – As the postponement of the attack was still further prolonged, a Battn of the 45th Bde was lent to each of the two assaulting Bdes. so as to spare the assaulting troops –

Copy No 1

SECRET.

Reference 1/10,000
Trench Map. Sheet
36.c.N.W. & 36.1.S.W.

15th Division Preliminary Operation Order No 8.

7th Sept, 1915.

1. The Division is to take a principal part in an attack on the German positions.

Objectives of Division.

2. The objectives allotted to the Division are:-

(a) German front line trenches from G.34.a.6.5. to sap at G.22.d.6.3. (Southern Sap).

(b) German second line trenches from LOOS cemetery in G.35.a (exclusive) to G.29.b.3.9.

(c) LOOS Village.

(d) Hill 70.

Objectives of 47th Division & 1st Division.

3. In order to form a defensive flank southwards to cover our advance, the 47th Division will attack with the following objectives:-

(a) The DOUBLE CRASSIER as far as point M.4.d.8.8.

(b) German front system of trenches from M.4.c.3.9. to G.34.a.6.5.

(c) German second line trenches from M.4.d.8.3. to the cemetery in G.35.a (inclusive).

(d) Enclosure in G.35.d.

(e) Fosse in G.33.

On our left the 1st Division will attack simultaneously from immediately north of the LE RUTOIRE-LOOS Road, with its right Brigade directed on PUITS No 14 bis. (inclusive)

Bombardment.

4. The attack will commence by a steady bombardment by all available guns day and night for four days up to the moment of the infantry assault on the 5th day. This bombardment will be distributed over the whole front of the 1st and 4th Corps.

Gas.

5. On the morning of the 5th day gas, interspersed and flanked by smoke from smoke candles, will be discharged for 40 minutes along the front; this discharge will be followed immediately by the infantry assault.

6. The attack of the Fourth Corps will be pushed home to the full extent of its power.

Preliminary Moves and sequence of events.

7. On the night of September 7th/8th the 44th and 46th Infantry Brigades will go into the front line under orders already issued.

8. The gas cylinders and candles will be placed in the recesses prepared for them on the nights of September 8th/9th, 9th/10th and 10th/11th. Special orders will be issued to those concerned for this operation, which, on the above nights, will take absolute precedence over all other work and traffic.

9. The artillery bombardment will begin on September 11th. During this and following three days troops will remain in their areas as already allotted, except that the western boundary of the 44th and 46th Brigade areas will not extend further west than the SAILLY line of trenches (inclusive).

During this period the trenches of the SAILLY line and of the GRENAY line (both branches) and the auxiliary trenches belonging to these systems, are reserved entirely for the Infantry Brigades (and attached troops) to whom they are allotted.

10. Troops will move into their forming up places on the night of September 14th/15th. Divisional orders will be issued for this move.

Forming up Places.

The areas allotted to Brigades and Divisional Troops for forming up are shown on the attached map;[x] the detailed placing of the troops (except Divisional Troops) in these areas will be left to Brigade Commanders. The different battle headquarters which are shown have been prepared for occupation.

x issued to 44th, 45th, 46th Inf. Bdes. and Divl Art. only.

Preparing Wire.

11. The 44th and 46th Infantry Brigades will be responsible for cutting our wire in their own front on the next night but one before the day of assault, (i.e. on the night of 13th/14th) and for preparing steps and pickets to help the assaulting troops to get out of the trenches.

The wire will be cut in diagonal strips, the loose wire being thrown over the uncut strips.

Rifle fire from our trenches will be kept up each night during the bombardment to prevent the Germans repairing their wire.

Assaulting Columns.

12. (a) The assault will be delivered by 4 columns, 2 from each of the leading Brigades. Each column will consist of one Battalion (with machine guns), one section R.E. and one Platoon of 9th Gordons, and will be formed up in depth on a front of two Platoons.

(b) The task of the assaulting columns will be to move straight forward to their ultimate objective.

Parties for cutting wire, blocking side trenches, and bombing down communication trenches, will be told off from the leading two companies.

Assaulting columns will not be entrusted with the tasks of occupying and consolidating positions won, nor of digging communications back to our own trenches; these tasks will be allotted to parties told off from the Brigade Reserves. The assaulting columns must push on -

(c) The 4th Company in each Column will carry a proportion of picks and shovels; the R.E. section will carry explosives for hasty demolitions; the platoon of the 9th Gordons will carry 6 sandbags per man, and tools.

(d) Each Company will move up at once into the place of the one in front of it directly this latter moves on-; connecting files will be placed along the communication trenches to enable this flow to be maintained.

(e) All ranks in the assaulting columns will wear their smoke helmets rolled up under their bonnets, ready to be lowered immediately should the men outrun the gas.

Objectives assigned to Brigades.

13. The objectives assigned to Brigades are as follows:-

<u>44th Infantry Brigade.</u>

1st. - German front trench from point of Salient at G.34.a.4.9. to the little cross trench at G.28.c.9.6., and support trench behind this line.

2nd. - Second line trench from G.35.a.3.3. to G.29.c.4.5. (i.e. in line with the cross roads at G.29.c.9.3.)

3rd. - LOOS Village.

4th. - PUITS No 15.

5th. - German work in H.31.d.

<u>46th Infantry Brigade.</u>

1st. - German front trench from G.28.d.0.7. to VERMELLES - LOOS road and communicating trenches behind it.

2nd. - Second line trench from left of 44th Infantry Brigade's 2nd objective to the sunken road at G.29.b.2.6.

3rd. - Trenches behind this to the third line from G.29.d.7.4. to G.30.a.2.7.

4th. - Road from G.30.c.4.2. to G.30.b.4.2.

5th. - Line from H.31 central to PUITS No 14 bis (exclusive).

The assaulting columns of the 46th Infantry Brigade must endeavour not to be drawn into a converging attack on LOOS, but to push straight on to their 4th objective.

They will better assist the 44th Infantry Brigade by outflanking the village, than by crowding into it.

The German trench running from G.35.a.3.3. to G.34.b central is allotted to the 47th Division, who will deal with it. This trench (exclusive) will be the right boundary of the 44th Infantry Brigade attack.

Flanks of line.

14. (a) The G.O.C.46th Infantry Brigade will detail parties of grenadiers to go forward simultaneously with the assault along the VERMELLES - LOOS and LE RUTOIRE - LOOS roads respectively, to work up the Southern Sap and northwards along the front and support trenches from the LOOS road REDOUBT. These parties will work on northwards till they join up with the grenadiers from the 1st Division, who will be working southwards from the Northern Sap.

The front between the VERMELLES - LOOS and LE RUTOIRE - LOOS roads will be occupied in the first instance by troops from the 46th Infantry Brigade reserve; these troops will be instructed to go forward and occupy the German front trench as soon as they can.

(b) The machine guns of the 9th Gordons will be attached to the 44th Infantry Brigade and will be used in the first instance for bringing fire to bear from Sap 18 on to the Southern faces of the LENS ROAD REDOUBT. These guns, together with No 3 Trench Mortar Battery and any other troops allotted by G.O.C. 44th Infantry Brigade to hold the front between the main road and Sap 18 (whence the left of the 47th Division assault starts) will be pushed forward as opportunity arises and as G.O.C. 44th Infantry Brigade may direct.

(c) The guns of No 63 $1\frac{1}{2}$" Trench Battery in position on the Divisional front will be pushed forward under the orders of the battery commander, as soon as the assaulting columns are clear of our trenches. The battery commander will have a call on the nearest infantry to help him move his guns.

Brigade Reserves.

15. As soon as the assaulting columns have cleared the German front trench, this trench will be occupied by the Brigade reserves, and parties told off to open up communication trenches to join up with our own line at the points shown on the attached map, where Russian Saps have already been commenced.

Divisional Reserve.

The Brigade in Divisional reserve (45th Infantry Brigade) will move up into our own front trenches as soon as these have been cleared by the two leading Brigades, but will not go further than these trenches without orders from Divisional Headquarters.

The Divisional Mounted Troops (including M.M.G. Battery and less special detachments), the headquarters and E+F companies 9th Gordons, and 74th Field Company R.E., will await orders in their forming up places.

Time of assault.

16. The exact time for the assault will be fixed by higher authority. There will be no rifle fire from our trenches during the gas discharge, but the artillery bombardment will not be interrupted.

Artillery programme.

17. The Divisional Artillery will act throughout under the orders of the Corps in accordance with a detailed programme, which will be communicated to G.O's C Brigades in due course.

Miscellaneous arrangements & precautions.

18. (a) Equipment to be carried.

(i) Packs and greatcoats will not be taken to the forming up positions on the night preceding the assault, but will be labelled and left under guard in selected houses or dugouts.

Every infantryman will carry:-

Rifle and equipment (less pack).
2 bandoliers of S.A.A. in addition to equipment amm: (220 rounds in all).
1 iron ration and unexpended portion of days ration.
2 sandbags in belt. (Pioneers, 6 sandbags.)
Smoke helmet.

N.B. Haversack will be carried on the back. Grenadiers will carry equipment amm: only.

(ii) 10 selected men per Platoon in the 44th and 46th Infantry Brigades will carry wire cutters (attached to a lanyard).

(iii) 8 selected men per Platoon in the 2 leading companies of the 44th and 46th Infantry Brigades will carry billhooks for destroying wire.

These men and men with wire cutters will be supplied with hedging gloves.

(iv) One man per Platoon throughout the Division will carry a yellow flag 2' x 2' on a 3' stick, to mark the progress of his Platoon in the attack; and one man per bombing squad will carry a yellow flag 1' x 1' on a 5' stick to mark the progress of his squad.

These flags will be carried, never stuck in the ground.

Note. The 47th Division will carry yellow flags with a black cross.

The 1st Division will carry red flags with a white stripe; and will also use a black screen with a white diagonal stripe for a special bomb supply party.

720 Ball grenades packed in boxes (which can be carried by one man) and 40 Rifle grenades will be stored in each of the 4 forward trench grenade stores (see sketch App. 2) ~~by the evening of [illegible]~~.

600 Battye grenades similarly packed and 40 Rifle grenades will be stored in each of the QUALITY Keeps, SOUTH, EAST, and NORTH. These are for use as Bde ~~[illegible]~~ reserves.

Grenades will be forwarded under Divisional arrangements from the Divisional grenade Dump at MAZINGARBE to Bde dumps on demand.

(b) Grenades.

500 grenades packed in boxes (which can be carried by one man) will be stored in each of the 4 forward trench depots (marked by red crosses on the map) by the evening of September 7th. This will be done by the Divisional Bombing Officer (Capt Lord Dudley Gordon, 9th Gordons) who will also be responsible for keeping these depots full during the action.

Grenades for bringing the equipment of grenadiers in the attack up to the full amount, will be available by 6 a.m. September 9th as follows:-

For 44th and 46th Brigades. - At Headquarters of 73rd Field Company R.E. at SAULCHOY FM.

For 45th Brigade. - At Divisional Bombing school at NOEUX -les-MINES.

These grenades must be drawn before the evening of the 14th, and will be issued direct to bombing squads of battalions (who will attend to draw them), under arrangements to be made by Brigades direct with the Divisional Bombing Officer.

(c) S.A. Ammunition.

(i) Web bandoliers to complete up to 220 rounds per man will be drawn by Brigades from the Brigade Ammunition Columns during September 9th and 10th; arrangements to be made direct with Divisional Artillery.

(ii) The S.A.A. now in the trenches and at Advanced Battalion Headquarters in Section X will be collected under Brigade arrangements and deposited in the trench depots which have been prepared at or near the trench grenade depots. 100 boxes (100,000 rounds) will be stored in each of those four depots, before the morning of September 11th. Extra boxes will, if necessary, be drawn by Brigades to complete to this amount. Care must be taken that only good ammunition is so stored.

The existing Brigade reserve store for section X (some 493,000 rounds) situated in QUALITY STREET, will not be drawn on for stocking the trench depots, but will be kept intact, made safe, ~~and~~ marked by a notice board, and put under a guard -

(d) R.E. Stores.

(i) Two advanced depots of R.E. Stores will be established near the junction of trenches 9.b and 26, and in trench 27 by the C.R.E. by the evening of September 7th. (see Sketch app. 2)

Each of these stores will contain:-

12,000 sandbags in double bundles of 25 for slinging.
200 picks.
200 shovels.
10 Crowbars.
50 wire cutters.
20 tracing tapes.
20 coils $1\frac{1}{2}$ rope 30' long.
20 coils plain wire - 35 lbs.
50 billhooks.
20 axes.

(ii) A large central store will be established by same date at the R.E. Store in QUALITY STREET.

(iii) The main Divisional R.E. Depot will be at LE SAULCHOY FM; a proportion of wagons will be kept there ready loaded with materials for constructing bridges for guns and vehicles over the trenches.

(iv) The following stores (to be taken by the infantry to their forming up places) will be ready for issue at the 91st Field Company R.E. Headquarters in MAZINGARBE from September 7th and will be drawn

Under Brigade arrangements:-

	44th I.B.	45th I.B.	46th I.B.
Large Yellow flags	64	64	64
Small do:	64	64	64
* Wire Cutters	448	80	448
* Hedging Gloves	620	160	320
* Billhooks.	128	32	128
Sandbags.	8000	8000	8000

* The allowance to 45th I.B. will be increased if possible.

(e) Water.

~~Eight~~ Nine 100 gallon + one 200 gallon tanks of water have been placed in the support trench at intervals along the Divisional front. (See Sketch app. 2) When these have been filled, Brigades in occupation of the trenches will be responsible for posting sentries to see that this water is not touched before the attack takes place.

Instructions will be issued later showing at what places in the forming-up areas, water from wells or pipes is available.

(f) Rations.

A reserve of one days iron ration per man is stored in the CORON de FOSSE 7, close to QUALITY STREET. This is a Divisional reserve and cannot be touched without permission from Divisional Headquarters.

(g) Medical.

Advanced dressing stations will be established in QUALITY ST., just behind FOSSE 7, and in the Brewery at LE PHILOSOPHE.

Communications. 19. (a) Advanced telephone and visual signalling stations are marked T. and V. respectively on the map (app 2) and will be kept open, if possible, throughout the bombardment and the attack, so that messages may be received there.

The central visual receiving station will be on FOSSE 3.

(b) Wires have been multiplied and buried.

(c) At least two light wires will be taken forward by each Battalion in the advance, for communication back to Brigade Headquarters.

(d) To supplement the above (all of which may fail), Battalion Commanders will arrange a system of runners to keep up communication with Brigade Headquarters and with their companies. 4 selected men per company and 6 per Battalion Headquarters have been found satisfactory numbers to detail for this purpose.

Police & Prisoners. 20. (a) The A.P.M. with the military police and ~~two~~ Three ~~troops (dismounted) of the Divisional Squadron~~ Cyclist platoons Div. Md Troops, will establish a line of posts along the VERMELLES-GRENAY Railway across the Divisional area and at other selected points to collect stragglers, assist wounded, direct messengers, and generally police the area behind the advancing Brigades.

(b) Prisoners will be sent to LE PHILOSOPHE, where arrangements will be made by the AP.M to take them over.

Miscellaneous instructions. 21. (a) Dugouts and cellars in the German lines may be found full of gas, and should not be entered without smoke helmets being lowered. Arrangements should be made to take forward VERMOREL Sprayers with the troops.

(b) All papers and orders are to be destroyed before the advance. No papers will be carried by officers and men taking part in the attack, except the new 1/10000 trench map recently issued, showing the German trenches only, and the 1/40000 map, Sheet ~~36.c.N.W.~~ 36C + 36B N.W. + the LENS sheet 1/100000

All messages and reports will refer to one or other of these maps.

(c) Men in the ~~trenches~~ ranks will not fall out to bring back wounded.

(d) Hand grenades are difficult to replenish; they must not be thrown indiscriminately.

(e) Any guns captured, which are in danger of being lost again, must be rendered useless by damaging the sights and breech mechanism. Captured machine guns must be collected or broken.

J B Burnett Stuart
Lieut Colonel.
General Staff.

Issued at 4 pm by St Lacc.
through signals.

To 44th Inf. Bde
45th ——
46th ——
Divl. Art.
4th Corps
1st Div
47th Div.
} Under secret cover.

1 copy for A office
1 Copy for G. office
1 Copy for War diary

(12) Copies sent 17/9/15 to 9th Gordons
(13) —————— Div. Md Troops.

"A" Form. Army Form C. 2121.

MESSAGES AND SIGNALS.

No. of Message

Prefix .... Code .... m.	Words / Charge	This message is on a/c of:	Recd. at .... m.
Office of Origin and Service Instructions. [illegible]	Sent At .... m. To .... By	.... Service. (Signature of "Franking Officer.")	Date .... From .... By ....

TO 44th Bde
46th Bde

SECRET

Sender's Number.	Day of Month	In reply to Number	AAA
* G. 776	11th		

Reference 15th Div Preliminary operation order No 8 of Sept 7th para 18 c (ii) AAA. The existing Brigade reserve store of SAA in QUALITY STREET will be checked marked & guarded by the 44th Bde, who will report to Div Hd. Qrs the exact number of boxes & rounds which it contains ✗ AAA This reserve will be available as an emergency reserve for Section X until the time for offensive action arrives AAA As soon as the attack commences this reserve will come under Divisional control as an extra reserve – AAA Addressed 44th Bde repeated 46th Bde.

✗ 585 boxes 1000
17 —— 850 } = 599450

½ million to be kept in store remainder distributed in trenches

From 15th Div
Place
Time 1.15 pm

The above may be forwarded as now corrected. (Z) J Burnett Stuart Lt Col.

Censor. Signature of Addressor or person authorised to telegraph in his name.

* This line should be erased if not required.

(688-9) —McC. & Co. Ltd., London.— W 14142/641. 225,000 4/15. Forms C 2121/10.

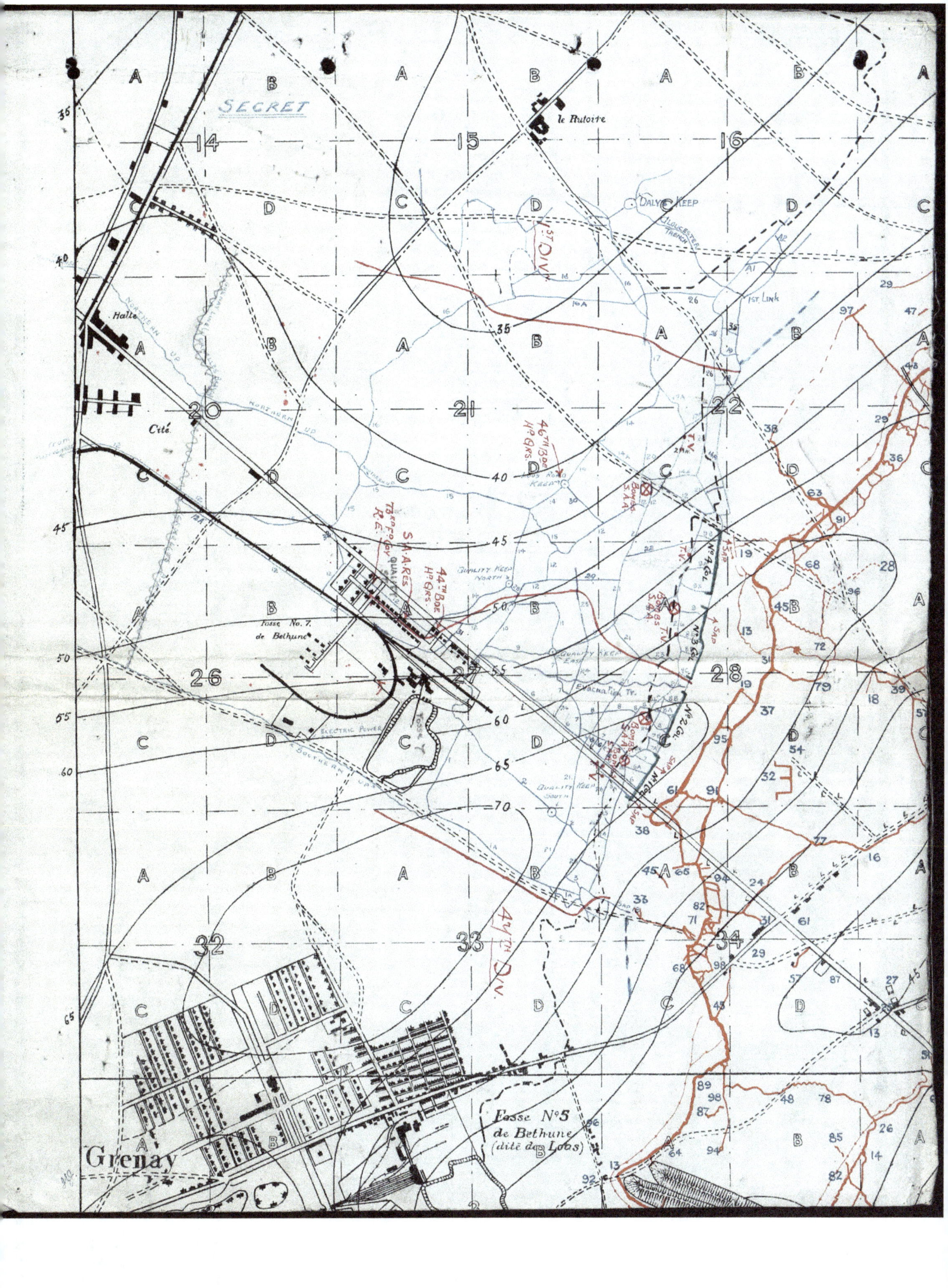
SECRET
le Rutoire
Daly's Keep
Gloucester Trench
1st Div
1st Link
Halte
Cité
Northern Up
Fosse No. 7 de Bethune
Electric Power
Southern Up
Quality Keep North
Quality Keep East
Quality Keep South
Loos Road Keep
Evacuation Tr.
46th Bde Hd Qrs
44th Bde Hd Qrs
S.A.A. Res
No 4 Col
No 3 Col
No 2 Col
Bombs S.A.A.
47th Div
Grenay
Fosse No 5 de Bethune (dite de Loos)

Copy No 6.

SECRET.

Reference 1/10,000
Trench Map. Sheet
36.c.N.W. & 36.1.S.W.

15th Division Preliminary Operation Order No 8.

7th Sept, 1915.

1. The Division is to take a principal part in an attack on the German positions.

Objectives of Division.

2. The objectives allotted to the Division are:-

(a) German front line trenches from G.34.a.6.5. to sap at G.22.d.6.3. (Southern Sap).

(b) German second line trenches from LOOS cemetery in G.35.a (exclusive) to G.29.b.3.9.

(c) LOOS Village.

(d) Hill 70.

(e) Cite ST AUGUSTE

(f) High ground N of LOISON - SOUS - LENS.

Objectives of 47th Division & 1st Division.

3. In order to form a defensive flank southwards to cover our advance, the 47th Division will attack with the following objectives:-

(a) The DOUBLE CRASSIER as far as point M.4.d.8.8.

(b) German front system of trenches from M.4.c.3.9. to G.34.a.6.5.

(c) German second line trenches from M.4.d.8.3. to the cemetery in G.35.a (inclusive).

(d) Enclosure in G.35.d.

(e) Fosse in G.33.

On our left the 1st Division will attack simultaneously from immediately north of the LE RUTOIRE-LOOS Road, with its right Brigade directed on PUITS No 14 bis. (inclusive)

Bombardment.

4. The attack will commence by a steady bombardment by all available guns day and night for four days up to the moment of the infantry assault on the 5th day. This bombardment will be distributed over the whole front of the 1st and 4th Corps.

Gas.

5. On the morning of the 5th day gas, interspersed and flanked by smoke from smoke candles, will be discharged for 40 minutes along the front; this discharge will be followed immediately by the infantry assault.

6. The attack of the Fourth Corps will be pushed home to the full extent of its power.

Preliminary Moves and sequence of events.

7. On the night of September 7th/8th the 44th and 46th Infantry Brigades will go into the front line under orders already issued.

8. The gas cylinders and candles will be placed in the recesses prepared for them on the nights of September 8th/9th, 9th/10th and 10th/11th. Special orders will be issued to those concerned for this operation, which, on the above nights, will take absolute precedence over all other work and traffic.

9. The artillery bombardment will bdgin on September 11th. During this and following three days troops will remain in their areas as already allotted, except that the western boundary of the 44th and 46th Brigade areas will not extend further west than the SAILLY line of trenches (inclusive).

During this period the trenches of the SAILLY line and of the GRENAY line (both branches) and the auxiliary trenches belonging to these systems, are reserved entirely for the Infantry Brigades (and attached troops) to whom they are allotted.

10. Troops will move into their forming up places on the night of September 14th/15th. Divisional orders will be issued for this move.

Forming up Places. The areas allotted to Brigades and Divisional Troops for forming up are shown on the attached map*; the detailed placing of the troops (except Divisional Troops) in these areas will be left to Brigade Commanders. The different battle headquarters which are shown have been prepared for occupation.

*issued to 44th, 45th, 46th Inf. Bdes, and Div. Art. only.

Preparing Wire. 11. The 44th and 46th Infantry Brigades will be responsible for cutting our wire in their own front on the next night but one before the day of assault, (i.e. on the night of 13th/14th) and for preparing steps and pickets to help the assaulting troops to get out of the trenches.

The wire will be cut in diagonal strips, the loose wire being thrown over the uncut strips.

Rifle fire from our trenches will be kept up each night during the bombardment to prevent the Germans repairing their wire.

Assaulting Columns. 12. (a) The assault will be delivered by 4 columns, 2 from each of the leading Brigades. Each column will consist of one Battalion (with machine guns), one section R.E. and one Platoon of 9th Gordons, and will be formed up in depth on a front of two Platoons.

(b) The task of the assaulting columns will be to move straight forward to their ultimate objective.

Parties for cutting wire, blocking side trenches, and bombing down communication trenches, will be told off from the leading two companies.

Assaulting columns will not be entrusted with the tasks of occupying and consolidating positions won, nor of digging communications back to our own trenches; these tasks will be allotted to parties told off from the Brigade Reserves. The assaulting columns must push on.

(c) The 4th Company in each Column will carry a proportion of picks and shovels; the R.E. section will carry explosives for hasty demolitions; the platoon of the 9th Gordons will carry 6 sandbags per man, and tools.

Will back-[illegible] with 2nd line?

(d) Each Company will move up at once into the place of the one in front of it directly this latter moves on-; connecting files will be placed along the communication trenches to enable this flow to be maintained.

(e) All ranks in the assaulting columns will wear their smoke helmets rolled up under their bonnets, ready to be lowered immediately should the men outrun the gas.

Objectives assigned to Brigades.

13. The objectives assigned to Brigades are as follows:-

44th Infantry Brigade.

1st. - German front trench from point of Salient at G.34.a.4.9. to the little cross trench at G.28.c.9.6., and support trench behind this line.

2nd. - Second line trench from G.35.a.[illegible].3. to G.29.c.4.5. (i.e. in line with the cross roads at G.29.c.9.3.)

3rd. - LOOS Village ~~(less the buildings in G35. b.2.2 & the d.1.8)~~ [illegible]

Less the buildings in G35. b.2.2 and d.1.8 & the new School at G35. d.7.8 all of wh are allotted to 47th Div.

4th. - PUITS No 15.

5th. - German work in H.31.d.

46th Infantry Brigade.

1st. - German front trench from G.28.d.0.7. to VERMELLES - LOOS road and communicating trenches behind it.

2nd. - Second line trench from left of 44th Infantry Brigade's 2nd objective to the sunken road at G.29.b.2.3.

This 2nd objective will be extended N to include the road junction at G29. b.2.9. A bombing Squad will be detailed to work up from that point along the trench called NORTH LOOS AVENUE to connect with grenadiers of 2nd Bde who will be working down it.

3rd. - Trenches behind this to the third line from G.29.d.7.4. to G.30.a.2.7.

4th. - Road from G.30.c.4.2. to G.30.b.4.2.

5th. - Line from H.31 central to PUITS No 14 bis ~~(inclusive)~~. (Exclusive)

The assaulting columns of the 46th Infantry Brigade must endeavour not to be drawn into a converging attack on LOOS, but to push straight on to their 4th objective.

go on

They will better assist the 44th Infantry Brigade by outflanking the village, than by crowding into it.

The German trench running from G.35.a.3.3. to G.34.b central is allotted to the 47th Division, who will deal with it. This trench (exclusive) will be the right boundary of the 44th Infantry Brigade attack.

Flanks of line.

14. (a) The G.O.C.46th Infantry Brigade will detail parties of grenadiers to go forward simultaneously with the assault along the VERMELLES - LOOS and LE RUTOIRE - LOOS roads respectively, to work up the Southern Sap and northwards along the front and support trenches from the LOOS road REDOUBT. These parties will work on northwards till they join up with the grenadiers from the 1st Division, who will be working southwards from the Northern Sap.

The front between the VERMELLES - LOOS and LE RUTOIRE - LOOS roads will be occupied in the first instance by troops from the 46th Infantry Brigade reserve; these troops will be instructed to go forward and occupy the German front trench as soon as they can.

2 Coys

(b) The machine guns of the 9th Gordons will be attached to the 44th Infantry Brigade and will be used in the first instance for bringing fire to bear from Sap 18 on to the Southern faces of the LENS ROAD REDOUBT. These guns, together with No 3 Trench Mortar Battery and any other troops allotted by G.O.C. 44th Infantry Brigade to hold the front between the main road and Sap 18 (whence the left of the 47th Division assault starts) will be pushed forward as opportunity arises and as G.O.C. 44th Infantry Brigade may direct.

allot troops bivouacs for the

G 707

(c) The guns of No 63 $1\frac{1}{2}$" Trench Battery in position on the Divisional front will be pushed forward under the orders of the battery commander, as soon as the assaulting columns are clear of our trenches. The battery commander will have a call on the nearest infantry to help him move his guns.

Brigade Reserves.

15. As soon as the assaulting columns have cleared the German front trench, this trench will be occupied by the Brigade reserves, and parties told off to open up communication trenches to join up with our own line at the points shown on the attached map, where Russian Saps have already been commenced.

Divisional Reserve.

The Brigade in Divisional reserve (45th Infantry Brigade) will move up into our own front trenches as soon as these have been cleared by the two leading Brigades, but will not go further than these trenches without orders from Divisional Headquarters.

The Divisional Mounted Troops (including M.M.G. Battery and less special detachments), the headquarters and ~~2 companies 9th Gordons, and 73rd Field Company R.E., will await orders in their forming up places.~~ E & F Coys 9th Gordon Hghrs & 74th Fd Co R.E. will await orders in their forming up places

Time of assault.

16. The exact time for the assault will be fixed by higher authority. There will be no rifle fire from our trenches during the gas discharge, but the artillery bombardment will not be interrupted.

Artillery programme.

17. The Divisional Artillery will act throughout under the orders of the Corps in accordance with a detailed programme, which will be communicated to G.O's C Brigades in due course.

Miscellaneous arrangements & precautions.

18. (a) Equipment to be carried.

(i) Packs and greatcoats will not be taken to the forming up positions on the night preceding the assault, but will be labelled and left under guard in selected houses or dugouts./

Every infantryman will carry:-

Rifle and equipment (less pack).
2 bandoliers of S.A.A. in addition to equipment amm: (220 rounds in all).
1 iron ration and unexpended portion of days ration.
2 sandbags in belt. (Pioneers, 6 sandbags.)
Smoke helmet.

N.B. Haversack will be carried on the back. Grenadiers will carry equipment amm: only.

R.E. ✓ 640 wire cutters required for Bde.

(ii) 10 selected men per Platoon in the 44th and 46th Infantry Brigades will carry wire cutters (attached to a lanyard).

R.E. ✓ 128 64 billhooks

(iii) 8 selected men per Platoon in the 2 leading companies (of each column) of the 44th and 46th Infantry Brigades will carry billhooks for destroying wire.

H.L.?

704 Hedging gloves

These men and men with wire cutters will be supplied with hedging gloves. (coming)

R.E. 64 yellow flags 2'x2' on 3' stick

(iv) One man per Platoon throughout the Division will carry a yellow flag 2' x 2' on a 3' stick, to mark the progress of his Platoon in the attack; and one man per bombing squad will carry a yellow flag 1' x 1' on a 5' stick to mark the progress of his squad.

R.E. 64 = 1 bombing squad per platoon 1'x1' on 5' stick

These flags will be carried, never stuck in the ground.

Note. The 47th Division will carry yellow flags with a black cross.

The 1st Division will carry red flags with a white stripe.

The 1st division will also use a black screen with white diagonal stripe for a special bomb supply party.

(b) Grenades. 720 ball grenades packed in boxes (which can be carried by 1 man) & 40 rifle grenades are stored in each of the 4 forward trench depots (See map. App 2). 500 Battye grenades similarly packed & 40 rifle grenades are stored in each of the Quality keeps - South - East & North. These are for use as Brigade reserve - Grenades will be forwarded under Divisional arrangements from the Div'l Reserve at Mazingarbe, to Brigade Dumps, on demand.

(b) Grenades.

500 grenades packed in boxes (which can be carried by one man) will be stored in each of the 4 forward trench depots (marked by red crosses on the map) by the evening of September 7th. This will be done by the Divisional Bombing Officer (Capt Lord Dudley Gordon, 9th Gordons) who will also be responsible for keeping these depots full during the action.

Carriers?

Grenades for bringing the equipment of grenadiers in the attack up to the full amount, will be available by 6 a.m. September 9th as follows:-

What is amount?

For 44th and 46th Brigades.	- At Headquarters of 73rd Field Company R.E. at SAULCHOY FM.
For 45th Brigade.	- At Divisional Bombing school at NOEUX -les-MINES.

These grenades must be drawn before the evening of the 14th, and will be issued direct to bombing squads of battalions (who will attend to draw them), under arrangements to be made by Brigades direct with the Divisional Bombing Officer.

Dudley Gordon. 79

(c) S.A. Ammunition.

(i) Web bandoliers to complete up to 220 rounds per man will be drawn by Brigades from the Brigade Ammunition Columns during September 9th and 10th; arrangements to be made direct with Divisional Artillery.

100 extra

(ii) The S.A.A. now in the trenches and at Advanced Battalion Headquarters in Section X will be collected under Brigade arrangements and deposited in the trench depots which have been prepared at or near the trench grenade depots. 100 boxes (100,000 rounds)

[illegible] 12-17.

will be stored in each of these four depots, before the morning of September 11th. Extra boxes will, if necessary, be drawn by Brigades to complete to this amount. Care must be taken that only good ammunition is so stored.

The existing Brigade reserve store for section X (some 493,000 rounds) situated in QUALITY STREET, will not be drawn on for stocking the trench depots, but will be kept intact, made safe and marked by a notice board.

(d) R.E. Stores.

(i) Two advanced depots of R.E. Stores will be established near the junction of trenches 9.b and 26, and in trench 27 by the C.R.E. by the evening of September 7th.

Each of these stores will contain:-

12,000 sandbags in double bundles of 25 for slinging.
200 picks.
200 shovels.
10 Crowbars.
50 wire cutters.
20 tracing tapes.
20 coils 1½ rope 30' long.
20 coils plain wire - 35 lbs.
50 billhooks.
20 axes.

(ii) A large central store will be established by same date at the R.E. Store in QUALITY STREET.

(iii) The main Divisional R.E. Depot will be at LE SAULCHOY FM; a proportion of wagons will be kept ready loaded with materials for constructing bridges for guns and vehicles over the trenches.

(iv) The following stores (to be taken by the infantry to their forming up places) will be ready for issue at the 91st Field Company R.E. Headquarters in MAZINGARBE from September 7th and will be drawn

Under Brigade arrangements:-

	44th I.B.	45th I.B.	46th I.B.
Large Yellow flags	64	64	64
Small do:	64	64	64
* Wire Cutters	448	80	448
* Hedging Gloves	620	160	320
* Billhooks.	128	32	128
Sandbags.	8000	8000	8000

* The allowance to 45th I.B. will be increased if possible.

(e) Water.

Eight 100 gallon tanks of water have been placed in the support trench at intervals along the Divisional front. When these have been filled, Brigades in occupation of the trenches will be responsible for posting sentries to see that this water is not touched before the attack takes place.

Instructions will be issued later showing at what places in the forming-up areas, water from wells or pipes is available.

(f) Rations.

A reserve of one days iron ration per man is stored in the CORON de FOSSE 7, close to QUALITY STREET. This is a Divisional reserve and cannot be touched without permission from Divisional Headquarters.

(g) Medical.

Advanced dressing stations will be established just behind FOSSE 7 and in the Brewery at LE PHILOSOPHE.

Communications. 19. (a) Advanced telephone and visual signalling stations are marked T. and V. respectively on the map and will be kept open, if possible, throughout the bombardment and the attack, so that messages may be

3 in own Section

received there.

The central visual receiving station will be on FOSSE 3.

(b) Wires have been multiplied and buried.

(c) At least two light wires will be taken forward by each Battalion in the advance, for communication back to Brigade Headquarters.

(d) To supplement the above (all of which may fail), Battalion Commanders will arrange a system of runners to keep up communication with Brigade Headquarters and with their companies. 4 selected men per company and 6 per Battalion Headquarters have been found satisfactory numbers to detail for this purpose.

8/Lt Fox to see.

Police & Prisoners. 20. (a) The A.P.M. with the military police and two troops (dismounted) of the Divisional Squadron, will establish a line of posts along the VERMELLES-GRENAY Railway across the Divisional area and at other selected points to collect stragglers, assist wounded, direct messengers, and generally police the area behind the advancing Brigades.

(b) Prisoners will be sent to LE PHILOSOPHE, where arrangements will be made by the AP.M to take them over.

Miscellaneous instructions. 21. (a) Dugouts and cellars in the German lines may be found full of gas, and should not be entered without smoke helmets being lowered. Arrangements should be made to take forward VERMOREL Sprayers with the troops.

(b) All papers and orders are to be destroyed before the advance. No papers will be carried by officers and men taking part in the attack, except the new 1/10000 trench map recently issued, showing the German trenches only, and the 1/40000 map, Sheets ~~36c.N.W.~~ 36C & 36B & the Lens Sheet 1/100,000.

All messages and reports will refer to one or other of these maps.

(c) Men in the trenches will not fall out to bring back wounded.

(d) Hand grenades are difficult to replenish; they must not be thrown indiscriminately.

(e) Any guns captured, which are in danger of being lost again, must be rendered useless by damaging the sights and breech mechanism. Captured machine guns must be collected or broken.

J. Burnett Stuart

Lieut Colonel.

General Staff.

Issued at ___________

through signals.

To 44th Inf Bde
45th —
46th —
Divl Art.
4th Corps.
1st Div.
47th Div
} Under Secret cover.

1 copy for G. Office
1 copy for War diary.

"A" Form.

Army Form C. 2121.

MESSAGES AND SIGNALS.

No. of Message

Prefix ... Code ... m.	Words	Charge	This message is on a/c of:	Recd. at ... m.
Office of Origin and Service Instructions.	Sent		... Service.	Date
ARLS	At ... m.			From
	To			By
	By		(Signature of "Franking Officer.")	

TO ~~44th Bde~~ 46th Bde.

SECRET

Sender's Number.	Day of Month	In reply to Number	AAA
G. 776	11th		

Reference 15th Div. Preliminary operation order no 8 of Sept 7th para 18 C (ii) AAA. The existing Brigade reserve store of SAA in QUALITY STREET will be checked marked + guarded by the 44th Bde, who will report to Div. Hd. Qrs. the exact number of boxes + rounds which it contains AAA This reserve will be available as an emergency reserve for Section X until the time for offensive action arrives AAA As soon as the attack commences this reserve will come under Divisional control as an extra reserve - AAA Addressed 44th Bde repeated 46th Bde.

acknowledged 14/1

From 15th Div

Place

Time 1.15 pm

The above may be forwarded as now corrected. (Z) Burnett Stuart Lt Col.

Censor. Signature of Addressor or person authorised to telegraph in his name.

* This line should be erased if not required.

(688-9) —McC. & Co. Ltd., London.— W 14142/641. 225,000 4/15. Forms C 2121/10.

— Map Showing —

Forming Up Places for Night of 14th/15th

Scale :- 1/10,000.

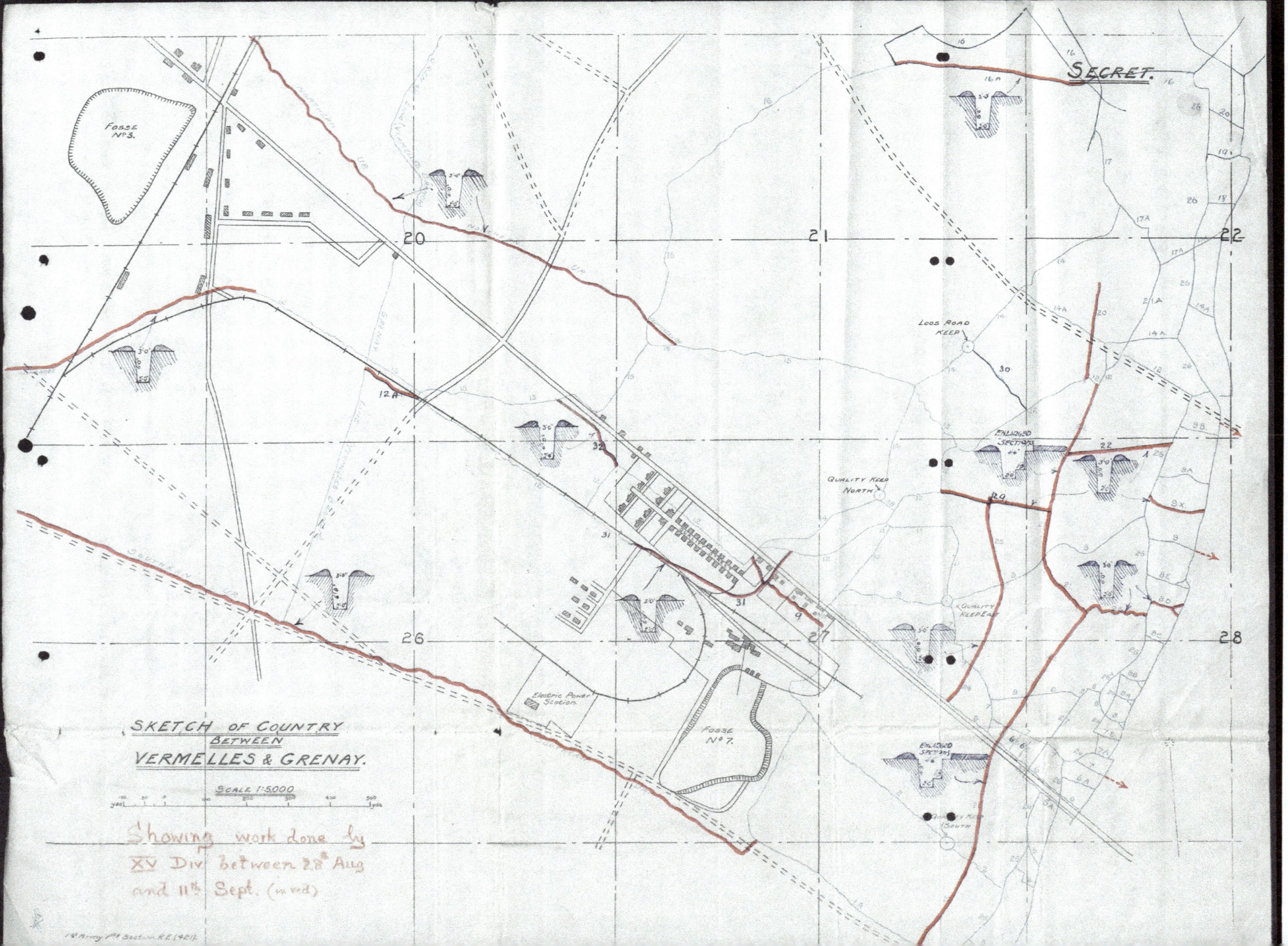
SECRET.
SKETCH OF COUNTRY
BETWEEN
VERMELLES & GRENAY.
SCALE 1:5000
Showing work done by
XV Div between 28th Aug
and 11th Sept. (in red)
Fosse No 3.
Fosse No 7.
Electric Power Station.
Loos Road Keep
Quality Keep North
Quality Keep East
Enlarged Sections
20
21
22
26
27
28

9 App V

CONFIDENTIAL

BILLETS, 15th DIVISION, 8th SEPT. 1915.

Divnl. Headquarters.	Chau. VAUDRICOURT.
2nd Echelon.	HESDIGNEUL.
Signal Coy.	VAUDRICOURT.
H.Qrs. 44th Inf. Brigade.	Chau. MAZINGARBE.
9th Black Watch.	MAZINGARBE.
8th Seaforth Hrs.	NOEUX-LES-MINES.
7th Cameron Hrs.	X.1.
10th Gordon Hrs.	MAZINGARBE.
H.Qrs. 45th Inf. Brigade.	LABEUVRIERE.
6th Cameron Hrs.	LABEUVRIERE.
13th Royal Scots.	VERQUIN.
7th R.Scots Fus.	LABEUVRIERE.
11th A. & S. Hrs.	LABEUVRIERE.
H.Qrs. 46th Inf. Brigade.	MAZINGARBE.
7th K. O. S. Bs.	PHILOSOPHE.
8th K. O. S. Bs.	X.2.
10th Scottish Rifs.	MAZINGARBE.
12th H. L. I.	NOEUX-LES-MINES.
9th Gordon Hrs (Pioneers)	
H.Qrs. & 2 Coys.	NOEUX-LES-MINES.
2 Companies.	MAZINGARBE.
15th Div. R.A. H.Qrs.	MAZINGARBE.
70th Bde. H.Q.	Saulchey Fm. MAZINGARBE.
,, A.C.	VAUDRICOURT.
71st Bde. H.Q.	Chau. MAZINGARBE.
,, A.C.	VERQUIN.
72nd Bde. H.Q.	MAZINGARBE.
,, A.C.	VERQUIN.
73rd Bde. H.Q.	NOEUX-LES-MINES.
,, A.C.	VAUDRICOURT.
No 3. T.M.Battery.	X.1.
15th D. A. C.	HESDIGNEUL.
15th Div. R.E. H.Qrs.	Chau. VAUDRICOURT.
73rd Field Coy.	MAZINGARBE.
74th Field Coy.	NOEUX-LES-MINES.
91st Field Coy.	MAZINGARBE.
Mtd Troops. Squadron.	VAUDRICOURT.
Cyclists.	VAUDRICOURT.
No 11 M.M.G.Battery.	VAUDRICOURT.
Divisional Train.	GOSNAY (1 Coy. at HESDIGNEUL)
Laundry.	HESDIGNEUL.
45th Field Ambulance.	NOEUX-LES-MINES.
46th Field Ambulance.	VAUDRICOURT.
47th Field Ambulance.	NOEUX-LES-MINES.
Fld. Amb. Workshop Unit.	HESDIGNEUL.
Convalescent Coy.	VAUDRICOURT.
32nd Sanitary Section.	HESDIGNEUL.
No 27 Mob. Vet. Section.	HESDIGNEUL.
Divnl. Supply Column.	LILLERS.

9

CONFIDENTIAL

TRANSPORT & WAGON LINES, 15TH DIVISION, Sept. 8th.

44th Inf. Brigade.) 73rd Field Coy.R.E.) 91st Field Coy.R.E.)	VERQUIN.
45th Inf. Brigade.-	
13th Royal Scots.	VERQUIN.
6th Cameron Hrs.) 7th R.Scots Fus.) 11th A.&.S. Hrs.)	LABEUVRIERE.
46th Inf. Brigade.-	NOEUX-LES-MINES.
9th Gordon Hrs (Pioneers)	NOEUX-LES-MINES.
74th Field Coy. R.E.	NOEUX-LES-MINES.
70th Bde. R.F.A. Wagon Lines.) 71st Bde. R.F.A. ,,) 72nd Bde. R.F.A. ,,) 73rd Bde. R.F.A. ,,)	VAUDRICOURT.

File

15th Division 4/9.

VII

~~44th Inf Bde.~~
~~45th Inf Bde.~~
~~46th Inf Bde.~~

The following steps should be taken by you in the event of any of your troops entering a town vacated by the enemy:-

(a) Search for concealed German soldiers.

(b) Collect and send in to Divl. Headquarters any papers and documents left behind by the enemy.

(c) Search for hostile telephones and carrier pigeons.

(d) Ascertain from inhabitants the composition and disposition of the enemy's forces in the neighbourhood.

2. Dead soldiers should be searched for papers.

3. It is suggested that an Officer should be appointed temporarily in each Brigade to carry out this work.

H. F. Baillie
Major
~~Captain~~ G.S.
15th Division.

11th September 1918.

A.K. see

Sew

SH

Copy for War Diary

App VIII

15th Division No 12.

File

Fourth Corps.

Reference your H.R. I/S 12.

The position of the advanced collecting station for this Division will be in PHILOSOPHE about G.19.b.9.8.

The route to the Corps collecting station will be MAZINGARBE - L.21.a. - NOEUX-LES-MINES - DROUVIN.

(signed) H.F.Baillie, Major,
for Major General,
commanding 15th Division.

10th Sept, 1915.

394

HEADQUARTERS,
15th DIVISION
12 SEP. 1915
Reg. No.

SECRET

IVth Corps
H.R.I/S.12

~~1st Division.~~

15th Division.

~~47th Division.~~

Reference IVth Corps No. H.R.I/S.12 dated 9th inst.

In order to lessen requirements as regards escorts for prisoners of war, it has been decided that prisoners collected at the 1st Division and 15th Division Collecting Stations at PHILOSOPHE will be sent to the 47th Division Collecting Station West of MAZINGARBE, the wired in grass enclosure at L.21.D.8.9., where all prisoners will be taken over by escorts provided under Corps arrangements, and evacuated to the Corps Collecting Station at VAUDRICOURT.

Sent to Bdes

R. ack

G795

H.W. Stenhouse Major

H.Q., IVTH Corps. for Brigadier General,

12th September, 1915. General Staff, IVTH Corps.

HYB

Copy for War Diary App. VII

CONFIDENTIAL. 15th Division 41/7/G.

15th Divl. R.A.
44th Inf. Bde.
45th Inf. Bde.
46th Inf. Bde.
A.P.M.

Herewith one copy of general instructions issued by Fourth Corps regarding disposal of Prisoners of War.

The Corps Collecting station for the forthcoming operations will be at the school in VAUDRICOURT, Sheet 36B. square E.28.c.18.

The Divisional collecting station will be in PHILOSOPHE about G.19.b.9.8.

The route to the Corps collecting station will be MAZINGARBE - L.21.a. - NOEUX-LES-MINES - DROUVIN.

(Sd) H.J. Baillie

Major, G.S.

11th September 1915. 15th Division.

CONFIDENTIAL.

PRISONERS OF WAR.

I. During operations advanced collecting stations are established at convenient well defined places where prisoners are taken over from the fighting troops by escorts specially detailed fot the purpose by the Division in whose Area the advanced collecting station is situation.

2. From the advanced stations prisoners are sent in to the Corps collecting station which is generally at or near the Corps Report Centre.

3. When it is known that prisoners have been captured an Officer of the "I" Branch of the General Staff ofthe Corps will generally proceed to the advanced collecting station to conduct a preliminary examination or he may intercept the prisoners on the way from units to the advanced collecting station or on the way to the Corps Collecting Station. Prisoners should not, however, be delayed pending his arrival.

4. The Officers in charge of advanced stations will arrange that the first prisoners taken are sent in at once to the Corps station. After this prisoners may be sent in in suitable batches according to the rate at which they arrive and the escorts available. They will be taken over at the Corps collecting station by a guard detailed under Corps arrangements.

5. Formations reporting the capture of prisoners should ascertain their Regiments providing no delay is thereby incurred, but beyond this no preliminary interrogation of prisoners will be made other than that mentioned in 3. nor is any one to be allowed to converse with them except on duty.

6. Maps, papers, documents, etc., should be taken off prisoners as early as possible and sent in with each batch, but other articles should be left in their possession as they will be searched at the Corps Collecting Station.
Before wounded prisoners are handed over to the Medical authorities all documents should be taken from them.

7. Officers should be seperated from the other ranks as soon as possible after capture.

8. The position of advanced and corps collecting stations will be notified to all concerned. The route by which escorts are to move from the advanced to Corps stations will also be indicated. In order to prevent delay, it is important that this route should be adhered to, but if it is found necessary to alter it, a message should be at once sent in to the Intelligence Officer at the Corps Collecting Station.

W.L.WHITE. Brigadier General.
D.A.& Q.M.G., IV Corps.

8th September 1916.

For War Diary

15th Division 41/7/G.

App VIII

S E C R E T.

15th Divl. Artillery.
44th Infantry Brigade.
45th do. do.
46th do. do.
A.P.M.

The last paragraph of my 41/7/G dated 11th September, 1915 is cancelled.

Prisoners of war will be taken from the Divisional Collecting Station in PHILOSOPHE to the 47th Division Collecting Station, the wired enclosure west of MAZINGARBE at L.21.d.8.9., where they will be taken over by the Fourth Corps.

(Sd) H.F. BAILLIE.
Major. G.S.
15th Division.

12th September, 1915.

App IX

15th Division G/806.

War Diary

SECRET. Copy No: 6

13th September, 1915.

With reference to 15th Division Preliminary Operation Order No 8 of 7/9/15, the following instructions are issued regarding Grenadier Squads:-

1. Grenadier Squads will consist of one N.C.O. and seven men from each Platoon.

2. The following table shows the way in which each Squad is organised for action:-

(1) Bayonet man	carries	no bombs.
(2) Bomb thrower	-	10 bombs in bandolier.
(3) N.C.O. in charge	-	10 bombs in bandolier.
(4) 1st carrier	-	10 bombs in bandolier. 15 bombs in box.
(5) 2nd carrier	-	6 bombs in bandolier. 8 bombs in box.
(6) 1st spare man	-	6 bombs in bandolier.
(7) 2nd spare man	-	do.
(8) 3rd spare man	-	do.
	Total	77 bombs.

3. Parties drawing bombs should bring one canvas bandolier for each grenadier. These have been issued to Brigades. Additional bandoliers will be issued with the bombs to those men carrying 10 bombs.

Bludgeons will also be issued at the same time as the bombs.

HMS

Lieut Colonel.

General Staff.

Issued at 3.0 pm
through Signals to
44th, 45th & 46th Inf. Bdes.
Divl. Bombing Officer.
1 for File.
1 for War Diary.

15th Division G/832.

Appx X

S E C R E T.

44th Infantry Brigade.
45th do. do.
46th do. do.

The attached copy of instructions issued to his Brigade commanders by the G.O.C. No 1 Group H.A.R. is forwarded for your information and that of your Battalion commanders.

Brigadier General Franks is anxious that we should feel quite satisfied that the Heavy Artillery are doing everything in their power to support and assist us.

JMS

Lieut Colonel. G.S.
15th Division.

14th September, 1915.

15th Division G/331.

SECRET.

1st Group H.A.R.

Thankyou for your No 38/4 of the 13th inst.

All my Brigade and Battalion commanders will be made acquainted with the instructions which you have issued; though they have already complete confidence in the readiness and ability of the Heavy Artillery to prepare and support their attack.

[signature]

Major General,

14th September, 1915. Commanding 15th Division.

CR
45

SECRET

15th Division

Herewith a copy of instructions issued by No.1 Group, Heavy Artillery Reserve.

Brigadier General Franks is most anxious that Infantry Brigade and Battalion Commanders should realize that the Heavy Artillery are doing everything in their power to assist them.

The C.R.A. would be glad if these instructions could in some way be made known to the Infantry.

H.Q.IVth Corps Arty. Geo. J. Boscawen Capt.R.F.A.

13-9-15 Staff Officer IVth Corps Artillery.

SECRET

Copy No: 16

Brigade Commanders, H.A.R.

INSTRUCTIONS

(1) No: 1 Group H.A.R. will help to prepare and support the attack of the 1st and 4th Corps in the forthcoming Operations by the bombardment of certain selected points, by keeping down the fire of hostile batteries, and in some cases by cutting wire which is inaccessible to the Field Artillery.
(") The programme of the bombardment has been issued to the brigades concerned, as has that of the wire cutting and special tasks allotted to counter batteries.

(2) It is of great importance that the assistance given to the infantry should be immediate and effective, and that the infantry should feel assured that it will be immediate and effective. With this in view the Officers Commanding brigades of heavy howitzers have been placed in direct communication with the Divisions whose attacks they are supporting, and will maintain communication with them throughout the battle. Similarly the Officers Commanding Sub-groups of Counter Batteries are in direct communication with with the C.R.A's of Divisions and through them with the Infantry Brigades in action. Officers Commanding will not hesitate to act upon their own initiative in answering any calls for assistance, merely reporting to Group Headquarters any serious modification of the programme.

(3) It is of great importance that wireless calls should be rapidly answered by the counter batteries. Officers Commanding should therefore arrange that one gun at least in each battery is always available to take up a wireless call. In dealing with enemy batteries in the area covered by both the French and British Counter Batteries, precedence is to be given to the battery which first engages the enemy battery. It will generally be better to leave that battery to complete its task undisturbed unless assistance is asked for

J B Walker

13th September 1915 Captain R.G.A.
Brigade Major No: 1 Group H.A.R.

Copies Nos: 1 & 2	filed		Copy No: 3	1st Bde R.G.A.	
Copy No: 4	2nd Bde R.G.A.		" " 5	3rd " "	
" " 6	15th " "		" " 7	22nd " "	
" " 8	Phipp's " "		" 9	du Vignaux Groupe	
" " 11	Advanced 1st Wing		)		
Copies Nos: 12, 13, 14, 15		1st Corps	)	for information	
" " 16, 17, 18, 19		4th Corps	)		

SECRET. **Administrative Instructions.** App XI

The following instructions are issued with reference to Divisional Operation Order No 8. of 7th instant.

\- - -

Baggage Wagons. 1. All baggage wagons of units will be loaded with their mobilization stores as for a move, and returned to the Divnl. Train by noon on 18th instant.

Surplus Stores and Blankets. 2. Any surplus stores (including blankets) will be collected under Brigade arrangements (in the case of Infantry and R.A.) in selected buildings or barns in MAZINGARBE and NOEUX-LES-MINES, the following places excepted.-

The Abattoir at MAZINGARBE.

The Divnl. Bath House at NOEUX-LES-MINES.

The Divnl. Bomb School at NOEUX-LES-MINES.

The Salvage Coy. main store building at NOEUX-LES-MINES.

One building if possible, or 2 adjacent buildings, should be arranged for each Brigade. All arrangements to be completed, and blankets stored by noon, 18th instant.

A guard, rationed for 6 days, should be placed over the building.

Other units will make arrangements on similar lines near their present quarters.

Ordnance. 3. The D.A.D.O.S. will arrange to have all Ordnance Stores collected in the Depot at HESDIGNEUL ready to load on to Ordnance lorries by 18th instant.

Shops. 4. All regimental shops will be closed, and contents disposed of either under 1 or 2 above.

Laundry. 5. The Divisional Laundry will be closed from 17th inst., and arrangements made by A.D.M.S. in conjunction with D.A.D.O.S. for disposal of stock of underclothing, &c.

Bath House. 6. The Divisional Bath House will be closed from 8.p.m. 18th instant. The accessories will be stored and a caretaker left in charge, under arrangements to be made by A.D.M.S.

[signature]

14.9.1915.

Lieut Colonel.,
A.A. & Q.M.G. 15th Division.

9

S E C R E T. **Administrative Instructions.**

The following instructions are issued with reference to Divisional Operation Order No 8. of 7th instant.

- - -

Baggage Wagons. 1. ~~All baggage wagons of units will be loaded with their mobilization stores as for a move, and returned to the Divnl. Train by noon on 18th instant.~~ cancelled

Surplus Stores and Blankets. 2. Any surplus stores (including blankets) will be collected under Brigade arrangements (in the case of Infantry and R.A.) in selected buildings or barns in MAZINGARBE and NOEUX-LES-MINES, the following places excepted.-

The Abattoir at MAZINGARBE.

The Divnl. Bath House at NOEUX-LES-MINES.

The Divnl. Bomb School at NOEUX-LES-MINES.

The Salvage Coy. main store building at NOEUX-LES-MINES.

One building if possible, or 2 adjacent buildings, should be arranged for each Brigade. All arrangements to be completed, and blankets stored by noon, ~~18th instant~~ 4th day of bombardment.

A guard, rationed for 6 days, should be placed over the building.

Other units will make arrangements on similar lines near their present quarters.

Ordnance. 3. The D.A.D.O.S. will arrange to have all Ordnance Stores collected in the Depot at HESDIGNEUL ready to load on to Ordnance lorries by ~~18th instant~~. 4th day of bombardment -

Shops. 4. All regimental shops will be closed, and contents disposed of either under 1 or 2 above.

Laundry. 5. The Divisional Laundry will be closed from 17th inst., and arrangements made by A.D.M.S. in conjunction with D.A.D.O.S. for disposal of stock of underclothing, &c.

Bath House. 6. The Divisional Bath House will be closed from 8.p.m. 18th instant. The accessories will be stored and a caretaker left in charge, under arrangements to be made by A.D.M.S.

[signature]

Lieut Colonel.,

16.9.1915. A.A. & Q.M.G. 15th Division.

SECRET.

Administrative Instructions.

The following instructions are issued with reference to Divisional Operation Order No.8. of 7th instant.

Baggage Wagons.

1. The authorized contents of baggage wagons of 44th, 45th, and 46th Infantry Brigades, and 9th Gordon Hrs. (Pioneers), will be collected and stored in selected buildings, with the exceptions referred to in para 2 of the Instructions at MAZINGARBE and NOEUX-Les-MINES (for 45th Brigade and 9th Gordons), under Brigade arrangements. Baggage wagons of units will be used for facilitating this collection, and when it is completed, will be returned empty to Officer Commanding Divisional Train, who will arrange to Park them by Brigades, each under an A.S.C. Officer of the Train, in a position at NOEUX-LES-MINES which has been selected at L.7.c.

Baggage wagons of Artillery will remain with their Units.

Baggage wagons of other units will be sent to the Divisional Train loaded with their authorized contents by noon, on the fourth day of bombardment.

Surplus Stores & Blankets.

2. Any surplus stores (including blankets) will be collected under Brigade arrangements (in the case of Infantry and R.A.) in selected buildings or barns in MAZINGARBE and NOEUX-LES-MINES, the following places excepted :-

The Abattoir at MAZINGARBE.

The Divl. Bath House at NOEUX-LES-MINES.
The Divl. Bomb School at NOEUX-LES-MINES.

The Salvage Coy. mainstore building at NOEUX-LES-MINES.

One building if possible, or 2 adjacent buildings, should be arranged for each Brigade. All arrangements to be completed, and blankets stored by noon, 4th day of bombardment. A guard rationed for 6 days, should be placed over the building.

Other units will make arrangements on similar lines near their present quarters.

Ordnance. 3. The D.A.D.O.S. will arrange to have all Ordnance Stores collected in the Depot at HESDIGNEUL ready to load on to Ordnance lorries by 4th day of bombardment.

Shops. 4. All regimental shops will be closed, and contents disposed of either under 1 or 2 above.

Laundry. 5. The Divisional Laundry will be closed from 17th instant, and arrangements made by A.D.M.S. in conjunction with D.A.D.O.S. for disposal of stock of underclothing, etc.

Bath House. 6. The Divisional Bath House will be closed from 8 p.m. 18th instant. The accessories will be stored and a caretaker left in charge, under arrangements to be made by A.D.M.S.

14/9/15. E.T. Lt.Col.

A.A. & Q.M.G. 15th. Division.

S E C R E T.

With reference to Administrative Instructions issued on 14.9.1915, para 1 thereof is cancelled, and the following substituted.

Baggage Wagons. 1. The authorized contents of baggage wagons of 44th, 45th, and 46th Infantry Brigades, and 9th Gordon Hrs. (Pioneers), will be collected and stored in selected buildings, with the exceptions referred to in para 2 of the Instructions at MAZINGARBE and NOEUX-LES-MINES (for 45th Brigade and 9th Gordons), under Brigade arrangements. Baggage wagons of units will be used for facilitating this collection, and when it is completed, will be returned empty to Officer Commanding Divisional Train, who will arrange to Park them by Brigades, each under an A.S.C. officer of the Train, in a position at NOEUX-LES-MINES which has been selected at L.7.c.

Baggage wagons of Artillery will remain with their Units.

Baggage wagons of other units will be sent to the Divisional Train loaded with ~~its~~ their authorized contents by noon, on the fourth day of bombardment.

2. Para 2. and para 3. For 18th instant, read fourth day of bombardment.

Lieut Colonel.,

17. 9. 1915. A.A. & Q.M.G., 15th Division.

XII

SECRET. Copy No 1

15th Division Operation Order No 9.

~~15~~ 17th September, 1915.

The following orders are issued in continuation of Preliminary Operation Order No 8 of 7. 9. 15:-

Moves. 1. (a) On day before the Bombardment begins.

The two Battalions of the 45th Infantry Brigade now in front trenches will be relieved by Battalions of the 44th and 46th Infantry Brigades respectively, and will go into billets in NOEUX-les-MINES.

The Battalions of the 44th and 46th Infantry Brigades now in NOEUX-les-MINES will move up into MAZINGARBE or into the trenches of the GRENAY line as the G.Os.C. Brigades may decide.

These moves to be completed by 8:30 p m.

(b) On the second night of the bombardment:-

The Battalions of the 44th and 46th Infantry Brigades at VERQUIN and LABEUVRIERE respectively will move into their respective Brigade areas, east of the SAILLY line (inclusive), as follows:-

The 8th K.O.S.Bs will march by GOSNAY - HESDIGNEUL to the park at VAUDRICOURT and rest there. The march to be by platoons at suitable intervals and as far as possible off the roads to avoid aerial observation; to be completed by 10 a.m.

The 7th Camerons will march by the Red Road (see sketch App: 1), the head passing the cross roads S of VAUDRICOURT park (K.4 central) at 8 p.m.

The 8th K.O.S.Bs. will follow the 7th Camerons.

Brigades will issue their own orders as to the

destinations of these Battalions within their respective areas.

(N.B. The SAILLY line is divided between Brigades as shown on map (App:1').

(c) On the third night of the bombardment:-

The two Battalions of the 45th Infantry Brigade at LABEUVRIERE will move up into billets and bivouac in VAUDRICOURT and DROUVIN.

Route - GOSNAY - HESDIGNEUL.

To be clear of LABEUVRIERE by 7 p.m.

(d) On the last night of the bombardment:-

All troops will move into their forming up places, as follows:-

(i) 44th and 46th Infantry Brigades and attached troops to be clear of the 45th Infantry Brigade forming up area by midnight.

(ii) 45th Infantry Brigade to be in position by 4 a.m., using the Red Road (see sketch App:1).

(iii) H.Q., and "E" and "F" Companies, 9th Gordon Highlanders will march at 6:45 p.m. by the Red Road, (see sketch App:1), to their forming up place ~~as shown on sketch (App:1.)~~

(iv) Divisional Mounted Troops will march to their forming up places as shown, using either the Red Road or the main road.
Move to be after dark and to be completed by 10 p.m.

All troops whether in movement or at rest will use all available cover and take all possible precautions to guard against aerial observation.

R.E. and Pioneers. 2. 73rd Field Company R.E. and "G" Company 9th Gordon Highlanders are placed under orders of G.O.C. 44th Infantry Brigade from receipt of these orders, and 91st Field Company R.E. and "H" Company 9th Gordon Highlanders under orders of the G.O.C. 46th Infantry Brigade.

The 74th Field Company R.E. will be distributed under the orders of the C.R.E.

12 mins. gas — followed by

8 mins smoke "
(4 candles, 1 at a time in each partition)

12 minutes gas "

8 mins smoke
(4 candles, 1 at a time in each partition) "

assault

At 0.38 the smoke is to be thickened by the use of 2 candles + 1 triple candle in each partition.

In order that the gas may come as a complete surprise no candles, phosphor bombs, phosphor grenades, or [illegible] phosphor should be lighted or thrown before 12 mins after the discharge of gas begins

This procedure will be explained the day before the assault to every the men taking part in it.

Time of Assault. 3. The gas and smoke discharge will last exactly 40 minutes. The last two minutes will be smoke only, so as to cover the deployment and give the gas time to get well ahead.

The time for the assault will be taken from the Special Company R.E. (all of whom have watches which will be carefully set). The assault will take place at the end of the 40th minute.

The 40 minutes are allotted as follows:-

10 minutes gas followed by
4 minutes smoke " "
6 minutes gas " "
4 minutes smoke " "
14 minutes gas " "
2 minutes smoke.

This procedure will be explained on the day before the assault to the men taking part in it.

amended see 5-9-15 See slip.

Reserve. 4. The XIth Corps will be in reserve behind the IVth Corps with its leading troops about NOEUX-les-MINES.

First Line Transport. 5. (a) From the first day of the bombardment until the day of the assault (both inclusive) only such essential vehicles as G.Os.C. Brigades, the C.R.E., O.C. 9th Gordon Highlanders, or the A.D.M.S. may direct will be kept at, or brought up to, MAZINGARBE.

(b) No animals will be kept at MAZINGARBE during the four days bombardment, but a proportion of animals for the above vehicles (as few as possible) may be brought up on the night preceding the day of assault and placed under cover; the walled-in triangle south of MAZINGARBE Chateau being reserved for vehicles and animals of the 45th Infantry Brigade, LE SAULCHOY

FARM for those of the R.E., and the bit of road under the western wall of the Chateau garden for the 9th Gordon Highlanders.

(c) All other first line transport of the R.E., Infantry, 9th Gordon Highlanders, and Divisional Mounted Troops will be parked by the last night of the bombardment at NOEUX-les-MINES in the area shown on the attached map (App:1) under Brigade Transport Officers.

Regimental transport officers will be either at NOEUX-les-MINES or MAZINGARBE, as the commanders mentioned in (a) may direct.

A mounted or cyclist orderly from the first line transport of each Infantry Brigade and from Divisional Train (see para:7) will be at the White House in NOEUX-les-MINES at 6 p.m. on the last day of the bombardment.

Brigade & Divisional Amm; Cols.

6. The Field Artillery Brigade Ammunition Columns will get into touch with the Brigade S.A.A. reserves of the Infantry Brigades which they supply, viz:- 70th with 44th, ~~71st~~ 72nd with 45th, ~~72nd~~ 71st with 46th.

The Divisional Ammunition Column will remain at HESDIGNEUL.

<u>Divisional Train.</u>

7. The Divisional Train will remain at HESDIGNEUL and GOSNAY.

<u>Fld. Ambs & Medical.</u>

8. (a) On the night preceding the bombardment Dressing Stations will be established as follows:-

Advanced Dressing Station.	QUALITY STREET.	1 bearer Sub Div. 46th Fld. Amb.
" " "	FOSSE 7	1 bearer Sub Div. 47th Fld. Amb.
Dressing Station	BREWERY, PHILOSOPHE.	1 tent Sub. Div. 46th ~~47th~~ Fld. Amb.

(b) On the last night of the bombardment, the medical arrangements as shown in App: (iii) will be completed.

Veterinary. 9. The A.D.V.S. will establish an advanced Collecting Station at the Mine, VERQUIN. The present collecting Station at HESDIGNEUL will remain open.

Supply of S.A.A. during action. 10. The trench depots of S.A.A. in the areas of the 44th and 46th Infantry Brigades will be regarded as S.A.A. reserves for those Brigades to supplement the ordinary Battalion and Brigade supply, and arrangements made by Brigades to forward ammunition from them.

The reserve at QUALITY STREET will be regarded as a forward "dump" from, [illegible], the Brigade Ammunition Columns and will be drawn on under Brigade arrangements.

The 44th Infantry Brigade will detail an officer to take charge of this reserve on the day of assault; ~~who~~ This officer will arrange with the Brigade Ammunition Columns for ~~its~~ the replenishment of the reserve.

Trench traffic arrangements. 11. Trenches will be reserved as follows:-

(a) For "up" traffic only:-

"Northern Up", 15, 14, 14a.

"Southern Up", 1a.

(b) For "down" traffic only:-

6- 31 through QUALITY STREET, -12 as far as junction with 15.

N.B. 12, west of junction with 15, is available for both "up" and "down" traffic.

(c) For casualties only:-

New ~~casualty~~ evacuation trench from 8c; ~~2.~~ trench 2

Troops in occupation will be responsible for policing these trenches.

Staff Officers and linemen repairing lines will be allowed to use communication trenches in any direction.

<u>Amendments.</u> 12. The following amendments will be made to 15th Divisional Preliminary Operation Order No 8 of 7. 9. 15.

(a) Last line of para:3, after "bis" add "(inclusive)".

(b) Para:13. The 5th objective assigned to the 46th Infantry Brigade should read:- "Line from H.31 central to PUITS No 14 bis (exclusive)".

(c) Para: 15 Delete last two lines and substitute "and E and F Companies 9th Gordon Highlanders and 74th Field Company R.E. will await orders in their forming up places" (see sketch App:1).

(d) Para:18 (a). Note at foot of page:- The 1st Division will also use a black screen with white diagonal stripe for a special bomb supply party.

(omit)

(e) Para: 18 (b). Delete 1st para: and substitute:- "720 Ball Grenades packed in boxed (which can be carried by one man) and 40 rifle grenades are stored in each of the 4 forward trench depots (see map, App: 2). 500 Battye Grenades similarly packed and 40 rifle grenades are stored in each of the QUALITY KEEPS, SOUTH, EAST and NORTH.

These are for use as Brigade reserves.

Grenades will be forwarded under Divisional arrangements from the Divisional Reserve at MAZINGARBE to Brigade Dumps, on demand.

(f) Para:21 (b) line 5. Delete "Sheet 36.C" and substitute "Sheets 36C and 36B, and the LENS sheet 1/100,000".

<u>Y.H. & Y.1.</u> 12 13. The G.O.C. 1st Division will take over command of the Y.O. - Y.1 front at 6 p.m. on the third day of the bombardment. 23rd

<u>Refilling Point.</u> 13 14. The refilling point for supplies will remain at HESDIGNEUL Common and for ammunition at HESDIGNEUL Racecourse till further notice.

Reports. ~~15.~~ 14 Reports to VAUDRICOURT to 6 p.m. on last day of bombardment, after that hour to MAZINGARBE BOULEVARD.

J Burnett Stuart
Lieut Colonel.
General Staff.

Issued at 10 am
through ~~Signals~~. Maj Henderson & Lt Lace.

Copies to

Divl. Mtd. Troops. (As for Preliminary op order)
Divl. Artillery.
C.R.E.
44th Inf. Bde.
45th Inf. Bde.
46th Inf. Bde.
9th Gordons.
A.D.M.S.
4th Army Corps.
1st Division.
47th Division.

15th Division G/915.

SECRET.

In consequence of later instructions received from the Corps, paragraph 3 of Operation Order No 9 of 17. 9. 15 will be amended as follows:-

Delete from line 9 to the end of para:& substitute:-

"The 40 minutes will be allotted as follows:-

12 minutes gas ....followed by

8 minutes smoke.
(4 candles, one at a time
in each partition).......... " "

12 minutes gas.................... " "

8 minutes smoke.
(4 candles, one at a time
in each partition).......... " "

Assault.

At "0.38" the smoke is to be thickened by the use of 2 candles and one triple candle in each partition.

In order that the gas may come as a complete surprise, no candles, phosphor bombs, phosphor grenades or free phosphor should be lighted or thrown before 12 minutes after the discharge of gas begins.

This procedure will be explained the day before the assault to the men taking part in it".

Major. G.S.
for Lieut Colonel,
General Staff.

Issued at 5.40pm

through Signals to

Mounted Troops.
Divl. Artillery.
C.R.E.
Infantry Brigades.
9th Gordons.
IVth Corps.
1st Division.
47th Division.

Acknowledged

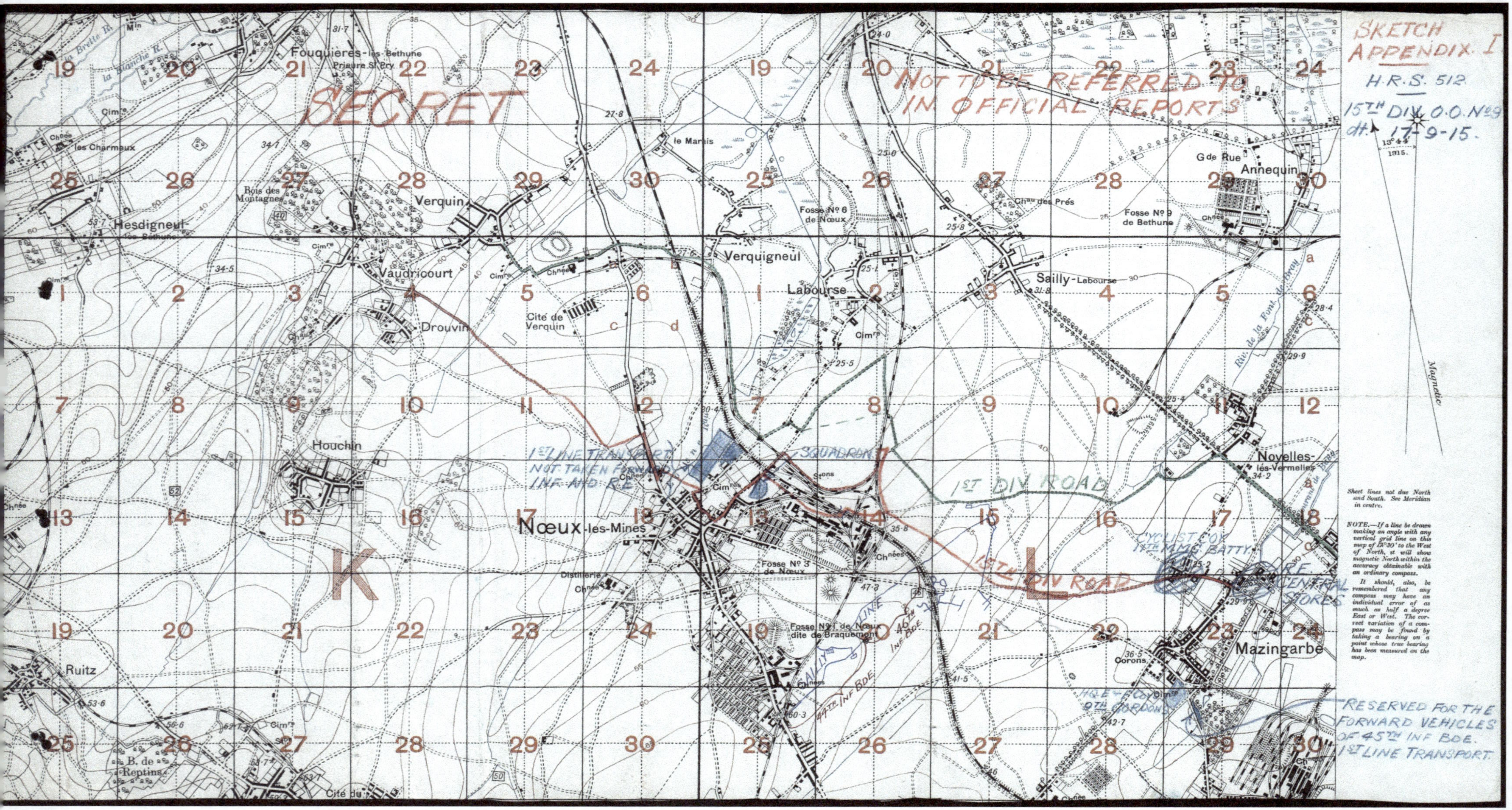
SKETCH APPENDIX. I
H.R.S. 512
15TH DIV O.O. No 9
dt. 17-9-15.
SECRET
NOT TO BE REFERRED TO IN OFFICIAL REPORTS
Magnetic
13°44'
1915.
Sheet lines not due North and South. See Meridian in centre.
NOTE.—If a line be drawn making an angle with any vertical grid line on this map of 12°30' to the West of North, it will show magnetic North within the accuracy obtainable with an ordinary compass.
It should, also, be remembered that any compass may have an individual error of as much as half a degree East or West. The correct variation of a compass may be found by taking a bearing on a point whose true bearing has been measured on the map.
RESERVED FOR THE FORWARD VEHICLES OF 45TH INF BDE. 1ST LINE TRANSPORT.
1ST LINE TRANSPORT NOT TAKEN FORWARD INF AND R.E.
SQUADRON
1ST DIV ROAD
15TH DIV ROAD
CYCLIST COY 15TH MMG BATTY
R.E. CENTRAL STORES
H.Q. & 4 COYS 9TH GORDONS
44TH INF BDE
46TH INF BDE
K
L
Fouquières-lès-Bethune
Prieuré St Pry
Verquin
Vaudricourt
Drouvin
Cité de Verquin
Houchin
Nœux-les-Mines
Distillerie
Fosse No 3 de Nœux
Fosse No 1 de Nœux dite de Braquemont
Fosse No 6 de Nœux
Fosse No 9 de Bethune
Verquigneul
Labourse
Sailly-Labourse
Chau des Prés
Gde Rue
Annequin
le Marais
Noyelles-lès-Vermelles
Mazingarbe
Corons
Hesdigneul-lès-Bethune
Bois des Montagnes
les Charmaux
Ruitz
B. de Reptins
Cité du
Rau de la Font de Bray
la Blanche R.
la Brette R.

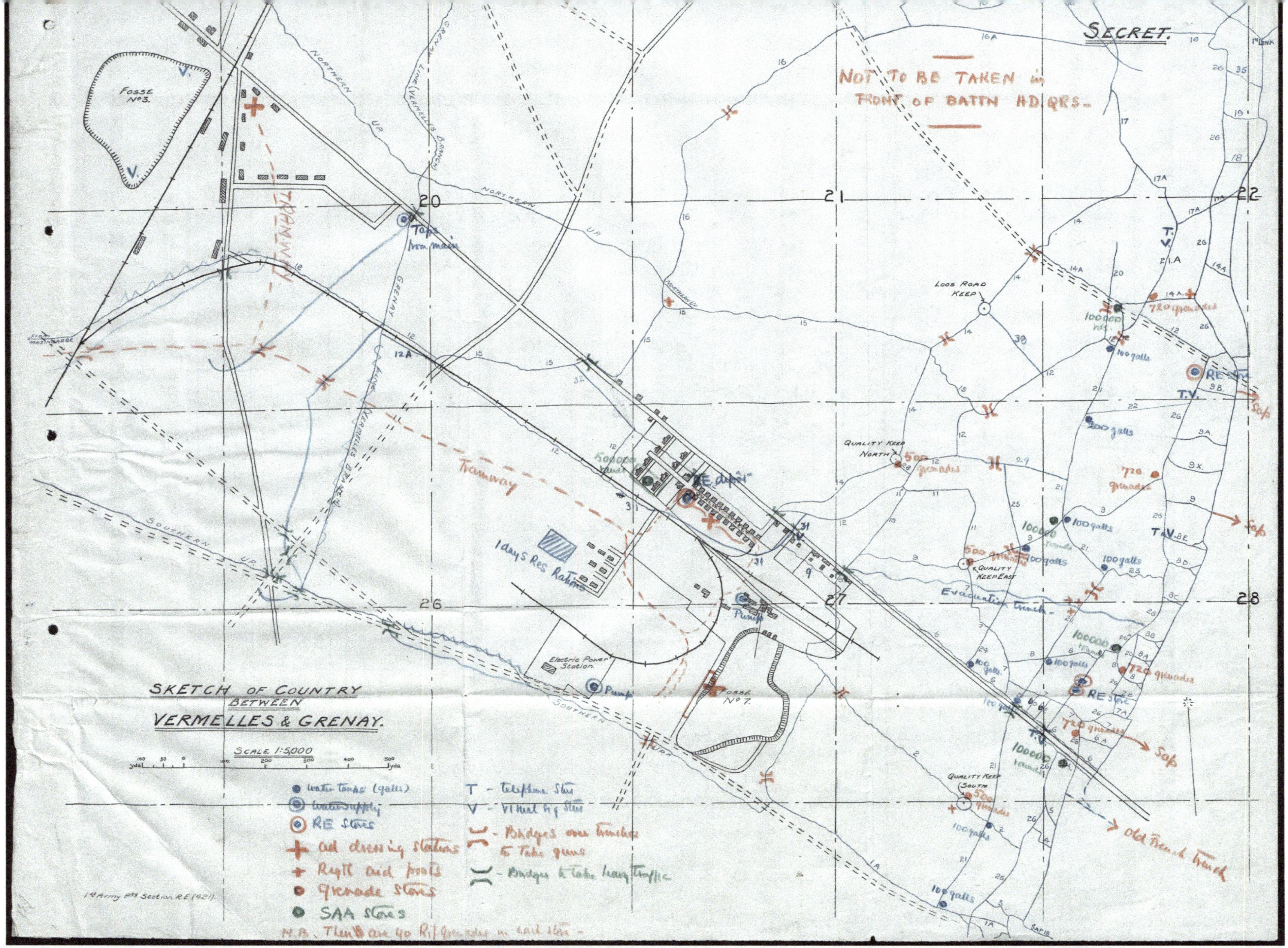
SECRET.
NOT TO BE TAKEN in FRONT OF BATTN HD. QRS.
SKETCH OF COUNTRY BETWEEN VERMELLES & GRENAY.
SCALE 1:5000
Fosse No3.
Fosse No7.
Loos Road Keep
Quality Keep North
Quality Keep East
Quality Keep South
Electric Power Station
Evacuation trench
Tramway
1 days Res Rations
RE depôt
Taps from main
Old French trench
Sap
water tanks (galls)
water supply
RE Stores
Advd dressing stations
Regtl aid posts
Grenade Stores
SAA Stores
T - telephone Stn
V - Vi[illegible] Stn
Bridges over trenches to take guns
Bridges to take heavy traffic
N.B. There are 40 Rif. Grenades in each store.
1st Army Ptg Section R.E. (421).

"A" Form.

Army Form C. 2121.

MESSAGES AND SIGNALS.

No. of Message

Prefix Code m. / Office of Origin and Service Instructions	Words / Charge / Sent At m. To By	This message is on a/c of: Secret Service. (Signature of "Franking Officer.")	Recd. at m. Date From By
[illegible]			

TO				
	Mtd Tps.	44th Inf Bde	9th Gordons	1st Div
	Div Art.	45th —	ADMS	47th Div
	CRE	46th —	4th Corps	Q A & Dmg [illegible]

* Sender's Number	Day of Month	In reply to Number	AAA
G 952	20		

The position of SAA Stores in the trenches are as shown on the attached tracing and not as shown on appendix 2 of operation order No 9 of 17-9-15

From 15th Div

Place

Time 10-20 pm

The above may be forwarded as now corrected. (Z) [illegible] Major GS

Censor. Signature of Addressor or person authorised to telegraph in his name.

* This line should be erased if not required.

(15491) S & Co Ltd. W 14142/641 20,000. 4/15. Forms C 2121/10.

13th DIV. No G. 952. dt. 20-9-15

SECRET.

"A" Form. Army Form C. 2121.

MESSAGES AND SIGNALS. No. of Message

Prefix ... Code ... m.	Words	Charge	This message is on a/c of:	Recd. at ... m.
Office of Origin and Service Instructions. SECRET	Sent At ... m. To ... By ...		... Service. (Signature of "Franking Officer.")	Date ... From ... By ...

TO

Sender's Number.	Day of Month.	In reply to Number	AAA
* G874	17th.		

With reference to 15th Div Operation Orders No 8 of 7-9-15 and No 9 of 17-9-15;
(1) The first day of the bombardment will be September 21st
(2) The cylinders will therefore be put into the trenches on the nights of 18/19th 19th/20th 20/21st.
(3) The assault will take place on the 25th.

From 15th Div.
Place
Time

The above may be forwarded as now corrected. (Z)

Censor. Signature of Addressor or person authorised to telegraph in his name. Montagu Stuart Lt Col G.S.

* This line should be erased if not required.

(B10. 11)—Wt. W 14142/61—2,000,000—3/15. S. & S., Ltd.

...GES AND SIGNALS. No. of Message

Prefix Code m.	Words	Charge	This message is on a/c of:	Recd. at m.
Office of Origin and Service Instructions	Sent		Secret	Date
BRLS	At m.		Service.	From
	To			
	By		(Signature of "Franking Officer.")	By

TO All recipients of Opⁿ Order No 9. of 17 9/15

Sender's Number	Day of Month	In reply to Number	AAA
G 903	18		

With reference to 15th Div Operation Order No 9 of 17.9.15

(1) Bde and Bn HQ will ~~be provided with~~ take the following maps in addition to those mentioned in para 21(3) of Operation Order ~~of~~ No 8 of 7.9.15

1/100,000. Sheets 5.5a, 12.

(2) App III of Opⁿ Order No 9 is cancelled and the attached Appendix III is substituted.

From 15 Div.

Place

Time 1030 pm

The above may be forwarded as now corrected. (Z)

Censor. Signature of Addressor or person authorised to telegraph in his name

*This line should be erased if not required.

5762 M. & Co. Ltd. Wt. W929/549—100,000. 6/14. Forms C2121/10.

"A" Form.

Army Form C. 2121.

MESSAGES AND SIGNALS.

No. of Message

Prefix Code m. Words Charge

Office of Origin and Service Instructions.

DRLS

Sent At m. To By

This message is on a/c of: Secret Service.

(Signature of "Franking Officer.")

Recd. at m. Date From By

TO IVth Corps ~~AAG Inds~~ ~~First Div~~ 47th Div

Sender's Number.	Day of Month.	In reply to Number	AAA
* 4903	18		

With reference to 15th Div operation order No 9 of 17-9-15

(1) Bde & Bn H.Q. will take the following maps in addition to those mentioned in para: 21 (b) of operation order No 8 of 7-9-15 1/100,000 sheets 5, 5a, 12.

(2) App III of operation order No 9. is cancelled and the attached appendix III is substituted

From 15th Div.

Place

Time 10.30 pm

The above may be forwarded as now corrected.

(Z) [signature] Major GS.

Censor. Signature of Addressor or person authorised to telegraph in his name.

* This line should be erased if not required.

(B10(11)—Wt. W 14142/611—2,000,000—8/15. S. & S., Ltd.

MEDICAL ARRANGEMENTS ON DAY OF ASSAULT. APP. (iii). SECRET

	Station.	Personnel.	Situation.	Remarks.
45th Field Ambulance.	(a) Adv. Dressing Station.	(a) 2 bearer Sub. Divns.	(a) Abbatoir, MAZINGARBE.	To be in reserve; orders as to disposal will be issued by the A.D.M.S.
	(b) Main " " and Hd. Qrs.	(b) 2 tent " "	(b) NOEUX-les-MINES (1) Bomb School. (2) Salvage Coy buildings. (3) Mairie. (4) Divl.Bath Hse.	At NOEUX-les-MINES a complete section is to be ready to move at a moments notice on receipt of orders. Ambulances at NOEUX-les-MINES Dressing Station.
46th Field Ambulance.	(a) Adv. Dressing Station.	(a) Bearer Division.	(a) QUALITY STREET.	Will receive wounded and sick for further evacuation by Motor Ambulance Convoy to Casualty Clearing Stations.
	(b) Rest Post and Divl. Collecting Station.	(b) 1 Tent Sub. Div. No 32 Sanitary Section.	(b) BREWERY, PHILOSOPHE.	Ambulances at NOEUX-les-MINES.
	(c) Main Dressing Station.	(c) 2 Tent Sub.Divns.	(c) VAUDRICOURT.	
47th Field Ambulance.	(a) Adv. Dressing Station.	(a) Bearer Division.	(a) FOSSE 7	Will receive wounded & sick for further evacuation by Motor Ambulance Convoy to Casualty Clearing Stations.
	(b) Main " "	(b) Tent "	(b) NOEUX-les-MINES (Schools now occupied)	Ambulances at Abbatoir, MAZINGARBE.

"A" Form.　　　　　　　　　　　　　　　　Army Form C. 2121.

MESSAGES AND SIGNALS.　　　　No. of Message..........

Prefix........ Code........ m. Office of Origin and Service Instructions.	Words	Charge	This message is on a/c of:	Recd. at........ m.
Special DR [?]	Sent At........m. To........ By........		SECRET Service. (Signature of "Franking Officer.")	Date........ From........ By........

TO ~~44th I Bde~~ [?] ~~45th~~ [?] 46th [?]

Sender's Number.	Day of Month.	In reply to Number	AAA
* G 905	17th		

Reference Bde Operation Order No. 9 of the 17th inst para 6 aaa 72nd Bde Amm Col will supply 45th I Bde and 71st Bde Amm Col will supply 46th I Bde aaa Please amend accordingly aaa Addressed all Bdes repeated Div Art. aaa Acknowledge

784

From	15th Div.
Place	
Time	9.5 am

The above may be forwarded as now corrected.　(Z)　J Burnett Stuart [?] Lt Col.

Censor.　Signature of Addressor or person authorised to telegraph in his name.

* This line should be erased if not required.

(B10 11)—Wt. W 14142/G.1—2,000,000—8/15. S. & S., Ltd.

15th Division G/908. App XIV

SECRET.

44th Infantry Brigade.
45th " "
46th " "

Herewith map showing the Corps arrangements regarding the lifting of Artillery fire during the various stages of the Infantry Attack.

not attached. This will be with War Diary of IV Corps Artillery

2. "0" is the moment at which the discharge of smoke and gas begins.

"0.40" is the moment at which the Infantry assault commences.

3. After "1.15" the Artillery will lift its fire in accordance with the requirements of the Infantry and the general situation.

4. Should the Infantry attack be checked at any period prior to "1.15", and more Artillery preparation of any particular locality be required, a special bombardment of this locality may be demanded. This may entail an alteration of the programme shown on the map, in which case the sanction of the Corps Commander will have to be obtained. The Infantry will be informed whether the special bombardment will take place, and the precise hour at which it will cease.

5. Any special bombardment asked for before or after "1.15" will last exactly 30 minutes of which the last 5 minutes will be intense. The Officer asking for a special bombardment should specify the hour at which he wishes it to start; if the message reaches the Artillery in time the bombardment will start at that hour; but if the message is late in arriving the 30 minutes bombardment will be reckoned from the time it was asked for - that is the actual bombardment will only last for the unexpired portion of the 30 minutes, and will cease at the 30th minute from the time it should have started - the last five minutes being intense in every case.

Sd. J. Burnett-Stuart

Lieut Colonel,

19th September, 1915. General Staff.

SECRET

HEADQUARTERS 4th CORPS
18 SEP 1915
GENERAL STAFF

IVth Corps No. H.R.S. 517

~~IVth Corps Artillery.~~
~~1st Division.~~
15th Division.
~~47th Division.~~
~~1st Corps.~~)
~~No.1 Group H.A.R.~~) For information.

Sent out

Copy of map in out file 1183

1919

Herewith map showing the Corps arrangements regarding the "lifting" of artillery fire during the various stages of the infantry attack.

2. 0 is the moment at which the discharge of gas and smoke begins.

0.40 the moment at which the infantry assault commences.

3. After 1.15 the artillery will lift its fire in accordance with the requirements of the infantry and of the general situation.

4. Should the infantry attack be checked at any period prior to 1.15, and more artillery preparation of any particular locality be required, a special bombardment of this locality may be demanded. This will in all probability entail a departure from the Corps programme shown on the map.

5. If such is the case, sanction will be obtained from the Corps Artillery Commander before such bombardment is arranged by the Divisional Artillery Group Commander. The infantry will then be informed that the re-bombardment will take place and definitely when it will end.

6. Such re-bombardment will consist of a bombardment of 30 minutes, the last five minutes of which will be intense.

7./

7. The infantry must be prepared to take instant advantage of this bombardment the moment the intense period ceases.

8. Application for artillery fire on any locality so long as it does not entail a departure from the Corps artillery programme need not be referred to the Corps Artillery Commander, but will be dealt with by the Commander of the Divisional Artillery Group concerned.

R A K Montgomery

H.Q.1Vth Corps. Brigadier General.

18th September, 1915. General Staff, 1Vth Corps.

Reference Trench Map.
36.c.S.W.1.
1/100,000 LENS map.

Copy No 1

SECRET.

15th Division Operation Order No.10.

21. 9. 15.

1. Paragraph 16 of Preliminary Operation Order No 8 of September 7th is amplified as follows:-

(a) The third objective of the 44th Infantry Brigade will be LOOS VILLAGE, less the buildings in G.35.b.2.2. and d.1.8., and the new school at G.35.d.7.8., all of which are allotted as objectives to 47th Division.

(b) The second objective of the 46th Infantry Brigade will be extended northwards so as to include the road junction at G.29.b.2.9.; a bombing squad will be detailed to work up from that point along the trench called "NORTH LOOS AVENUE" to connect with the grenadiers of the 2nd Brigade who will be working down it.

2. The objectives allotted to the Division (see paragraph 2 of Divisional Preliminary Operation Order No 8 of September 7th) are now extended to include:-

(e) CITE ST. AUGUSTE.

(f) High ground north of LOISON-SOUS-LENS.

It is the intention of the Divisional Commander to push on to these objectives with all the offensive power of the Division.

Brigade and Battalion Commanders will therefore be prepared to act in accordance with this intention.

The Brigade which first reaches HILL 70 will be responsible for detailing a sufficient force to consolidate and hold it, until troops from the Divisional Reserve can be pushed up to take it over.

The remaining troops will go forward with their left on the road marked "Metalled but poor"; the German third line trenches in front of the FME.DES MINES DE LENS and of the CITE ST. AUGUSTE will be their next objective, and the high ground north of LOISON-SOUS-LENS their final objective.

The 1st Division on our left will cooperate in this advance, moving with its right through the BOIS HUGO, and directed on PONT-A-VENDIN.

The Heavy Artillery will continue to shell the German trenches from the Dynamitiere in N.1. central to N.2.b. and thence northwards, during and after the lifting of the Corps Artillery fire from the "1.15" line; and batteries of the Divisional Artillery will be brought forward in support.

The development of this operation depends on events, but it is essential that all Commanders should know the intention of the General Commanding, so that the forward movement may be maintained with determination and confidence.

3. (a) The Artillery of the 1st., 15th., and 47th Divisions, 4 batteries of 6" Howitzers., 2 batteries (4.5) 109th Brigade, and 2 batteries (18 pr.) 107th Brigade, divided into three Divisional Groups will be under the command of Brigadier General Budworth M.V.O., and will support the 1st., 15th., and 47th Divisions in their respective attacks under instructions already issued.

(b) The following guns of the 1st Group H.A.R. also will carry out the bombardment and support the attacks of the 1st., 15th., and 47th Divisions:-

1 15" Howitzer.
4 9.2" Howitzers.
8. 8" do.
4 6" Mark VII Guns.
7 batteries 60 prs. (28 guns).
3 " 4.7" (12 guns).
2 9.2" guns on railway trucks.
4 batteries 18 prs. (24th Div.)

(c) Several batteries of the French Heavy Artillery will also cooperate.

(d) As soon as possible after the German advanced trenches have been captured, the Divisional Artillery will be placed again under the direct control of the Divisional Commander. Two batteries of 6" Howitzers will be allotted to the 15th Division at the same time.

[signature]
Lieut Colonel,
General Staff.

Issued at 11-20 am
through Signals to
A.
Mounted Troops.
Divl. Artillery.
C.R.E.
44th, 45th &46th Inf. Bdes.
9th Gordons.
A.D.M.S.
Copies to
IVth Corps.
1st Division.
47th Division.
No 1 Group H.A.R.
~~IVth Corps Artillery.~~

– as for Prelim op order + to No 1 group HAR.

Copy No 1

15th Division Operation order No. 11.
27th Sept, 1915

1 The Division (less the Artillery which still remains in action, and the Fld. Ambs:) will move tomorrow into billets and bivouacs at DROUVIN, HOUCHIN and HAILLICOURT, and become G.H.Q reserve.

2. Billeting areas are allotted as follows:-
DROUVIN to RE. and Divl: Mtd Tps.
HOUCHIN to 44th Inf Bde and 9th Gordon Hdrs.
HAILLICOURT to 45th and 46th Inf Bdes.

3. The route will be by the Red Road as far as NOEUX-LES-MINES; thence direct to HOUCHIN and DROUVIN; and to HAILLICOURT ~~and~~ VIA HOUCHIN and through ~~E/~~ F of FOUR-A-CHAUX.

4. The road from NOEUX-LES-MINES through K.17.d - 16 d, 15. central, 14 b, 13 a, will not be used.

5. The 45th Inf Bde less two battns will march off from MAZINGARBE at 9 a.m; the two Battns at NOEUX will march at the same time.

6. The 44th Inf Bde and 9th Gordons will leave MAZINGARE at 9-30 am.

The 46th Inf Bde will leave MAZINGARBE at 10-30 am.

2

R.E. will leave MAZINGARBE at 11-15 a.m.
Div. Mtd Tps " " " " noon.
First Line Transport will accompany Units.

7. Refilling point tomorrow – HESDIGNEUL at 11am.

8. Divl Hd. Qrs will close at MAZINGARBE and open at DROUVIN CHATEAU. at noon.

[signature] Lt Col
GS

Issued at 3-45 pm.
Through Signals.

Copies to.

1.		
2	1	Mtd Tps.
3	2	Divl Artillery
4	3	CRE.
5	4	44th Inf Bde.
6	5	45th " "
7	6	46th " "
8	7	A.D.M.S.
9	8	
10	9	4th Corps.
11	10	~~G.H.Q.~~ War Diary
12		"A"
13		Signals
14		Train.

Prefix .... Code .... m.	Words	Charge	This message is on a/c of:	Recd. at .... m.
Office of Origin and Service Instructions	Sent		.... Service.	Date
	At .... m.			From
	To			
	By		(Signature of "Franking Officer.")	By

TO { Div Mtd Trps — 44th Inf Bde — 9th Gordons
RA — 45th " — ADMS — IVth Corps
CRE — 46th " — Train — Signals }

Sender's Number	Day of Month	In reply to Number	AAA
* G 118	27		

Ref 15th Div Operation order No 11 of today AAA It has been found necessary to alter the billeting arrangements of the REs as follows AAA Major [illegible]'s company will billet at Houchin with the 44th Bde and Major Mahon and Major Pollard Lowsley's Coys at Haillicourt with the 45th and 46th Bdes respectively AAA Bdes will allot accommodation accordingly AAA The RE will march independently as stated in the order AAA addressed all recipients of operation order

From 15th Div
Place
Time 8.35 pm

The above may be forwarded as now corrected. (Z)

.... Censor.

(Sd) J S Burnett-Stuart
Lt Col GS

Signature of Addressor or person authorised to telegraph in his name.

* This line should be erased if not required.

(15491) S. & Co. Ltd. W 14142/641. 90,000. 4/15. Forms C 2121/10.

15th Division G/167.

XVI

SPECIAL DIVISIONAL ORDER.

The following message has been received from Sir Henry Rawlinson:-

"The Corps Commander is anxious that you should communicate to all ranks of the 15th Division his high appreciation of the admirable fighting spirit which they displayed in the attack and capture of LOOS Village and HILL 70.

Sir Douglas Haig has also desired the Corps Commander to convey his congratulations to the Division ".

The Major General Wishes to say that he is very proud of his Command.

(Sd) J.S. Burnett-Stuart

Lieut Colonel,

27th September, 1915. General Staff.

IVth Corps No. 1082

Special Divisional order

15th Division.

The following message has been received ~~from the Corps Commander~~ from Sir Henry Rawlinson :—

" The Corps Commander is anxious that you should communicate to all ranks of the 15th Division his high appreciation of the admirable fighting spirit which they displayed in the attack and capture of LOOS Village and HILL 70.

Sir Douglas Haig has also desired the Corps Commander to convey his congratulations to the Division."

[signature]

Brigadier General.

27th September, 1915.

General Staff, IVth Corps.

The Major Gen. wishes to say that he is very proud of his Command.

15th Division G/989.

S E C R E T .

C.R.E.
44th Inf. Bde.
45th Inf. Bde.
46th Inf. Bde.
9th Gordon Hdrs.

The 2nd. French Cavalry Corps will wear helmets without crests. The helmet is covered by a cover of the same colour as the uniform.

To avoid all danger of mistakes, the alteration in uniform will be communicated to all ranks.

H.F.BAILLIE. Major, G.S.,
15th Division.

22nd. September 1915.

A to see.

seen

Special Order of the Day.

The Field-Marshal Commanding-in-Chief has received the following message from Field-Marshal Right Hon. H.H. Earl Kitchener of Khartoum, Secretary of State for War:—

To—

27th September, 1915.

"SIR JOHN FRENCH,

General Headquarters.

My warmest congratulations to you and all serving under you on the substantial success you have achieved and my best wishes for the progress of your important operations.

KITCHENER."

Distribution as Intelligence Summaries

1st Printing Co., R.E. G.H.Q. 1612

G. 755.
G. 977.
G. 12.
G. 13.
G. 14.
G. 28.

(<u>Note:</u> All G. Papers mentioned in the Diary with the exception of G. 755, G. 977 and G. 28 are <u>MISSING</u>)

"A" Form. Army Form C. 2121.

MESSAGES AND SIGNALS.

No. of Message ______

Prefix ______ Code ______ m. | Words | Charge

Office of Origin and Service Instructions

Sent
At ______ m.
To ______
By ______

This message is on a/c of:
______ *Service.*
(Signature of "Franking Officer.")

Recd. at ______ m.
Date ______
From ______
By ______

TO
45th I. Bde.
44th I. Bde.
46th I. Bde.

Sender's Number	Day of Month	In reply to Number	AAA
* G 755	10th		

On 12th inst. 45th Bde will place one Battn at disposal of 44th Bde and one at disposal of 46th Bde. ~~AAA~~ for duty in the front line AAA Battns of 44th and 46th Bdes thus released will go into billets in 45th Bde. area and come under ~~Command~~ 45th Bde for purposes of accommodation only AAA details will be arranged between Bde. commanders concerned. AAA Addressed 45th 44th & 46th Bdes.

A/Tosell. 9/ [illegible]

From 15th Div
Place
Time 9.38 am

The above may be forwarded as now corrected. (Z)
______ *Censor*

Signature of Addressor or person authorised to telegraph in his name. [illegible]

* This line should be erased if not required.

(15491) S. & Co. Ltd. W 14142/641. 90,000. 4/15. Forms C 2121/10.

15th Division G.977.

SECRET.

187 Coy. R.E.

1. The 187 Coy. R.E. will move to MAZINGARBE on the 24th inst. to billets arranged by 44th Infantry Brigade.
The company will march by the RED ROAD in small parties at suitable intervals so as to escape as far as possible aerial observation.
The march to be completed by 10 a.m.

2. The sections under Lieutenants Thomas and Walker, and 2nd Lieutenant Lefebure with half his section will meet an officer and guides detailed by 44th Infantry Brigade at MAZINGARBE CHATEAU ~~AVENUE~~ at 5 p.m. on the 24th., and will move,

(a) by trenches 12-31-9,
(b) then by 2 for Lieutenant Thomas' section, and by 36 for Lieutenant Walkers and 2nd Lt Lefebure's half section.

3. The remainder of 2nd Lieutenant Lefebure's Section, and the sections under Lieutenants Smeaton, Charles, and Shalcross will assemble 5 minutes before the hour of starting at MAZINGARBE CHURCH where they will be met by guides as below:-

(a) Men for bays 116-8 will be met by guides of the 10th Bn. Sco. Rif.; hour of start 5.0.p.m.
(b) Men for bays 10-36 will be met by guides of the 7th Bn. Sco. Bord.; hour of start 5.10.p.m.
(c) Men for bays 41-99 will be met by guides of the 12th Bn. High. L.I.; hour of start 5.20.p.m.

The 46th Infantry Brigade will arrange the routes to be followed.

4. Table showing allotment of Bays is attached.

5. After the leading Brigades have advanced to the assault, the sections of 187 Coy. R.E. will move under their own officers using trenches 2, 6, and 36 to QUALITY STREET whence they will proceed to billets at MAZINGARBE, either across the open or by trench 12.

Major, G.S.
15th Division.

21st September 1915.

Copies to 44th Infantry Brigade.
" " 46th Infantry Brigade.

		BAYS. 15th Div. Nos.	187 Coy. R.E. Nos.	Section of 187 Coy.
44th Infantry Brigade.	10th Bn Gordon Highlrs.	4 to 50	1 to 14	Lieut. Thomas.
		52 to 59	15 to 17	Lieut. Walker.
	9th Bn Black Watch.	61 to 85	18 to 26	
		88 and 91	27 and 28	
	8th Bn Seaforth Highlrs.	94 to 112	29 to 35	Half 2/Lieut. Lefebure's Section.
46th Infantry Brigade.	10th Bn Sco. Rif.	116 to 133	36 to 42	Half 2/Lieut. Lefebure's Section.
		1 to 8	43 to 46	Lieut. Smeaton.
	7th Bn K.O. Sco. Bord.	10 to 26	47 to 56	
		28 to 36	57 to 61	Lieut. Charles.
		41 to 61	62 to 70	
	12th Bn High, L&I	64 to 99	71 to 83	Lieut. Shalcross.

Sent to Sanders (187 C).

Prefix ____ Code ____ m. | Words | Charge | This message is on a/c of: ____ Service. | Recd. at ____ m. | Date | From | By

Office of Origin and Service Instructions.

DRLS

Sent At ____ m. To By

(Signature of "Franking Officer.")

TO 44 Inf Bde / 45 " " / 46 " " / Dvl. Art. / 9th Gordons

Sender's Number	Day of Month	In reply to Number	AAA
G12	23		

HQ of Inf Bdes Div Art and 9th Gordons will send an Officer to Adv. HQ to check watches at 6 pm 24th aaa Watches will be checked again by telephone at 3.am 25th except in case of 9th Gordons

From 15 Div

Place

Time 6.0 pm

The above may be forwarded as now corrected. (Z) E. [illegible] Maj GS

Censor. Signature of Addressor or person authorised to telegraph in his name

*This line should be erased if not required.

Prefix ____ Code ____ m. | Words | Charge | This message is on a/c of: SECRET Service. | Recd. at ____ m. | Date | From | By

Office of Origin and Service Instructions.

DRLS

Sent At ____ m. To By

(Signature of "Franking Officer.")

TO ADMS / 44 Inf Bde / 46 Inf Bde

Sender's Number	Day of Month	In reply to Number	AAA
G.13	23		

RAMC personnel to complete Advanced Dressing stations at QUALITY ST and FOSSE 7 to 1 Bearer Div each will move by trench 12 entering trench at MAZINGARBE at 8.30 pm on 24th aaa addressed ADMS repeated 44 and 46 IB

A to See [illegible]

From 15 Div

Place

Time 6.30 pm

The above may be forwarded as now corrected. (Z) E. [illegible] Maj GS

Censor. Signature of Addressor or person authorised to telegraph in his name

*This line should be erased if not required.

5

Prefix ______ Code ______ m. | Words | Charge | This message is on a/c of: ______ Service. | Recd. at ______ m. | Date | From | By

Office of Origin and Service Instructions. | Sent At ______ m. To By | (Signature of "Franking Officer.")

TO F Trench Battery
Dist Mtd Troops

Sender's Number	Day of Month	In reply to Number	AAA
G 14	~~23~~ 24		

F Trench Battery will move ~~to-day~~ to the forming up place allotted to the 11th M.M.G. Battery at which it will remain attached aaa

Addsd F Trench Batty and Dist Mtd Troops

A [illegible]

Seen [initials]

From 15 Div
Place
Time 9.0 am

The above may be forwarded as now corrected. (Z) [signature]

Censor. Signature of Addressor or person authorised to telegraph in his name

---

Prefix ______ Code ______ m. | Words | Charge | This message is on a/c of: ______ Service. | Recd. at ______ m. | Date | From | By

Office of Origin and Service Instructions. | Sent At ______ m. To By | (Signature of "Franking Officer.")

TO Div Art | 46th Inf Bde.
44th Inf Bde
45th Inf Bde

Sender's Number	Day of Month	In reply to Number	AAA
G 28	24th		

there is a possibility of the attack being postponed for 24 hours AAA We shall know as to this between 6 and 7 tonight AAA If attack is so postponed it will be necessary to stop troops going into the trenches and if possible pull back those who have gone in AAA If we are told at 6 pm "to carry on" troops will go in as arranged AAA Between 9 and 10 pm we shall know nature of attack to be made tomorrow AAA If weather is unfavourable we alone shall attack and shall do so at 10 a.m to capture German front trenches at and between the two salients AAA No other attack will be made that day by 4th Corps, but 9th Div of 1st Corps will attack at dawn AAA Addressed 44th 45th & 46th Bdes repeated Div Art AAA acknowledge

From 15th Div
Place
Time

The above may be forwarded as now corrected. (Z) [signature]

Censor. Signature of Addressor or person authorised to telegraph in his name.

4

3.

GENERAL INSTRUCTIONS & PAPERS RE ATTACK ON
21ST SEPTEMBER.

SECRET

HEADQUARTERS, 15th DIVISION
2 - SEP. 1915
Reg. No.

IVth Corps No. H.R.S. 506/3(X).

~~1st Division.~~
15th Division.
~~47th Division.~~

1. It will not be possible to reserve definite Divisional areas after the fourth day of the bombardment, that is to say, from the night 11th/12th September (inclusive).

2. The following localities will be reserved on night 11/12:-

(a) For reserve battalions of the brigade of the 1st Division holding Y.1 - VERMELLES branch line from CORONS DE RUTOIRE KEEP (inclusive) to railway crossing at G.8.d.3.0.

(b) For a brigade of the 1st Division - SAILLY LABOURSE line from LONE KEEP southwards.

(c) For a brigade of the 1st Division - VAUDRICOURT (K.28). This brigade will be in Corps Reserve.

(d) For reserves of leading brigades of the 15th Division - VERMELLES branch south of CORONS DE RUTOIRE KEEP (exclusive).

(e) For reserve brigade of the 15th Division - the GRENAY line from the BETHUNE - LENS road to MAZINGARBE - ANCIEN MOULIN road.

(f) For reserve brigade of 47th Division - the GRENAY line south of the MAZINGARBE - ANCIEN MOULIN road.

3. The G.O.C. 1st Division will take over command of the battalions of the 1st Division holding Y.1. from 15th Division on the night of 11th/12th September.

Exact time to be settled between 1st and 15th Divisions, and reported to this office.

4. The

4. The 1st Division is establishing an Advanced Head-quarters at MARSDENS KEEP.

Brigadier-General,
General Staff, IVth Corps.

H.Q. IVth Corps.
2nd September, 1915.

SECRET

IVth Corps No. H.R.S. 506/5(S).

HEADQUARTERS 4th CORPS
3 SEP 1915
GENERAL STAFF

~~1st Division.~~
15th Division.
~~47th Division.~~

The G.O.C. wishes to remind divisions regarding the following points which require attention in orders to be issued for the attack.

1. Smoke helmets to be worn rolled up by all ranks, to be ready to be lowered should troops enter trenches or localities in which gas is still hanging.

2. Troops to be warned that the cellars in LOOS may be found full of gas, and should not be entered without smoke helmets being lowered.

3. Arrangements for bringing up vermoral sprayers for spraying captured hostile trenches and dug-outs.

4. Preparation of steps in the parapet, and posts on the parapet, to assist men to get out of our trenches for the attack.

5. Arrangements for cutting our own wire without disclosing to the enemy more than is possible that it has been cut.

6. Arrangements for telephone wires being taken forward with the attacking troops.

7. Arrangements for keeping up the supply of grenades to the attacking troops.

all done

Brigadier-General,
General Staff, IVth Corps.

H.Q. IVth Corps.
3rd September, 1915.

SECRET

IVth Corps No. H.R.S. 506/11

15th Division.
~~47th Division.~~

If you have not already done so, the G.O.C. wishes you to establish a Report Centre at your Advanced Head-quarters when your B.G.R.A. moves forward to his fighting station.

Reference IVth Corps No. H.R.S. 506/2 dated 2nd September, 1915.

R A Montgomery

Brigadier-General,
General Staff, IVth Corps.

H.Q. IVth Corps.
3rd September, 1915.

Settled – we need not put anyone up yet.

SECRET

IVth Corps No. H.R.S. 506/7(=).

~~1st Division.~~
15th Division.
~~47th Division.~~

During the four days' bombardment by the artillery it is hoped that many large gaps will be cut in the enemy's wire with shrapnel fire.

In order to prevent the enemy from repairing his wire during the hours of darkness, it will be necessary to maintain a more or less continuous fire of machine-guns and rifles on these points, and special orders should be given accordingly.

Included in prelim.y O/s Order 1110

R.
9668

Brigadier-General,
General Staff, IVth Corps.

H.Q. IVth Corps.
3rd September, 1915.

327

SECRET

H.R.S. 506/4

HEADQUARTERS 4th CORPS
3 SEP 1915
GENERAL STAFF

~~1st Division.~~
15th Division.
~~47th Division.~~
~~G.O.C. IVth Corps Artillery.~~
~~1st Group H.A.R.~~
~~O.C. Gas Company.~~

1. Under instructions received from the 1st Army the date of the infantry attack will be postponed from 12th to 15th instant.

2. The programme will otherwise remain the same, that is to say, three nights will be devoted to bringing up cylinders and candles - September 8/9, 9/10, 10/11. There will be four days' preliminary bombardment - September 11th, 12th, 13th, 14th.

3. It may be necessary for the 15th Division to commence bringing up gas on the night 7th/8th, but this will not interfere with the arrangements made by 1st and 47th Divisions.

4. The Gas Company will arrive on the 4th as before arranged, and will be billeted in VERQUIN from 4th to 10th, and from 11th to 15th at MAZINGARBE.

5. The dates in IVth Corps No. H.R.S. 506/3 of 2nd September will be amended accordingly.

R
G668

A Montgomery

3rd September, 1915.

Brigadier General,
General Staff, IVth Corps.

SECRET

IVth Corps No. H.R.S. 399 (G).

~~1st Division.~~
15th Division.
~~47th Division.~~

The dividing point between the 4th and 1st Corps on the rearward lines of defence will be as follows:-

<u>VERMELLES Branch of the GRENAT Line.</u>

Where crossed by LE RUTOIRE ALLEY. (LE RUTOIRE ALLEY inclusive to 4th Corps).

<u>GRENAY Line.</u>

Where crossed by the BETHUNE - LENS road. (Road inclusive to 4th Corps).

<u>SAILLY-LABOURSE Line.</u>

At a point half way between LONE KEEP NORTH and LONE KEEP SOUTH.

The dividing point between the 15th and 47th Divisions on the GRENAY and SAILLY-LABOURSE lines, up to night 14/15 will be the NOEUX - MAZINGARBE - ANCIEN MOULIN road. (Road inclusive to 15th Division).

Brigadier-General,
General Staff, IVth Corps.

H.Q. IVth Corps.
4th September, 1915.

75

Secret

46. 1. B

Please detail men for work on night of Sept 8/9 in accordance with attached table.

2 Each man will carry a sling rifle and web. bandolier with 50 rds SAA.

3. Smoke helmets will be carried by all ranks, ready for instant use.

4. Detail for Sept 9/10 will be issued to morrow.

E Henderson
Major GS.
15 Div.

6.9.15

Captain Trouton, 10 S.R., to get in touch with Maj. Stewart, Blk W — 8th 9th & 11th — (Bru 620)

1 Bay = 15 C. (1st night 7 . 2nd night 8)

Last night will be asked for 2 men per bay to be placed under orders of G man. These will smoke — as soon as finished will rejoin Coys — (? from 2nd line, where remain till 2nd line comes up)

46th INFANTRY BRIGADE — SECRET.

Detail of Working Parties for Special duty

First Night.

Unloading: Time	Officers	N.C.O's	O.R	Carrying: Time	Officers	N.C.O's	O.R	Guides: No	To conduct to Bays No	Remarks
Nil				9.45 pm.	1	2	14	1	116. 119.	
						1	14			
						2	14	1	122. 125.	
						1	14			
						1	14	1	127. 130	
						1	14			
					1	8	84	3		
				10.15 pm.	1	2	14	1	133. 1.	
						1	14			
						1	14	1	4. 6.	
						1	14			
					1	2	14	1	8. 10.	
						1	14			
						1	14	1	12. 14.	
						1	14			
						2	14	1	17. 19.	
						1	14			
					2	13	140	5		
				10.45 pm.	1	2	14	1	20. 21.	
						1	14			
						1	14	1	22. 23.	
						1	14			
					1	2	14	1	26. 28.	
						1	14			
						1	14	1	29. 32.	
						1	14			
					1	2	14	1	34. 36.	
						1	14			
					3	13	140	5		
					1	2	14	1	41. 43.	
						1	14			
				10.45 pm.		1	14	1	44B. 46.	
						1	14			
						1	14	1	49. 52.	
						1	14			
					1	2	14	1	54. 58.	
						1	14			
						1	14	1	61. 64.	
						1	14			
					1	1	14	1	68. 70.	
					3	14	168	6		

Summary (a) unloading nil (b) carrying

1.	8.	84.
2.	13.	140.
3.	13.	140
3.	14.	168
9.	48	532

(c) guides. 19.

46 INFANTRY BRIGADE SECRET.

Detail of Working Parties for Special duty
Second Night. (page 1)

UNLOADING				CARRYING				GUIDES		REMARKS
Time	Officers	N.C.O.s	O.R	Time	Officers	N.C.O's	O.R	No	To conduct to Bays No	
Nil				8.15 pm	1	2	14.	1	74.76.	
						1	14.			
						1	14.	1	78.81.	
						1	14.			
						1	14	1	84.86.	
						1	14.			
					1	2	14.	1	Sap 10. 89.	
						1	14			
						1	14			
						1	14.	1	95.99.	
					2	12	140	5		

46th INFANTRY BRIGADE SECRET.

Detail of Working Parties for Special duty

~~Second~~ Night. (page 2)

UNLOADING				CARRYING				GUIDES		REMARKS
Time	Officers	N.C.Os	O.R	Time	Officers	N.C.Os	O.R	No	To conduct to Bays No	
Nil				9.45pm.	1	1 1	8 8	1	116. 119.	
						1 1	8 8	1	122. 125	
						1 1	8 8	1	127. 130.	
					1	1 1	8 8	1	133. 1.	
						1 1	8 8	1	4. 6	
					1	1 1	8 8	1	8. 10.	
						1 1	8 8	1	12. 14.	
						1 1	8 8	1	17. 19.	
					3	16	128.	8		
				10.15pm.	1	1 1	8 8	1	20. 21.	
						1 1	8 8	1	22. 23	
					1	1 1	8 8	1	26. 28.	
						1 1	8 8	1	29. 32.	
						1 1	8 8	1	34. 36.	
					1	1 1	8 8	1	41. 43.	
						1 1	8 8	1	44B. 46.	
						1 1	8 8.	1	49. 52.	
					3	16	128	8		
				10.45.	1	1 1	8 8	1	54. 58.	
						1 1	8 8	1	61. 64.	
						1 1	8 8	1	67. 70.	
					1	1 1	8 8	1	74. 76.	
						1 1	8 8	1	78. 81.	
						1 1	8 8	1	84. 86.	
					1	1 1	8 8	1	Sap10. 89.	
						1 2	8 8	1	95. 99.	
					3.	17	128	8		

SUMMARY (a) unloading Nil (b) Carrying

	Offrs	N.C.Os	O.R
	3.	16.	128
	3.	16.	128
	3.	17.	128
	9.	49	384
add from p.1.	2	12	140
Total	11.	61	524

(c) Guides 24 + 5 = 29.

46. INFANTRY BRIGADE SECRET.

Detail of Working Parties for Special duty
Third Night.

UNLOADING				CARRYING				GUIDES		REMARKS
Time	Officers	N.C.O.s	O.R.	Time	Officers	N.C.O.s	O.R.	No	To conduct to Bays No	
				9.15 pm	1	1 1	8 8	1	116. 119.	
						1 1	8 8	1	122. 125	
						1 1	8 8	1	127 130.	
					1	1 1	8 8	1	133. 1.	
						1 1	8 8	1	4. 6	
					1	1 1	8 8	1	8. 10.	
						1 1	8 8	1	12. 14.	
						1 1	8 8.	1	17. 19.	
					3.	16	128	8		
				9.45 pm.	1	1 1	8 8	1	20. 21.	
						1 1	8 8	1	22. 23.	
					1	1 1	8 8	1	26. 28	
						1 1	8 8	1	29. 32.	
						1 1	8 8	1	34. 36.	
					1	1 1	8 8	1	41. 43.	
						1 1	8 8	1	44/3 46.	
						1 1	8 8	1	49. 52.	
					3	16	128.	8		
				10.15 pm	1	1 1	8 8	1	54. 58.	
						1 1	8 8	1	61. 64.	
						1 1	8 8	1	68. 70.	
					1	1 1	8 8	1	74. 76.	
						1 1	8 8	1	78. 81.	
						1 1	8 8	1	84. 86.	
					1	1 1	8 8	1	Sap 10. 89	
						1 2	8 8	1	95. 99.	
					3	17	128	8		

Remarks:

Summary (a) Unloading N.L. (b) Carrying (c) Guides N.L.

	Offrs	N.C.Os	O.R.
	3.	16.	128
	3.	16.	128
	3.	17.	128
	9	49.	384

SECRET

IVth Corps No. H.R.S. 510/1

~~1st Division.~~
15th Division.
~~47th Division.~~

The following positions will be occupied by Divisions as Advanced Head-quarters:-

1st Division .. New Avenue, MAZINGARBE.

15th Division ,, ,, ,, ,,

47th Division .. Mine Offices, LES BREBIS.

Paragraph 4 of IVth Corps letter No. H.R.S. 506/3 of the 2nd September, 1915, is cancelled.

A A Montgomery

Brigadier-General,
General Staff, IVth Corps.

H.Q. IVth Corps.
8th September, 1915.

SECRET

365

IVth Corps No. H.R.S. 508/4

HEADQUARTERS, 15th DIVISION
10 SEP 1915
Reg. No. 365

HEADQUARTERS 4th CORPS
9 SEP 1915
GENERAL STAFF

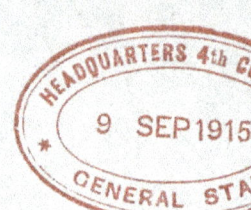

~~1st Division.~~
15th Division.
~~47th Division.~~

Previous to the attack, troops should be warned that no food or water found in the German trenches, after the gas attack, should on any account be used, as the gas may in all probability have a poisonous effect on both.

R.A.K. Montgomery

9th September, 1915.

Brigadier General,
General Staff, IVth Corps.

SECRET

1st Army No. 206 (IM)

Already in our orders

4th Corps.

It has been decided that the trench maps of the scale of 1/10,000 with the official maps to the scale of 1/20,000 and 1/40,000 are to be the maps for use during the forthcomingoperations.

Maps to the scale of 1/5,000 will not, therefore, be reproduced except under exceptional circumstances, the need for which should be specified in submitting the map for reproduction.

5-9-15. (Sd.) J.C. CHARTERIS, Lieut. Col.,
General Staff, 1st Army.

(2)

15th Division.

4th Corps
H.R.I./S.11

Forwarded for information.

H.W. Stenhouse Major
H.Q., IVTH Corps. for Brigadier General,
9th September, 1915. General Staff, IVTH Corps.

SECRET

1st Army No.
G.S. 169(a)

IVth Corps No. H.R.S. 507.

HEADQUARTERS, 15th DIVISION
9 - SEP. 1915
Reg. No. 371

GENERAL PRINCIPLES FOR THE ATTACK.

1. The enemy is to be beaten on a certain length of front and driven out of it, and must not be allowed time to reform in rear of the captured trenches.

For this a violent and continuous action is required.

The keynote of all the work, both as regards details and the general idea, is offensive action.

When once the enemy's front system of trenches is broken, delay is usually the chief cause of failure and heavy casualties.

Commanders must bear in mind that, once the enemy's line is broken, it is the intention to follow up by such action as will cause a general retirement of a great part of the enemy's line. Thus the operations will be continued during a considerable period.

Supports and Reserves.

2. Bearing the above in mind, it is of the highest importance that all commanders should consider carefully the handling of their reserves to maintain the forward movement.

Under the existing conditions, only one definite offensive blow can be expected from one body of infantry, and, therefore, fresh troops must be pushed through those making the first attack to develop the success won. Troops heavily engaged during the day should not ordinarily be expected to continue the offensive on the following day, but should be either actually relieved or arrangements made for fresh troops to pass through them. The organization of reserves in depth should be made with this object.

Supporting and reserve troops must be close up from the commencement of the operations, so that they can follow close on the heels of the troops in front. Commanders of such troops must clearly understand the objective and their role, and use their initiative.

Ample cover must be provided for the reserve troops well forward, with good and sufficient communicating trenches. Direction boards must be put up to prevent mistakes in the existing labyrinth of trenches.

The Infantry attack.

3. Forming up places for attacking troops and reserves must be carefully reconnoitred, and all troops should be rehearsed in detail beforehand in the actual way in which they are to get into and out of their forming up places.

The attack on the front trenches will probably not be equally successful all along the line. Support must be given at once to the units which have been successful to enable them to press on. Where unsuccessful a new attack must be organised from a flank where the line has been broken.

If a certain body of infantry fails to gain its own particular local objective, there is no reason why the troops on either flank should be held up. Every body of infantry must push on and thereby facilitate the task of the troops on the right and left.

The whole operation can be regulated with the greatest precision. Parties of infantry should be detailed beforehand for the capture of the several localities. The accuracy of the photographic maps permits of this being done.

We must /

We must not wait to be counter attacked, but must follow up our attack at once. Infantry must push on, and field guns, trench mortars, machine guns, etc., must be pushed forward in close support of the attacking infantry to batter down houses etc. The responsibility for supporting the attacking infantry in this way rests with Infantry Commanders, and special guns will be allotted to them for this purpose.

Localities must be seized promptly to act as supporting points to further advance, but only the necessary number of men will be left to entrench each of these points.

All ground gained will be secured (F.S.R. Part 1, Sec: 105 (5)).

Artillery.

4. The preliminary bombardment will be deliberate and carefully observed.

It will be directed chiefly with the following objects :-

(a) Wire cutting along the whole front of the First Army.

(b) Destruction of the enemy's observation posts.

(c) Destruction of the enemy's strong points in rear of the front line.

(d) Demolition of all obstacles to the infantry advance in certain zones of the enemy's front system of trenches, to assist the assault.

(e) Destruction of the enemy's batteries.

(f) Barrages on the enemy's communications and to prevent reliefs and supplies being brought forward, especially at night.

Once the infantry attack is launched, the task of the Artillery is :-

(a) The support of the infantry during its attack.

(b) To gain superiority of fire over the hostile artillery.

The guns must be registered beforehand on all the objectives and tactical localities as far forward as possible.

Similarly, the barrages of shrapnel must be arranged beforehand. These will be gradually expanded as the infantry advances.

The nature of the artillery support required by the infantry depends on the local conditions of the fight.

Infantry commanders must be in close touch with the artillery and the means of communication must be arranged beforehand and clearly understood.

Some field or horse artillery guns must be ready to push forward rapidly in support of the infantry as the latter get beyond the support of the remaining guns. (Field Artillery Training, Sec. 156 (4).)

Special Parties.

5. Special parties must be detailed for work subsidiary to the attack, such as bomb parties, sandbag parties, bayonet parties, entrenching tool parties. These parties must all be conversant with their various duties.

The idea of the offensive must be inculsated in the grenadier parties, so that their efforts are directed to bombing so as to assist the movement to front and flank, rather than to more defensive work and blocking approaches.

Special /

Special attention must be given to repairing roads, and detachments of R.E., with infantry working parties attached, must be organized and in position to follow up the attack, for clearing away obstacles and mending roads, to allow free passage for troops.

Special parties for extending and maintaining the telephone wires must also be organized beforehand (see paragraph 7).

R.E. Stores and Materials.

6. Advanced depots of R.E. stores must be established close up behind our own lines at short intervals along the front of the attack. These depots should contain material for entanglements, sandbags, trench-bridging material, tools, etc.

Parties of R.E. with infantry must be specially detailed to move forward with these stores to secure positions gained.

Communications.

7. In order that the offensive may be continued without interruption and be suited to the changing conditions of the fight, the several commanders must be kept in close touch with the situation; hence communications must be carefully organized beforehand and adequate means of getting information back from the front provided. Wherever possible, communications should be triplicated and arrangements made to carry on communications by flags, lamps, etc., when wires are broken. This is of the first importance, and all commanders will give this matter their close attention.

The ground over which the attack is to pass and the localities to be attacked can in most cases be seen and studied. So far as is possible, therefore, arrangements should be made beforehand between what points communication by flag or otherwise is to be established as the attack progresses.

The positions of commanders must be carefully thought out and suitably protected points organized for commanders near their troops.

Telegraph and telephone wires must be buried up to our front trenches, and arrangements made to push wires on as soon as possible after the attack has passed beyond them.

Staff Officers must be pushed well forward with the object of collecting information and keeping commanders regularly informed of the situation.

With this object in view, positions of observation and dugouts should be made, and special communications established beforehand with these places.

Special attention must be given to instructing signal companies in their duties and action during an advance, and all preparations must be made with a view to the forward movement being sustained.

Divisional Cavalry and Cyclists.

8. Divisional Cavalry and Cyclists must be kept handy to push on rapidly as opportunity offers, to anticipate the enemy in occupying houses and other tactical points, and so facilitating the advance after the enemy's main lines of defence have been broken.

Distribution

copies –
each I B – 4
RA – 5
RE – 3
MG Tps – 1
9th Gordons – 1

P.A. with orders
J.f.2.

15th Div:

Secret

This morning I saw the B.M. 2nd Inf Bde. In discussing our boundaries the question of how we were going to deal with "Southern Saps" arose.

I stated I did not think a direct attack by bombers only, on the West end of it would succeed and that I proposed to deal with it from the East or German end having once established a footing to the North of Loos Fort.

The BM pointed out to me that this would leave Southern Saps free to enfilade the 2nd Bde attack.

With this I agree but from the present position of my left flank party I do not see how a direct attack on this Sap head will be successful.

I think a Sap should be made out from our line between 12 & 14A so as to lie at right angles and across a line drawn in prolongation of the Southern Sap from which an

attack could be made on
a ½ platoon or platoon frontage
The latest photograph shows
the position clearly.

I shall come & see you about
this to morrow if you can
send a car for me.

I mentioned this to the G.O.C.
15 Div this afternoon.

T. G. Matheson
B.G.
11-9-15 46th Inf Bde

2.

G.792. 46th Bde.

The Maj. Gen. has considered this, and has decided that his original order must stand. A direct attack on the head of this Sap must be made simultaneously with the main assaults to south & north of it; but it is at your discretion to employ one or two platoons of infantry with the grenadiers.

As regards the possibility of pushing out a parallel towards the Sap head, he considers that the gas discharge would render any such parallel untenable & so useless as a starting place for the assault.

The artillery will be directed to pay particular attention to this Sap & to the wire in front of it.

15th Div. / 12.9.15

J. Bennett Stuart Lt Col.
G.S.

SECRET

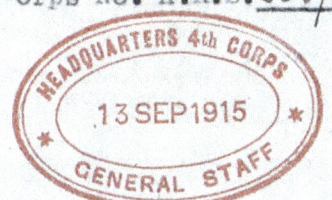

IVth Corps No. H.R.S. 508/2

~~1st Division.~~
15th Division.
~~47th Division.~~

1. No date has yet been fixed for operations to begin, but Divisions must be prepared for short notice.

2. As you know, there are four days of preliminary bombardment ending with the attack on the morning of the 5th day.

The 3 nights preceding the four days' bombardment have been set aside for taking up gas cylinders - a total of 7 days programme before the day of the attack.

Divisions should have their programmes during these 7 days cut and dried, as we shall probably not get more than 12 to 24 hours' notice.

3. The numbers of cylinders to be taken up are of course a difficulty in telling off working parties, etc., but it is recommended that the maximum of 15 per partition be provided for, with a small margin in case the number of cylinders should be increased at the last moment.

4. Arrangements must also be made to give warning, should it be necessary for any reason, to stop the gas being turned on at the last moment. It will probably be turned on between 7 and 10 in the morning, and we shall know probably 2 hours beforehand if the attack is postponed.

5 Divisions must make careful arrangements for conveying messages to the above effect all along their front line so that there shall be no risk of any cylinders being turned on.

13th September, 1915.

A. Montgomery
Brigadier General,
General Staff, IVth Corps.

(15 Div.
445)

lVth Corps No. H.R.S. 511/3.

SECRET

HEADQUARTERS 4th CORPS
16 SEP 1915
GENERAL STAFF

15th Division.

Reference attached copy of letter of 1st Division No. 509 G. dated 10th instant, and 4th Corps reply.

The Corps Commander wishes 15th Division to arrange for a signal on the same lines for capture of Hill 70.

H.Q.lVth Corps.
15th September, 1915.

[signature]
Brigadier General.
General Staff lVth Corps.

GOC saw Corps Cmdr 17th
who said we needn't.
[initials]

Cancelled by HRS 511
of 17/9/15

SECRET

1st Division 509 (G)

IVth Corps.

1. It is proposed to employ, subject to the Corps Commander's approval, the following ground signals in connexion with impending operations:-

By 1st Infantry Brigade.

i. The figure Λ pointing towards the enemy to indicate that our troops have captured HULLUCH.

ii. The figure V pointing away from the enemy, to indicate that our troops have been driven out of, and are no longer holding HULLUCH.

By 2nd Infantry Brigade.

i. The figure T to indicate that our troops have captured PUITS No. 14 bis.

ii. The figure ⊥ to indicate that our troops have been driven out of and are no longer holding PUITS 14 bis

2. These signals will consist of strips of white sheeting 15 feet long by 3 feet broad, and will be carried and laid by the Headquarters of a battalion detailed by the Brigadier in some open spot near his battalion headquarters.

8x2

D/

3. If approved, would you please inform the Flying Corps, and request the O.C. Squadron to direct his Officers to look out for, and report these signals.

(sd) R.H.Longridge. for Major Genl.
Commanding 1st Division.

10th September,1915.

H.R.S. 519.

SECRET

HEADQUARTERS 4th CORPS
16 SEP 1915
GENERAL STAFF

1st Division.

1. With reference to your letter No. 509 G. of 10th September, 1915, the Corps Commander considers that the signals could be reduced in size to about 8 feet by 2 feet.

2. He considers that the important signals are the ones shewing that HULLUCH and PUITS 14 bis has been captured.

3. It may not be possible, in the event of the positions being lost to reverse the signals, and the originals indicating their capture may remain down, even though the positikns have been lost.

Too much attention therefore should not be paid to them after the one indicating capture of the positions have been first put down.

(Sd) A.A. Montgomery

H.Q.1Vth Corps.
15th September, 1915.

Brigadier General.
General Staff 1Vth Corps.

SECRET

IVth Corps H.R.S. No. 515/2.

HEADQUARTERS 4th CORPS
16 SEP 1915
GENERAL STAFF

~~1st Division.~~
15th Division.
~~47th Division.~~
~~187th Coy. R.E.~~

---

1. The G.O.C. has decided that no signals to denote a postponement shall be sent up either by the Corps or by Divisions.

2. Sufficient notice will be given if the attack is to be postponed.

3. Divisions will make all possible arrangements to ensure that messages for the front line get through by means of telephones, runners, or visual signalling.

[signature]

H.Q. IVth Corps.
15th September, 1915.

Brigadier General.
General Staff IVth Corps.

"A" Form.

Army Form C. 2121.

MESSAGES AND SIGNALS.

No. of Message

Prefix ... Code ... m.	Words / Charge	This message is on a/c of:	Recd. at ... m.
Office of Origin and Service Instructions. D.R.L.S.	Sent At ... m. To ... By ...	SECRET. Service. (Signature of "Franking Officer.")	Date ... From ... By ...

TO

A.A. & Q.M.G.	C.R.E.	46th Inf. Bde.	~~[illegible]~~
~~[illegible]~~	44th Inf Bde	9th Gordons.	~~[illegible]~~
15 Div Art.	45th Inf Bde.	A.D.M.S.	~~[illegible] Div.~~

Sender's Number.	Day of Month.	In reply to Number	AAA
* G.882	17th		

It is probable that the supply of electricity from Mine No. 6 will be cut off during the days of bombardment AAA Offices, dugouts etc that are using electricity from this source should be warned

From 15th Div.

Place

Time 12 noon

The above may be forwarded as now corrected. (Z) [illegible signature]

Censor. Signature of Addressor or person authorised to telegraph in his name.

* This line should be erased if not required.

(810 11)—Wt. W 14142/611—2,000,000—8/15. S. & S., Ltd.

18th Division G/916.

SECRET MEMORANDUM.

1. The following notes indicate the kind of information which the Artillery want from the Infantry during the advance, when it is possible for the latter to give it:-

(a) Exact position on which fire is required, described with reference to the map.

(b) What is the actual object to be engaged - house, redoubt, machine gun, trench etc.

(c) Position of our own troops and distance from object.

(d) Position from which fire on the object can best be observed.

(e) Position of Officer making the report.

2. When reporting on hostile fire the points to be noted are:-

(a) Nature of projectile - whether field gun, field howitzer (generally large quantity of white smoke), or heavy howitzer (black smoke).

(b) Direction from which fire is thought to be coming.

(c) Position of the Officer making the report.

(d) If the guns themselves or flashes can be seen.

(e) The rate of fire i.e. number of rounds arriving per minute, and number of shell arriving at one time.

Lieut Colonel,
General Staff.

19/9/15.

Copies to:-

44th Infantry Brigade.
45th " "
46th " ".

RA. for information

SECRET

IVth Corps No. H.R.S. 524

HEADQUARTERS,
15th DIVISION
18 SEP. 1915
Reg. No. 466

~~1st Division.~~
15th Division.
~~47th Division.~~
~~IVth Corps Art.~~

1. The following maps will be carried during the forthcoming operations:-

1/100,000 .. Sheet 5.
,, 5a.
,, 11.
,, 12.

1/40,000 .. ,, 36c.

1/10,000 Trench map, Sheets 36c N.W. 3.
,, 36c S.W. 1.

2. No maps showing our trenches or billeting areas will be carried.

3. No documents of any sort that are likely to be of value to the enemy will be taken into the trenches prior to the attack.

R ack G 895

Order issued G.953 of 18/9.

Sent out 18/9

R.A. [illegible]

Brigadier-General,
General Staff, IVth Corps.

H.Q. IVth Corps.
18th September, 1915.

SECRET

Result of experiments carried out in the VERMELLES sector of line, held by Dismounted Division

---

(1) With suitable instruments, and proper arrangements, conversation by the enemy can be overheard, when his front line trenches are 100 yds distant from British front line trench.
(2) The overhearing of conversation by the enemy is considerably interfered with, owing to induction from our own buzzer circuits.
(3) Conversation can be overheard at a distance of 150 yards on metallic circuits, when the wires are six feet apart.
(4) There is every reason to believe that if the enemy is in possession of a suitable instrument, that all conversation and messages sent or spoken over earth return telephones circuits can be overheard. This is providing that the earth is placed under 1000 yards distant from British front line trench.
(5) There is a great deal of unnecessary conversations down telephones by operators. This leads to unnecessary interference, and interferes with overhearing the enemy.
(6) The enemy use their telephones far less than the British, there is very little conversation by their operators.
(7) The enemy test their circuits at 5a.m. in the morning by sending an O.K. call.

CONCLUSIONS

(a) It is quite clear that no earth return circuits should have their earths nearer the front line, than 1000 yards as a minimum, probably 2000 yards would be necessary to be safe.
(b) To be immune from overhearing, all telephonic communications for a distance of 2000 yards from the enemy should be on metallic circuits, composed of insulated wires, laid close together parallel, or twisted.
(c) Incidentally all conversations in the enemy's front line trenches can be overheardif interference from our own circuits is removed. This can be done by substituting metallic circuits as suggested in (b).
(d) In the event of a line from our own front line back to the brigade headquarters, being cut during a bombardment, a report of the situation in the front line can be overheard on a suitable instrument, if the line and earth terminals of the telephone in the front line trench are connected to earth. This can even be overheard, if the report is spoken down the telephone, after the wires have been cut.
Unbreakable emergency circuits have been established between the batallion or company headquarters (as required) and the headquarters of brigades. These consist of the following:-
(1) High frequency alternators worked by hand, and suitably geared, and connected up to a key.
One in the front line, one close to brigade headquarters.
These have only a very short line in the forward trench, and a suitable arrangement at the brigade headquarters.
The earth is ~~wired~~ used as a conducting media.
Experiments prove that these instruments are capable to communicating up to four kilometres. This circuit was used in the VERMELLES sector, where all lines were cut during a recent bombardment.
(2) The ~~continuation~~ combination of carrier pigeons, and a wireless receiving set.
The Pigeons are used as the means of transmission, and the wireless receives the acknowledgement of the arrival of the pigeons at the loft, and if desired can be utilized to send message in an emergency.
This circuit is only valuable during day, as at night pigeons cannot work, though a message can be sent forward if desired. The wireless receiving set, and the pigeons are placed in a company or batallion headquarters, and work together, a short length of ground aerial alone is used in the front line trench as a receiving aerial.
This circuit has also proved most useful. The acknowledgement of the arrival of the pigeons have been received in thirteen minutes at the company or batallion headquarters.
The back station is used for intercepting wireless messages when not working to the forward stations. Certain messages have also been picked up by the front aerial.

(Sgd) L.W. Sadleir-Jackson, Major,
Commanding Signals Cavalry Corps.

29/1/16

SECRET

EMERGENCY CIRCUITS

DISMOUNTED DIVISION

Right Battalion Headquarters	Wireless Receiving set Pigeons	"A"
Centre Battalion Headquarters	JACKOPHONE	"B"

Pigeons fly from Battalion Hd.Qtrs. to SAILLY LA BOURSE, where arrival is at once acknowledged by wireless set at loft.
JACKOPHONE works from centre battalion Hd.Qtrs to right Brigade Hd.Qtrs.

- EMERGENCY CIRCUITS -

"A" works from front to rear under orders of battalion commander, and arrival of pigeons is signalled automatically from pigeon loft on arrival i.e., pigeon No.495 arrives, clip at once taken off and despatched direct to staff.
Wireless sends at once No.495 arrived safely, or in Signal parlance "495 R D"
"A" does not work forward unless so ordered by staff in an emergency, but can do so if required.
"B" does ~~work~~ not work unless ordered to do so in an emergency, when wires are cut, orders being given for forward station to work by Battalion Commander, for back station to work, by Commander Brigade right Section.

INTERCEPTING

Intercepting wires are installed
(1) STICKY TRENCH
(2) KAISERIN TRENCH
(3) HAIRPIN
The original German of all messages, or communications of a military nature, is sent in duplicate to Right Brigade Signal Office, one copy being for use of Brigade intelligence officer, the second copy for transmission to the Intelligence of the Dismounted Division, and also to be repeated to Intelligence 1st Corps.
No mention is to be made by telephone of the existance of the intercepting station, and emergency circuits.

(Sgd) L. W. Sadleir-Jackson,
Major,
Commanding Signals Cavalry Corps.

29/1/16

4

DRAFT INSTRUCTIONS FOR ATTACK ON 21st SEPTEMBER.

COPY

G. 600 — S E C R E T

G.O.C. 44th I. Bde.

HEADQUARTERS.
12th September,1915.
No. S. 25
44th INFANTRY BRIGADE.

The attached draft instructions are for your own and your Bde. Major's information only.

The Divisional Commander will hold a conference at Div. Hd. Qrs. at 11 a.m. to-morrow, the 31st to discuss these draft instructions -

Please attend without your Bde. Major.

A Divl. car will be sent to fetch the G.O.C's. 44th and 45th Bdes.

Please acknowledge receipt.

(Sgd). F. BURNETT STUART,
Lt. Col.
G.S.

15th Division.
30/8/15.

DRAFT INSTRUCTIONS FOR ATTACK.

1. The Div. is to take a principal part in an attack on the German positions - probably within the next fort-night.

Objective of 15th Div.

2. The objectives allotted to the Div. are :-

(a) The front line trenches from G.34.a.6.5. to the German sap at G.22.d.6.3.

(b) The second line trenches from the cemetery in G.35.a. (exclusive) to G.29.b.3.9.

(c) LOOS Village.

(d) HILL 70.

These objectives are shaded in blue on the map.

Objectives of 47th Div. and I. Corps.

3. In order to form a defensive flank southwards to cover our advance, the 47th Div. will attack with the following objectives:-

(a) The Double Crassier as far as point M.4.d.8.8.

(b) The German front system of trenches from M.4.c.3.9. to G.34.a.6.5.

(c) The second line trenches from M.4.d.8.8. to the cemetery in G.35.a. (inclusive).

(d) Enclosure in G.35.d.

(e) FOSSE in G.36

These objectives are shaded in green on the map.

On our left, the I. Corps will attack the villages of BENIFONTAINE - HULLUCH and ST. ELIE.

Bombardment.

4. The attack will commence by a steady bombardment by all available guns day and night for 4 days up to the moment of the infantry assault on the 5th day. This bombardment will be distributed over the whole front of the 1st and 4th Corps.

Gas. 5. On the morning of the 5th day Gas, interspersed and flanked by smoke from smoke candles, will be discharged for 40 minutes along the front; this discharge will be followed immediately by the infantry assault.

6. The attack will be pushed home to the full extent of the 4th Corps power.

Preliminary action by 15th Div.

7\.
(a) Up to the night immediately preceding the opening of the action by the artillery, the front of XI, X2, and YI will continue to be held by the 45th Bde. with one X Battn. attached from the 1st Div. On this night the 45th Bde. will be relieved by the 44th and 46th Bdes. and will go into Divl. reserve at NOEUX LES MINES and in the trenches of the SAILLY line W. of that place.

(b) For the purpose of this relief the front will be divided up into 2 sectors) Right and Left.

The Right Sector will extend from the present southern boundary of XI to the line trench 12 - junction of 14 a with 14 - junction of new coms. trench with 16 (all inclusive) - house G.20 d central - level crossing G.20 a. MAZINGARBE Church (all exclusive): and will be taken over by the 44th Bde.

X An additional 1½ Battns. and 2 Fd.Coys.R.E. from 1st Div. will also be attached - all these are for work on the front from 14 a northwards, which becomes eventually the 1st Div. Battle front.- The work will be controlled by the 1st Div.

The Left Sector will extend from the above line to the northern boundary of the divisional area, and will be taken over by the 46th Bde. - plus X the Battn. of the 1st Div. which will remain in position

(c) During the following 4 days of bombardment the distribution of the troops in the right and left sectors will be :-

In front system	44th Bde.	46th Bde.
In PHILOSOPHE	1 Battn.	1½ Battns
CORONS DE RUTOIRE & trenches of GRENAY branch of VERMELLES line	1 Battn.	1½ Battns
In MAZINGARBE and in Trenches of main VERMELLES Line.	2 Battns. 1 Coy. R.E. 1 Coy.9th Gordons.	2 Battns. 1 Coy.R.E. 1 Coy.9th Gordons.

The Keeps will not be occupied during this period. Hd. Qrs. of these two Bdes. will be in the two houses in the new avenue at MAZINGARBE which have been prepared as Divl. and Divl. Art. advanced Hd. Qrs. respectively - (See paragraph 20) -

---

X

The other 1½ Battns. 1st Div. and the R.E. Coys. will be withdrawn under 1st Div. arrangements during the bombardment.

Action on night immediately preceding the assault.

8.

(a) During the night immediately preceding the day fixed for the assault, all troops will move up into their positions of readiness as shown on the attached map. The detailed arrangements for this move will be made by G.Os. Co Bdes, who will see that companies are told off to their places, guides provided, and sentries with written instructions posted beforehand at junctions of communicating trenches where necessary -

(b) The front from trench 14a to the left of Y 1 will be taken over on the night by the 1st Div. who will resume command of their detached Battn. and assume all responsibility for this front -

(c) Divl. Bde and Art. Hd. Qrs. will also move to their advanced stations on this night; and Divl. troops not allotted to Bdes. will move to their assigned positions under divisional orders.

Preparation of wire and exits from trenches.

9. The Bde. holding the Right Sector will be responsible that our won wire is cut opposite the points selected for assault on the last night but one before the day of assault. The wire will be cut close to the posts and diagonally - not straight, from front to rear.

This Bde. will also be responsible that steps are cut in the front walls of trenches at the forming up places.

Equipment.

10.

(a) Packs and great coats will not be taken to the forming up positions, but will be labelled and left under guard in selected houses and dug-outs before moving off.

Every infantryman will carry with him

Rifle and equipment (less pack)

2 bandoliers of S.A.A. in addition to equipt. ammnt.

1 ration and unexpended portion of days' ration.

2 sandbags (in belts)

smoke helmets.

Waterbottle

(haversack will be carried on back).

(b) 10 selected men per platoon in 44th and 46th Bdes. will carry wire cutters (attached to a lanyard) - Extra wire cutters to complete to this amount will be provided.

(c) 8 selected men per platoon in the two leading Coys. of each assaulting column will carry bill hooks for destroying wire. These men and men with wire cutters will be provided with hedging gloves.

(d) 1 man per platoon throughout the Div. will carry a yellow flag 2' x 2' on a 3' stick to mark the progress of his platoon in the attack. and 1 man per bombing squad will carry a yellow flag 1' x 1' on a 5' stick to mark the progress of his squad. These flags will be carried, not stuck in the ground. They will be supplied by the C.R.E.

Preparatory arrangements by Div.

11. The following arrangements will be made before the attack commences.

(a) Preparation of advanced dressing station at FOSSE 7.

(b) Establishment of depot of sandbags (20,000) at and R.E. stores at QUALITY ST.

(c) Placing of stores of grenades and S.A.A. at the forward ends of our communication trenches, suitable places are being selected. These will replenished during the action from Bde. Ammtn. Col. wagons in rear.

(d) Placing of gas cylinders and smoke candles in trenches. In addition to the gas specialist personnel on selected man will be told off by O.C. 9th Gordons to discharge the smoke candles in the proportion of one such man to each 15 cylinders.

(e) Making of new trenches, forming up places, durations round keeps, bomb proofs at various Hd.Qrs. and saps towards enemy's line.

(f) visual signal station in FOSSE 3

(g) Burying, duplicatinn and laddering of wires.

(h) Carfful labelling of all trenches and communication ways with labels low down so that they can be read by electric torch at night.

Organisation of Assaulting Columns.

12. There will be 4 assaulting columns (two from each leading Bde) consisting of 1 Battn. 1 Sect. R.E. and 1 platoon 9th Gordons in each column. These will be formed up in depth on a front of 2 platoons No. 4 column will include also a party of 50 picked grenadiers from the 45th Bde.
The Battn. Machine guns of the assaulting Battns. will go forward with them.

Tasks of Columns. 13.

(a) The task of assautling columns will be to go straight forward as fastas possible to their final objectives.

Parties for cutting wire, blocking side trenches and bombing dowm communication trenches will be told off from the two leading companies.

(b) Assaulting columns will not be entrusted with the task of occupying and consolidating positions won or of digging communications back to our own trenches, unless the whole column is hung up. These tasks will be allotted to parties told off from Bde. Reserves.

(c) The 4th Coy. in each column will carry a proportion of picks and shovels.

The R.E. section will carry explosives for hasty demolitions.

The platoon of Pioneers will carry 6 sand bags per man, and tools.

(d) In the two leading coys. of each column men will wear their smoke helmets rolled up under their bonnets ready to be let down at once should the men outrun the gas.

(e) Each company will move up at once into the place of the one in front of it directly this latter moves on.

Objectives of Bdes & plan of attack. 14.

(a) The objectives assigned to Bdes. are as follows:-

<u>44th Bde.</u>

1st Front trench E.F. and support trench behind.

2nd Second line Trench G.H.

3rd LOOS Village.

4th PUITS No. 15.

5th German work on HILL 70.

<u>46th Bde.</u> 1st Trench J.K. and rectangle of communication trenches behind it.

2nd Second Line trench L.H.

3rd Trench M.N.

4th road from G.36.b.1.6. to Puits No.14 bis inclusive.

5th Work on Hill 70.

(b) The assaulting columns of the 46th Bde. must endeavour not to be drawn into a converging attack on LOOS, but to push straight on to their 4th objective. They will this best assist the 44th Bde. whose attack will be supported from behind.

(c) The machine guns of the 9th Gordons will be placed at the disposal of G.O.C. 44th Bde., and will be used in the first instance, together with No.3 Trench mortar battery and 2 coys from the Bde. Reserve, to hold the front from Sap 18 to the LENS road - Sap 18 will be used as a communication trench by the 47th Div. but emplacements off the sap will be made for machine guns to fire on the southern face of the salient.

(d) The six Vickers guns of the M.M.G. Battery will be placed at the disposal of G.O.C. 46th Bde, and will be used in the first instance, together with ½ Coy. from the Bde. Reserve to hold the front from the left of No. 4 Column to trench 14 a. The fire of these guns will be directed on the northern face of the northern salient, and on the German sap G.22.d.6.3.

(e) The German trench running from G.35.a.6.3. to G.34.b central is allotted to 47th Div. who will deal with it. This trench (exclusive) will be the right boundary of the 44th Bde. attack.

(f) The party of picked grenadiers referred to in para 12 will go forward with the leading company of No. 4 Column, and will bomb northwards towards the HULLUCH road along the german front and support trenches, detailing parties to work down the communicating trenches running eastwards from his line. One ½ Coy. infantry will be told off by 46th Bde. as escort to these grenadiers. The troops holding the line on the left of No.4 column will move forward (with the machine guns) and occupy the German front trenches as soon as the grenadiers have cleared them. The troops of the 1st Divn. on our left will have orders to conform to this advance.

(g) As soon as the assaulting columns have cleared the German front trench, this trench will be occupied by the Brigade reserves and parties told off to open (up from both ends) communication trenches to join up with our own trenches. These parties will be left behind when the Bde. reserve moves forward, until relieved by other troops. The Bde. in divl. Reserve (45th) will move up into our own front trenches as soon as these have been cleared by the two leading Bdes., but will not leave these trenches without orders from Div.H.Q.

Signal for Assault.

15. Fixed time will be fixed for the assault, at which moment the leading companys will advance, simultaneously with those of the 47th Div.

Communication.

16.

(a) A visual signal station will be established on FOSSE 8 3 by the Divl. Signal Coy. Particulars as to this will be given to Bde. and Battn. Sign. Officers by O.C. 15th Signals.

(b) At least 2 light wires will be taken forward by each Battn. for communication back to Bde. Hd. Qrs. These wires will be in addition to those taken forward byt artillery observing officers.

(c) To supplement tha above(both of which may fail) Battn. commanders will arrange a system of runners to keep up communication with Bde. Hd. Qrs. and with their companies. 4 Selected men per company and 6 per Battn. Hd. Qrs. have been found satisfactory numbers to tell off for this purpose.

(d) In the forming up positions each company or party will keep in touch with the company in front by means of connecting files along the communicating trenches.

Artillery Support.

17. The artillery programme will be issued separately to all concerned.

During the gas discharge the artillery bombardment will not be interrupted. After the discharge, the artillery will continue to fire on any hostile troops beyond or retiring before the gas, and will prevent the enemy from forming up for a counter attack.

When the assault takes place, the artillery fire will be lifted to cover the infantry advance.

It is essential that the advancing infantry, by means of messages and of the flags provided for the purpose, should endeavour to keep the artillery informed of their progress.

The objects of the 4 days preliminary bombardment

will be :-

(i) Removing all obstacles in the hostile front system of Trenches opposite the points of assault, and cutting the wire entanglements along the whole line.

(ii) Destroying artillery observation stations.

(iii) Bombarding the defences and communications on the general line DOUBLE CRASSIER - LOOS - HULLUCH

(iv) Damaging defended buildings in rear of the hostile trenches to make them more susceptible to gas attack.-

(v) Lowering the moral of the enemys supports and reserves by a continuous bombardment.

During and after the launching of the attack, the task of the artillery is to establish curtains of fire in front of our infantry, and barrages on the exposed flanks of attack; while the counter batteries continue to engaged the German guns.

The R.E. will hold a party in readiness in each sector to go forward and prepare passage for guns over the trenches.

Disposal of Prisoners.

18. Any prisoners captured will be collected and sent back under escort to QUALITY St. when they will be taken over by the A.P.M. and the escorts relieved.

Special warnings to troops.

19. Troops will be warned :-

(a) Against relaxing the attack against an enemy who displays the white flag, unless it is quite certain that he has discarded his arms, and is out of reach of support.

(b) That all papers and orders are to be destroyed; no papers will be carried by officers and men taking part in the attack except the AUCHY - LENS map showing the German trenches. <u>All messages and</u>

reports will refer to this map.

(c) That men in the ranks will not fall out to bring back wounded.

(d) That any guns captured which are in danger of being lost again will be rendered unserviceable by destroying the sights and breech mechanism.

(e) That hand grenades are difficult to replenish, and must not be wasted. There must be a supply of grenades in hand to meet counter attacks.

Divl.Hd.Qrs. 20. Divl. Battle Hd. Qrs. will be established in the 3rd house from the northern end of the new avenue in MAZINGARBE. All reports will be sent there. Divl. Art. Hd. Qrs. will bein the next house to this.

Advanced Divl. Administrative Head Qrs. will be at the WHITE HO. in NOEUX LES MINES.

(Sgd) F. BURNETT STUART,

Lt. Col.
G.S.

15th Div.
30/8/15.

5

NOTES RE CONFERENCES.

SECRET

3v3

1st Army. G.S. 164/2 (a)   IVth Corps No. H.R.S. 398.

MEMORANDUM.

The G.O.C. 1st Army will hold a conference at Advanced 1st Army Headquarters at HINGES at 10-30 a.m. on Monday 6th September.

The following will attend;-

1st Army:- M.G.R.A., M.G.R.E., D.A.&Q.M.G., O.C.No.1 Wing R.F.C
Officer i/c Signals.

1st Corps:- G.O.C., S.G.S.O., G.O.C.R.A., C.E,

2nd Division:- G.O.C., S.G.S.O., C.R.A.
7th Division:- G.O.C., S.G.S.O., C.R.A.
9th Division:- G.O.C., S.G.S.O., C.R.A.

IVth Corps:- G.O.C., S.G.S.O., G.O.C.R.A., C.E.

1st Division:- G.O.C., S.G.S.O., C.R.A.
15th Division:- G.O.C., S.G.S.O., C.R.A.
47th Division:- G.O.C., S.G.S.O., C.R.A.

Indian Corps:- G.O.C., S.G.S.O., G.O.C.R.A., C.E.

Meerut Division:- G.O.C., S.G.S.O., C.R.A.

IIIrd Corps:- G.O.C., S.G.S.O., G.O.C.R.A., C.E.

8th Division:- G.O.C., S.G.S.O., C.R.A.

No. 1 Group H.A.R.:- G.O.C.

No. 4 " G.O.C.

No. 5 " G.O.C.

Adv. 1st Army.   (sd) R.Butler. Major General,
1st September, 1915.   General Staff, 1st Army.

(2)

~~1st Division.~~
15th Division.
~~47th Division.~~

Forwarded.

[signature]

2nd September, 1915.   Brigadier General,
General Staff, IVth Corps.

H.R.S. 525/1

SECRET

HEADQUARTERS 4th CORPS
21 SEP 1915
GENERAL STAFF

~~1st Division.~~
15th Division.
~~47th Division.~~
~~4th Corps Artillery.~~

Certain situations may arise which require previous consideration and discussion. The Corps Commander's views as to how he proposes to deal with the various likely eventualities are given below, and will be discussed by him at the Conference to-morrow.

1. If the weather conditions permit it is intended that the hour of zero is to be 4.50 a.m. The hour will be definitely notified to Divisions between 9 p.m. and 10 p.m. on the 24th September.

2. If the weather conditions do not admit of gas being used on the morning of the 25th, and circumstances do not admit of offensive operations being postponed, the great moral effect of a surprise gas attack will be eliminated, and it is not intended to attempt to carry the whole of the enemy's defences in one rush.

The advance will be made in stages until the final objectives are reached, but each stage will have to be systematically prepared.

3. Under these conditions, the 15th Division will attack the LOOS salients at 5 a.m. on the 25th without the use of gas, but with the employment of such smoke shells, etc., as can be employed to assist the assault.

We shall probably receive warning as regards unfavourable weather conditions about 1 p.m. on 24th.

4. The 1st and 47th Divisions will not attack at the same time as the 15th Division (see para. 6 below), but as soon as the 15th Division attack is launched will demonstrate all along their fronts.

5. The Corps Artillery and No. 1 Group H.A.R. will

/open

open intense fire as soon as the 15th Division attack is launched.

(a) <u>On the 47th Division Front</u>.

(i) On the front line system of trenches from the DOUBLE CRASSIER (inclusive) to G.34.a.8.2.

(ii) On all objectives whose destruction will afford the greatest assistance to the 15th Division.

(b) <u>On the 15th Division Front</u>.

(i) On the second line system of trenches between the cemetery G.35.b (inclusive) to G.29.b.3.9.

(ii) On all objectives in rear whose destruction will afford the greatest assistance to the 15th Division, especially LOOS Village.

(c) <u>On the 1st Division Front</u>.

(i) On the front line system of trenches from sap G.22.d.6.3 - 3.8 (exclusive) to LONE TREE.

(ii) On all objectives whose destruction will afford the greatest ássistance to the 15th Division.

3rd Division to start with the easing off

This <u>intense</u> fire to be continued until the 15th Division is firmly established in the enemy's first line system of trenches.

6. The attack on the LOOS salients by the 15th Division on the 25th will be followed later by attacks by the 1st and 47th Divisions, the nature and time of which will depend on the conditions that then obtain.

7. The 1st and 47th Divisions will, therefore, be prepared to act as follows:-

(1) If the wind remains unfavourable, and if the progress effected by the French makes such a course desirable, the 1st Division will attack with the object of capturing:-

(a)

(a) The hostile first line system of trenches from sap G.23.a.4.3 - G.22.b.9.7 (inclusive) to VERMELLES - HULLUCH road (exclusive).

(b) The hostile second line system of trenches from G.29.b.3.9 to G.12.d.6.0.

(c) The southern part of HULLUCH.

The 7th Division will at the same time attack the northern part of HULLUCH.

The 47th Division to make a demonstration at the same time.

The attack of the 1st Division will be made later in the day on the 25th September, and will be preceded by one hour's intense bombardment by all available guns of the 1st Group, H.A.R., and Corps Artillery, leaving only sufficient guns to cover the front of the 15th Division and to assist in the demonstration by the 47th Division.

or

(2) If the wind remains unfavourable, but the progress of the French does not render an early attack desirable, the ~~15th~~ 1st and 47th Divisions will attack after dark, night 25th/26th, at an hour to be notified later.

The objectives of the 1st Division will be the hostile front line system of trenches from sap G.23.a.4.3 - G.22.b.9.7 (inclusive) to VERMELLES - HULLUCH road, the enemy's second line trenches from G.29.b.3.9 to G.12.d.6.0 and the southern part of HULLUCH Village.

The objectives of the 47th Division will be the DOUBLE CRASSIER as far east as M.4.d.8.8, the front line system of trenches from M.4.a.1.3 to G.34.a.6.5, and the

second

second line trenches from M.4.d.8.8 to the cemetery (inclusive).

At the same time, the 15th Division will attack the second line trenches between the cemetery (exclusive) and G.29.b.3.9.

or

(3) If the wind becomes favourable during the 25th, the 1st, 15th and 47th Divisionswill attack under cover of gas on morning of 26th September. The objectives of the three Divisions being those laid down in Operation Order No. 35, paragraphs 6, 7, and 8.

A.A. MONTGOMERY, Brigadier-General,
General Staff, IVth Corps.

H.Q. IVth Corps.
21st September, 1915.

Wrote alternative orders on these lines - Subsequently destroyed them [illegible]

6.

ARTILLERY INSTRUCTIONS.

SECRET

HEADQUARTERS, 15th DIVISION 2 SEP. 1915 Reg. No.

322/

IVth Corps No. H.R.S. 506./2

HEADQUARTERS 4th CORPS 2 SEP 1915 GENERAL STAFF

15th Division.
~~47th Division.~~

The G.O.C. wishes your B.G.R.A. to move forward to his fighting station as early as possible.

Order conveyed personally by Gray – move 5.15 –

2. This station will be in communication with the fighting station of the Commander of the Corps Artillery, which is at VAUDRICOURT, where General Budworth has already moved.

3. It is presumed that the fighting station to be occupied by your B.G.R.A. will be at or near your own Advanced Head-quarters.

Would you inform me if this is so?

Done See G 660

Brigadier-General,
General Staff, IVth Corps.

H.Q. IVth Corps.
2nd September, 1915.

SECRET

IVth Corps No. H.R.S. 509/3

~~1st Division.~~
15th Division.
~~47th Division.~~
~~G.O.C. IVth Corps Artillery.~~

A copy of First Army letter No. G.S. 164/3 (d), dated 10th September, 1915, is forwarded herewith for your information.

Please acknowledge receipt.

HEADQUARTERS,
15th DIVISION
10 SEP. 1915
Reg. No. 376

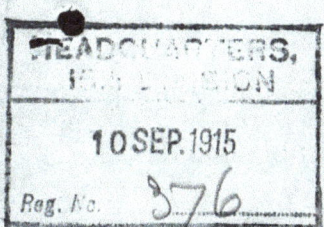

Brigadier-General,
General Staff, IVth Corps.

H.Q. IVth Corps.
10th September, 1915.

A

10/9

SECRET.

IVth Corps No. H.R.S. 509.

Head-qrs.,

1st Corps.
3rd Corps.
4th Corps.
Indian Corps.

No. 1 Group, H.A.R.
No. 4 Group, H.A.R.
No. 5 Group, H.A.R.

No. G.S. 164/3 (d). 10/9/15.

This minute cancels the whole of my minute No. G.S. 135 (d) of 3/9/15.

2. The numbers of rounds available for you for the fothcoming operations will be as follows:-

Nature.	x	4th Corps.	No. 1 Group H.A.R.	x
		ROUNDS PER GUN.		
13 pr. H.E.		354	-	
S.		544	-	
15 pr. B.L.C. S.		336	-	
18 pr. H.E.		230	-	
S.		682	-	
4.5" How. H.E.		450	-	
S.		15	-	
5" How. H.E.		600	-	
6" How. H.E.		569	-	
4.7" gun H.E. & C.P.		-	158	
S.		-	58	
60 pr. H.E.		-	354	
S.		-	180	
6" gun H.E.		-	158	
15" How.		-	113	
		TOTAL ROUNDS.		
8" How. H.E.		-	2640	
9.2" How. H.E.		-	2110	

3. As regards the 2.75" guns, there is not likely to be any ammunition beyond that now carried in all echelons in front of railhead. These echelons should not be depleted below 100 rounds per gun.

4. The numbers of rounds detailed in para: 1 represent the total amount of ammunition allotted for the forthcoming operations, which, for the purposes of a rough basis for calculations, may be put at:-

4 days' deliberate bombardment;

2 days' battle; and

4 days' subsequent fighting.

In the case of the 8" and 9.2" howitzers the allowance given in para: 1 will deplete the echelons in front of railhead by 50 and 40 rounds per howitzer, respectively.

5. The numbers of rounds which may be drawn by you, in excess of establishment, before the operations begin, have been communicated to you in my Q/343 of 4/9/15.

6. These rounds will be allotted to you gradually by Army Headquarters in such a manner as to regulate the flow of ammunition from the Base in a steady stream.

7. Unauthorised overdrawals have been frequent during past operations, in spite of repeated definite orders against the practice.

It must be clearly understood by all concerned that no rounds are to be drawn, in any circumstances, either now or in the future, in excess of establishment, without allotment by Army Headquarters.

It is not necessary to recapitulate the reasons for

/these

these orders. They should be known to, and appreciated by, all concerned; but, as it appears, from recent overdrawals, in spite of orders to the contrary, that there is still some doubt on the subject, it is to be clearly understood, and made known to all concerned, that the Army Commander intends to take severe disciplinary action in every future case of disobedience of these orders.

8. During the forthcoming operations no ammunition will be drawn until the rounds issued in excess of establishment have been fired, after which ammunition will be drawn to replace expenditure, that is to say, to the extent necessary to keep all echelons in front of railhead up to establishment.

(sd) R.BUTLER.

Maj-Gen., G.S.,

for General,

Advanced First Army. Commanding First Army.

HEADQUARTERS,
15th DIVISION.
14 SEP. 1915
Reg. No.........

15 BW
429

S/38

Secret.

15th Division

Herewith 4 copies of Special Instructions for Bombardment prior to, during, and after the assault.

Please acknowledge receipt.

done

14.9.15

H Sherbrooke
Major
for Br Genl Comd'g 15th D.A.

15th Division G/842.

SECRET.

44th Infantry Brigade.
45th do. do.
46th do. do.

Herewith copy of special instructions for bombardment prior to, during, and after the assault.

Major. G.S.
15th Division.

15th September, 1915.

Secret

Instructions re preliminary Bombardment. 1.

1. The zones allotted to the 18-pr Brigades will be as on the attached maps.

2. Brigades will cut wire on the front of their zones.

3. O.s C. Brigades will divide the front for wire-cutting between their Batteries

4. Wire-cutting will be carried on continuously during each day of the bombardment. It should be deliberate and every round should be observed. O.s C. Brigades should endeavour to arrange that for the first day at any rate not more that two Batteries of each Brigade are firing at the same time at the wire. If sufficient rpogress is not made on the first day this restriction will be removed, as the wire must be properly cut at all costs.

5. It is estimated that about 100 rounds shrapnel per gun per day will be enough for this purpose, but if necessary this must be increased.

6. At stated intervals (see Table A annexed) Batteries will open fire with H.E. on the front line parapet and saps in their allotted frontage. If they are wire-cutting they must change for the necessary interval. They should not as a rule fire directly behind where they have been wire-cutting, but should select strong points, machine-gun emplacements etc., towards one flank or other. They should endeavour to get direct hits, and, to avoid waste of H.E., can test their range with a few rounds of percussion shrapnel. Places that have been already destroyed by the fire of heavy guns should be avoided. Special attention should be paid to any new work or repairs done after the bombardment begins.

7. Guns employed in wire-cutting need not be used for the bombardment, but the other guns of the Battery employed.

8. In addition to the wire on the front line trenches O.C. 72nd Brigade will endeavour to cut as much as possible in front of the support trenches from G 34 a 6.5 to G 28 d 2.8.

9. Some of the points that evidently require special attention with H.E. are:-

Sap running to G 34 a 3.3

Copies to 44th 45th & 46th Bdes -

G 34 a 6.5

South edge of Southern Salient

G 28 c 6.1

G 28 c 9.5

G 28 d 1.9 to 3.7

G 28 b 3.1

G 28 b 4.5

South edge of Northern Salient

G 28 b 4.9

Sap running to g ~~28~~ 22 d 3.8, especially the head and near G 22 d 6.3

Table A

72nd Brigade. Batteries from the right.

			No. of rounds H.E.
1st	Battery	8 a.m.	25
2nd	"	9 "	25
3rd	"	9.30 "	25
4th	"	10 "	35
4th	"	10.30"	35
1st	"	12 noon	25
2nd	"	12.30 p.m.	25
3rd	"	2 p.m.	25
4th	"	3 "	35
3rd	"	4 "	25
2nd	"	4.30 "	25
1st	"	5.30 "	25
		Total	330

70th Brigade, Batteries from the right.

			No. of rounds H.E.
1st	Battery	7.30 a.m.	30
2nd	"	9. "	"
3rd	"	10. "	"
4th	"	11.30 "	"
4th	"	12 noon	"
3rd	"	1. p.m."	"
2nd	"	2. " "	"
1st	"	3. "	"
1st	"	4. "	"
2nd	"	4.30 "	"
3rd	"	5.30 "	"
4th	"	6. "	"
		Total	360

71st Brigade. Batteries from the right.

			No. of rounds H.E.
1st	Battery	8 a.m.	30
2nd	"	9 "	"
3rd	"	9.30 "	"
3rd	"	11. "	"
2nd	"	12.30 p.m.	"
1st	"	2. p.m.	"
1st	"	3. "	"
2nd	"	4. "	"
3rd	"	5. "	"
		Total	270

Note.

If it is considered necessary to fire more rounds at any time to finish off a job, they must be deducted from another period.

4

SECRET

Enfilade and oblique fire.

---

10. 72nd Brigade will also fire as follows on the front system of trenches between roads and communication trench from G 23 central to H 13 a 4.4.

11. The front line is to be divided into two parts: one Battery to be told off for each of these parts and one for the communication trenches mentioned above.

12. Each Battery will fire during the day between the hours 6 a.m. - 10 a.m., 10 a.m. - 2 p.m. and 2 p.m. - 7 p.m., i.e. one series in each period mentioned. Batteries will fire slowly for periods of at least 20 minutes, and will search along the whole front allotted to them. They will be allowed 50 rounds per battery of shrapnel for each period.

Total - 450 rounds.

---

13. Once during the morning and afternoon O.s C. 18-pr Brigades will detail one Battery each to search with shrapnel the communication and second line trenches in their zones West of LOOS. These Batteries will search along the trenches indicated to them by their Brigade Commanders. 50 rounds will be allowed for each period, and must be fairly evenly spread over half an hour.

Total - 300 rounds.

4.5" Howitzers.

14. O.C. 73rd Brigade will divide the 15th Divisional zone between his Batteries. Their principal duties during the bombardment will be to bombard the second line trenches and communication trenches in this area. 100 rounds per gun per day is allotted, but this must include night firing.

15. Batteries will endeavour to register important points not in their own zones before the bombardment starts.

15a. They will also deal with any hostile observation posts.

Siege Battery.

16. The 5th Siege Battery will bombard the front line trenches, paying special attention to saps and strong points. Important points behind the front line should be previously registered.

Night Firing.

17. The areas numbered on the maps are to be kept under fire at night. They will be allotted as follows:-

1 to 6.................	72nd Brigade)	
7,8,9,10 and 13........	70th ")	see map
11,12,14 and 15........	71st ")	

Each area is to be fired on once every 2 hours during the night at irregular intervals: 6 rounds each time for each area.

Total - 450 rounds shrapnel.

18. In addition to the above one Battery in each 18-pr Brigade must fire 20 rounds shrapnel at the front line system of their zones 3 times during the night. This should be scattered along the front.

Total - 180 rounds.

19. O.s C. Brigades will tell off Batteries for this purpose, but it will not as a rule be necessary to use more than one gun at a time for this purpose. Care should be taken to make

it as easy as possible for the detachments.

20. O.C. 73rd Brigade will also detail one Battery for the sa same purpose. This Battery will fire on points 4,6,9,16 and 17 (see map) once each at irregular intervals between the hours 7 p.m. to 10 p.m., 10 p.m. to 1 a.m. and 1 a.m. to 5 a.m. 6 rounds will be allowed for each place during each of these 3 periods.

Total - 90 rounds.

21. All Batteries must be prepared to prevent the enemy repairing wire etc. during the night. This will be the special duty of the 18-pr Brigades, but howitzers must be prepared to assist if called on. Necessary communications must be kept up at night with the infantry to ensure early information of work being done by the enemy.

S E C R E T

BATTERY COMMANDERS IN THE TRENCHES

A proportion of Battery C.O.s from each Brigade must be in the trenches before the assault takes place.

This B.C. will follow thw infantry attack when in his judgment it is reasonably safe for him to do so, and he thinks that he will be able to see the situation better by advancing. He should not expose himself unduly. His duty is to report on the situation to his own Brigade Commander, and to be able to bring fire to bear without delay on places from which the enemy are holding up, or are likely to hold up, our own infantry. He should be given a free hand to open fire from his own Battery at once, if he considers that the situation demands it. but if his Battery is already firing he must be prepared to justify his reasons for changiggon to a new objective. It is impossible to enumerate all the reasons which would justify his doing so, but a counter-attack by the enemy might be an example. If he considers that the fire of his own Battery is not enough to deal with the situation, he should report what he thinks necessary: for instance, a strong work would require to be dealt with by heavy howitzers. To enable him to carry out these duties, he will require plenty of light (D.1) wire, two or more telephones and at least three operators and instruments. These men should be armed with rifles, and provided with smoke-helmets and two days' rations.

The Battery Commander should never order a continuous fire, but always give a stated number of rounds, as then, if his wire is cut, ammunition will not be wasted.

SECRET

OFFICERS WITH INFANTRY

One Officer from 70th and 72nd Brigades is to remain with Headquarters of each attacking Brigade.

A line connecting them direct with H.Q. 15th Divl Arty is to be laid down. These Officers should be provided with at least 2 miles of light wire to enable them to advance with the Headquarters. They will not move away from Brigade Headquarters without an order from the Brigadier-General.

Their duties are to pass on all information they can gather of the situation to 15th D.A., and all requests of the Infantry Brigadier they are with for artillery assistance.

They will require 3 operators and 2 instruments. They should all be armed and provided with smoke-helmets and 2 days' rations.

lVth Corps No. H.R.S. 517.

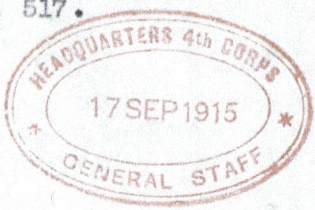

C.A. 64. SECRET

HEADQUARTERS 4th CORPS
17 SEP 1915
GENERAL STAFF

Headquarters, lVth Corps.

The attached tracing shows the proposed positions, on the day of attack, for the battery wagon lines and brigade ammunition columns, which it is considered expedient to move from their present positions.

In order that these positions may not interfere with other transport arrangements, they are forwarded for your information.

In all cases cover from view, except from balloons, is obtained, but the remainder of the ground is nearly all over-looked.

In the case of the 47th Division the batteries of the 1st Division, temporarily attached, are the only ones that may be required to move in the earlier stages and consequently the reserve batteries (15 pr.) of the 47th Division will move to the Corons L. 19. c., as soon as the wagon lines of the 1st Division move forward, and remain there ready to occupy the positions vacated by the 1st Division batteries - if necessary.

4th Corps Artillery. Sd. C.E.D.BUDWORTH. Br. General.
16-9-15. Commanding 4th Corps Artillery.

-2-

~~1st Division~~.
15th Division.
~~47th Division~~.

For your information.

H.Q.lVth Corps. Brigadier General.
17th September, 1915. General Staff lVth Corps.

Identification Trace for use with Artillery Maps.

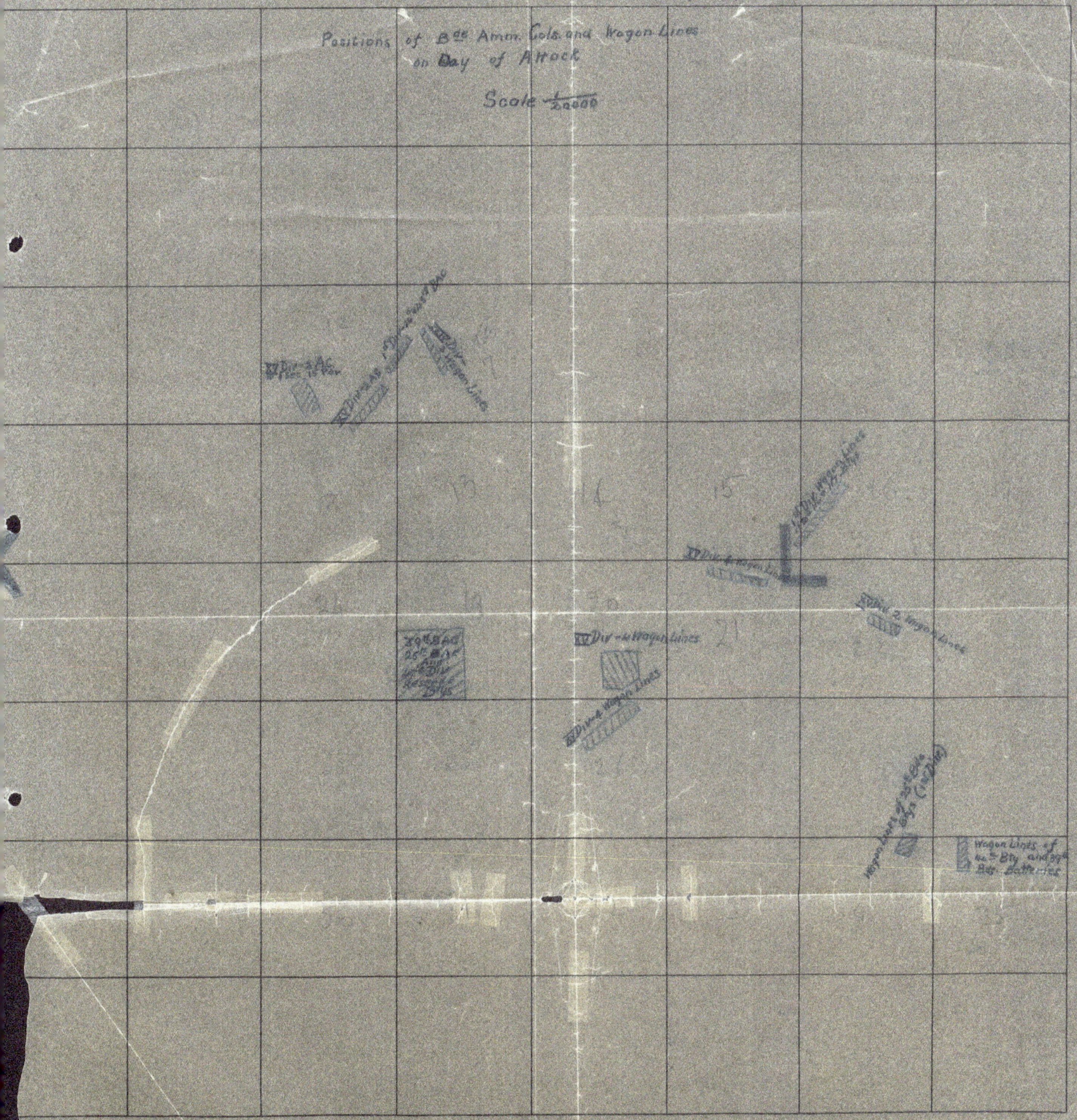

—(1). These traces are intended to facilitate the communication of information as to the position of targets, which have been located on a squared map.

(2). The squares on this trace are 1,000 yards in length on the 1/20,000 scale, and 2,000 yards in length on the 1/40,000 scale.

(3). The squares on the trace are fitted to the squares of the map showing the targets, which are then drawn on the trace. Sufficient letters and numbers must also be added to enable the recipient to place the trace in the correct position on his own map. A little detail may also be traced, but this is not essential. The name and scale of the map to which the trace refers must be always given. The trace can be used for either the 1/20,000 or 1/40,000 scale.

G.S.G.S. 3022

Tracing taken from Sheet 36 B N.E.

of the 1: 20,000 map of ....

Signature .... Date ....

Secret

15th Division G.976.

Fourth Corps.

Original handed to Bowley by me WDS 21/9/15

Your H.R.S. 517.

We have arranged with 1st Group H.A.R. to support our attack by firing on the German trenches from the Dynamitiere at N.1. central to N.2.b. central and thence northwards to H.26.d.3.6. Special attention will be paid to following points:-

Salients at N.1.b.1.3. and N.2.a.5.4.

Angle at N.2.b.5.4.

Work at N.3.a.3.3.

Pt. H.32.d.8.10.

Work at H.32.b.4.5. (especially strong)

Small work at H.26.d.3.1.

When the fire of the Corps Artillery is lifted from the "1.15" line, the fire of the H.A.R. on the further line given above will be increased, and will be kept there until we can get reports indicating that it should be lifted.

Sd (F W N McC.)

Major General,

21st September 1915. Commanding 15th Division.

Copied to all Bdes WDS

+ Copy sent to Div Art + 4th Corps Art. WDS. 22/9

Confirmed by 1st group HAR in their mess: J.B. 9/86 of 22/9 -

"A" Form. Army Form C. 2121.

MESSAGES AND SIGNALS.

No. of Message

Prefix / Code m. / Office of Origin and Service Instructions	Words / Charge / Sent At m. To By	This message is on a/c of: Service.	Recd. at m. / Date / From / By
		SECRET (Signature of "Franking Officer.")	

TO: 44th Bde, 3rd Bde, 46th Bde, 47th Div., Div Art.

* Sender's Number	Day of Month	In reply to Number	AAA
G991	22		

A demonstration will be made on the front of the Div tomorrow AAA at 3-55 pm the Divl Artillery Groups will open intense fire on the enemy's trenches in front of the 44th Bde as follows:-

(a) Five minutes on the front line trenches

(b) Lift on to the second line trenches for 3 mins:

(c) Come back on to front line for 3 mins.

During period (b) the infantry holding the front trenches of the 46th Bde will open rapid rifle and machine gun fire for 2 or 3 mins. The Infantry holding the front trenches of the 44th Bde will do everything possible to make the enemy believe an attack is imminent in order to induce them to man their trenches before the artillery begin period (C) AAA acknowledge AAA addressed 44th & 46th Bdes & Divl Art. repeated 3rd Bde & 47th Div.

From 15th Div.

Place

Time 4 pm

The above may be forwarded as now corrected. (Z) (Sd) J.B.S.

Censor. Signature of Addressor or person authorised to telegraph in his name.

Lt Col. GS

* This line should be erased if not required.

(15491) S. & Co. Ltd. W 14142/641. 90,000. 4/15. Forms C 2121/18.

7

LETTERS AND INSTRUCTIONS RE GAS.

308

IVth Corps No. H.R.S. 506

of 31.8.15

~~1st Division.~~
15th Division.
~~47th Division.~~
~~O.C. Gas Company.~~

Instructions for the bringing up and reception of gas cylinders and smoke candles.

1. The division of the IVth Corps front into "smoke" or "gas" fronts is shown on the attached plan "A".

(a) The fronts on which the infantry attacks will be made, and a length of from 300 to 500 yards on either flank of each attack, are termed "gas" fronts, and on these fronts gas and smoke will be discharged as follows:-

	10 minutes gas followed by		(5 cylinders)
	4 minutes smoke	,, ,,	(2 candles)
	6 minutes gas	,, ,,	(3 cylinders)
	6 minutes smoke	,, ,,	(3 candles)
	14 minutes gas		(7 cylinders)
Total	40 minutes = per partition		(15 cylinders) (5 candles).

R 9626

(b) The remaining fronts (with the exception of B - B.1) will be termed "smoke" fronts, and

gas

gas and smoke will be discharged as below:-

	6 minutes gas followed by	(3 cylinders)
	34 minutes smoke	(17 candles)
Total	40 minutes = per partition	(3 cylinders) (17 candles).

(c) Between B and B.1 nothing will be discharged as it may involve danger to the troops holding A - B.

2. Arrangements for the reception of gas cylinders in the trenches are to be completed by the evening of 5th September.

Storage protected from hostile artillery fire will be required in the trenches for 18* or 3 cylinders in each partition, according as the front is a "gas" or a "smoke" front.

* (See para. 4 (c) as regards this figure).

3. The number of partitions given in Plan "A" is only approximate.

To enable exact numbers to be definitely fixed before the cylinders are distributed, Divisions will forward as early as possible to this office, the exact number of partitions on the fronts for which they will

be

be responsible. These are as follows:-

47th Division - E - F and D - E.

15th Division - C - D, B.1. - C, B - B.1.

1st Division - A - B.

4. (a) The exact number of cylinders that will actually be available for the attack is not yet definitely known. The probable number is ~~2250~~ 2260. 84 39.
Plan "A" and attached notes are worked out on this figure.

(b) On the above figure the allotment will be approximately:-

1st Division	..	~~180~~.	168
15th Division	..	~~1116~~.	1245
47th Division	..	~~948~~.	846
			2259 lt 39

(c) Should more cylinders be available, the number of cylinders in each partition of the "gas" fronts will be increased and the time during which gas will be discharged increased accordingly, and that during which smoke is discharged decreased. The proportion on "smoke" fronts will remain the same. To provide for this, each partition on the gas fronts should be prepared for the reception of 18 cylinders.

CDR informed

(d)

(d) Should less cylinders be available, there will be no change in the "gas" and "smoke" fronts nor in the total time (40 minutes) during which smoke and gas will be discharged, but the strength of the discharge of gas will be adjusted so that cylinders will last for more than two minutes, thus necessitating less cylinders in each partition.

5. In order to meet these possibilities, the O.C. Gas Company and Divisions will arrange that the number of cylinders taken up on the first night to each partition on both descriptions of front is kept approximately equal.

On the "gas" fronts on the first night each partition should be given 7 cylinders. On the "smoke" fronts the full number 3 can be put in. The number of cylinders that go into partitions on the second and third nights will be regulated according to the number of cylinders available.

6. Candles will be available at Railhead as shown below on the first night and can be taken up as desired

by

by divisions, but it is recommended that the bulk should go up on the third night.

1st Div.	~~1050~~ 952	(allowing ~~30~~ 48 spare).	= 1000
15th Div.	~~750~~ 415	(allowing ~~26~~ 35 spare).	450
47th Div.	~~920~~ 794	(allowing ~~28~~ 56 spare).	850
			2300
Total.	~~2720~~ 2		

Total No. of Candles 3500 / 2300 / 1200

Remainder 1200 will be kept in Corps Reserve and be kept at MINX under C.E.

7. Three nights are being allowed for the bringing up of cylinders and candles from Railhead to their position in the trenches.

The approximate allotment of gas cylinders will be :-

	1st Div.	15th Div.	47th Div.	Total
1st night.	-	500	500	1000
2nd night.	180	500	448	1128
3rd night.	-	~~116~~ 245	-	116
	~~180~~ 168	~~1116~~ 1245	~~948~~ 846	~~2244~~ 2259

Exact numbers to be settled between O.C. Gas Company and Divisions as soon as the exact number of partitions has been ascertained by divisions, and the number of cylinders available is known to O.C. Gas Company.

8.

8. A Gas Company, under Captain Sanders, R.E., has been allotted to the IVth Corps and will arrive on 4th September. It consists of approximately ~~13~~ 15 officers and 400 men, divided into ~~13~~ 15 sections. These will be allotted to :-

1st Div. ~~2~~ 3 Sections = ~~2~~ 3 officers, 60 men.
15th Div. 6 sections = 6 officers, 180 men.
47th Div. ~~5~~ 6 sections = ~~5~~ 6 officers, 140 men.
380

From the 4th to 7th September they will be billeted in, or bivouac at, VERQUIN, and from 8th to 12th at MAZINGARBE. During the whole period 4th to 12th they will be rationed by 15th Division.

9. H.Q. of O.C. Gas Company will remain throughout at "Railhead", and will be connected up direct with Corps Advanced Head-quarters.

10. "Railhead" for cylinders and candles will be at MINX (Fosse 8 - K.6.a.).

Divisional dumps will be at:-

1st Div. LE RUTOIRE (G.15.b.).
15th Div. FOSSE 7. Quality Street (G.27.c.).
47th Div. ST. PANCRAS ROAD KEEP, MAROC, (M.2.b.).

11. Divisions will supply wagons for transporting cylinders and candles from Railhead to Divisional dumps. The wheels of these wagons will be muffled. Wagons will be at Railhead each evening at 7 p.m.

12. The working party for unloading cylinders from the train and loading into wagons will be found by the Gas Company. The Gas Company, before loading the cylinders into the wagons, will see that all the screws except one are taken out of the boxes, one screw being left in at one end to keep the lid attached to the box.

The boxes, with lids, will be returned to Railhead in the empty wagons as soon as the cylinders have been taken out of them at Divisional dumps.

13. The loading parties at the Divisional dump, and the carrying parties up to the trenches from the dumps, will be found by divisions.

14. The O.C. Gas Company will be responsible for the distribution of cylinders to divisions at Railhead on the lines laid down in paragraph 7.

He

He will also be responsible for the distribution of candles to divisions in accordance with paragraph 6.

Divisions will arrange with him how many candles they want sent up each night.

15. An R.E. officer has been detailed by 1st Division to assist O.C. Gas Company in the above work.

An A.S.C. officer has been detailed by 1st Division to marshal the wagons at Railhead.

16. Each division will have a separate unloading and loading place at Railhead. A plan of these will be issued to those concerned.

17. The officers and N.C.Os. of the Gas Company will be available from 8th September (inclusive) to supervise the arrangement of the cylinders in the trenches, and ensure that the cylinders are ready for working on the morning of 12th September.

18. . The actual time at which the discharge of gas will commence will be notified later, but it will be a question of very careful timing. The Gas Company are

responsible

responsible that the correct times are kept and all watches will be synchronized with those of the Gas Company.

19. Section Commanders of the Gas Company are to have free use of the telephone line for sending back messages to Army Head-quarters.

Their messages will be treated as "priority" at Divisional and Corps Head-quarters.

20. Divisions will furnish men for the discharge of smoke candles at the rate of 2 men per partition; in case of casualties amongst the Gas Company, these men will also be available for assisting in the discharge of gas, and will receive instruction accordingly.

21. Poles and slings for carrying up the cylinders will come with the cylinders up to the Divisional dumps. O.C. Gas Company will be responsible for the correct number going up with each group of wagons.

22. When done with, the poles and slings will be collected by Divisions and returned to the Gas Company at MAZINGARBE.

23. The personnel of the Gas Company will be withdrawn from the trenches as soon as possible after the infantry assault has commenced and rejoin their company at MAZINGARBE.

24. A table showing the measurements of cylinders is attached.

Brigadier-General,
General Staff, IVth Corps.

H.Q. IVth Corps.
31st August, 1915.

Plan A

Not drawn to scale. Partition = 25 yards. Gas / Smoke

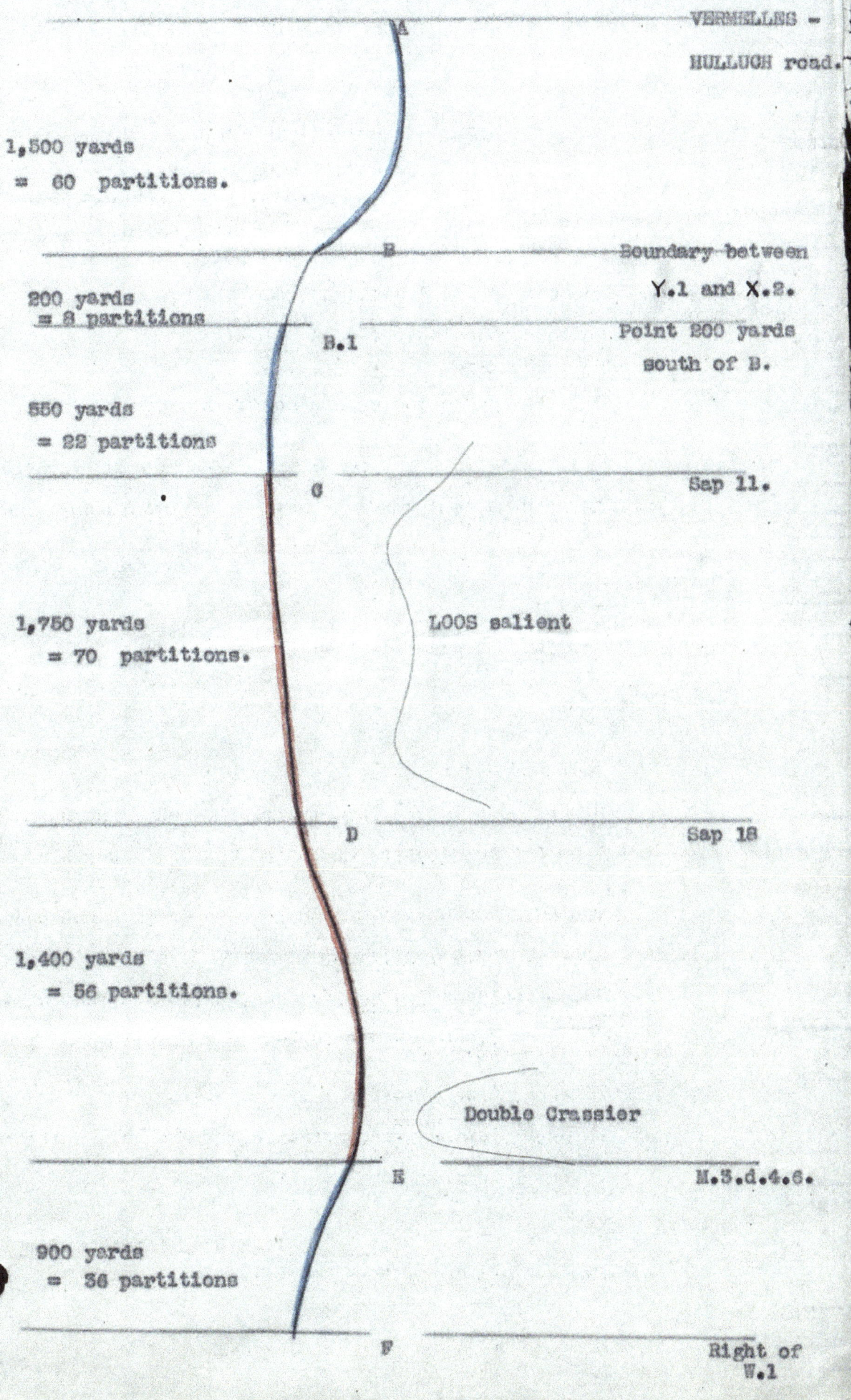

SECRET

Notes to explain Plan "A".

			Cylinders.	Candles.
A - B.	60 partitions - smoke	=	180.	1020.
B - B.1.	8 partitions - nothing. (Any discharge of gas or smoke in this length of front might seriously affect our own troops in A - B if the wind was at all variable).			
B.1 - C.	22 partitions	=	66.	374.
C - D.	70 partitions	=	1050.	350.
D - E.	56 partitions	=	840.	280.
E - F.	36 partitions	=	108.	612.
	Total	=	2244.	2636.

SECRET

DIMENSIONS OF CYLINDERS.

First type:-

Circumference	2'	3"
Diameter		8½"
Total height.	3'	2½"
Height to top of shoulder	2'	8½"
Handles of cylinder project		2½"

Second type with cap:-

Circumference	2'	2"	
Diameter		8¼"	
Height with cap	3'	7"	or 3' 8½"
" without cap	3'	4½"	
" to top of shoulder	2'	10½"	
Handles of cylinder project		2½"	

Average weight of cylinder, without box = 125 lbs.
" " with box = 167 lbs.

Length of jet pipe	10'	0"
Right-angled bend		6½"
Length of iron connecting pipe	6'	4½"
" copper pipe (straight)	7'	0"
" " (with bend)	6'	4½"
" flexible pipe	7'	0"

"A" Form. Army Form C. 2121.

MESSAGES AND SIGNALS. No. of Message

Prefix ... Code ... m.	Words	Charge	This message is on a/c of ... Service.	Recd. at ... m.
Office of Origin and Service Instructions.	Sent			Date
	At ... m.			From
	To			By
	By		(Signature of "Franking Officer.")	

TO CRE SECRET.

* Sender's Number.	Day of Month	In reply to Number	AAA
	First		

1. Each Bay should be prepared for 18 cylinders between Sap 18 and C.T. 14a. (+ c)

2. From C.T. 14a places ~~for~~ should be prepared for 3 cylinders @ 25^x interval up to a point 200 yards South of the Northern Boundary of X2. – 3 + plan A.

3. Storage should be protected from hostile artillery fire as far as possible

4. Bays should be ready by morning of Sept 5th

(Companies start 6 pm Sept 4)

From

Place

Time 9.30 am

The above may be forwarded as now corrected. (Z)

Censor. C. Hewitt [illegible] Major GS 15 Div.

Signature of Addressor or person authorised to telegraph in his name.

* This line should be erased if not required.

(688-9) —McC. & Co. Ltd., London.— W 14142/641. 225,000 4/15. Forms C 2121/10.

"A" Form. Army Form C. 2121.

MESSAGES AND SIGNALS.

No. of Message

Prefix ... Code ... m.	Words	Charge	This message is on a/c of:	Recd. at ... m.
Office of Origin and Service Instructions.	Sent		... Service.	Date
	At ... m.			From
	To			By
	By		(Signature of "Franking Officer.")	

TO CRE
187th Co RE

SECRET

Sender's Number.	Day of Month	In reply to Number	AAA
* special.	3rd.		

There are 69 large Bags
26 Small Bags
in the trenches.
2 In accordance with instruction received from IV Corps please arrange to provide 1 pick
1 shovel
per partition for the use of the gas company.
3. Addressed CRE. repeated O.C. 187th (Gas) Co RE.
4. Acknowledge.

R
CM [illegible]

From 15 Div.
Place
Time 9.50 am.

The above may be forwarded as now corrected.

(Z) E. [illegible] Major GS
15 Div.

Censor. Signature of Addressor or person authorised to telegraph in his name.

* This line should be erased if not required.

(688-0) —McC. & Co. Ltd., London.— W 14142/641. 225,000 4/15. Forms C 2121/10.

SECRET

HEADQUARTERS 4th CORPS
1 SEP 1915
HRS 506
GENERAL STAFF

311

HEADQUARTERS, 15th DIVISION.
1 SEP 1915
Reg. No.

~~1st Division.~~
15th Division.
~~47th Division.~~
~~[struck-through line]~~

1. Reference paragraph 11 of H.R.S. 506 of 31/8/15.
Wagons will report to Captain Butler, A.S.C. at 7 p.m. each evening in the stubble field at E.29.D.8.3., and will afterwards enter Fosse No.8 at Western Gate at K.5.B.5.8.

2. Divisionswill arrange for conducting wagons back from MINX to Divisional Dumps.

3. Wagons should work in Groups of 5 so as to facilitate leading arrangements at MINX.

4. Reference paragraph 16 of H.R.S. 506 of 31/8/15.
As all the arrangements at MINX will be made by the Corps, plans of MINX will not be issued to Divisions.

5. 1st Division will arrange that such Officers and N.C.O's as Captain Butler may require shall be placed at his disposal on 5th, 6th and 7th September.

6. Divisions will arrange that 1 pick and 1 shovel for each partition in the trenches are provided for the use of the Gas Company.

7. Reference paragraph 8 of H.R.S. 506 of 31/8/15.

Line 3 - for 13 Officers read 15 Officers.
4 - for 13 Sections read 15 Sections.
6 - for 2 Sections = 2 Officers read 3 Sections = 3 Officers.
8 - for 5 Sections = 5 Officers read 6 Sections = 6 Officers.

[signature]
for Brigadier General.
General Staff 1Vth Corps.

H.Q.1Vth Corps.
1st September, 1915.

SECRET

IVth Corps No. H.R.S. 506/9

~~1st Division.~~
15th Division.
~~47th Division.~~
~~O.C. Gas Coy.~~

With reference to IVth Corps No. H.R.S. 506 dated 31st ultimo, paragraph 3, the exact number of partitions has now been ascertained and involves certain changes in the lengths of the 'gas' and 'smoke' fronts.

These are explained in a new 'Plan "A" ' (with Notes) which is issued herewith to supersede the original one. This will involve amendments in other paragraphs of the above quoted letter.

Para. 4 (a). The latest number of cylinders due to arrive is 2260

Para. 4 (b). Allotment:-

1st Division	=	168	cylinders
15th Division	=	1245	" + 5 Candles.
47th Division	=	846	"
Total		2259	

R
2669

Para. 6.

1st Division	- 952	plus	48	spare	=	1,000
15th Division	- 415	"	35	"	=	450
47th Division	- 794	"	56	"	=	850
						2,300

The total number of candles coming up will be 3,500. The remaining 1,200 will be kept in Corps reserve and be kept at MINX under the Chief Engineer.

Para.7. The allotment of gas cylinders each night will be settled between Divisions and O.C. Gas Company direct.

A A Montgomery
Brigadier-General,
General Staff, IVth Corps.

H.Q. IVth Corps.
3rd September, 1915.

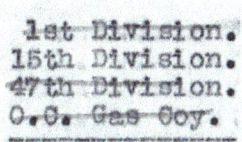

P L A N "A"

Not drawn to scale Partition = 25 yds.

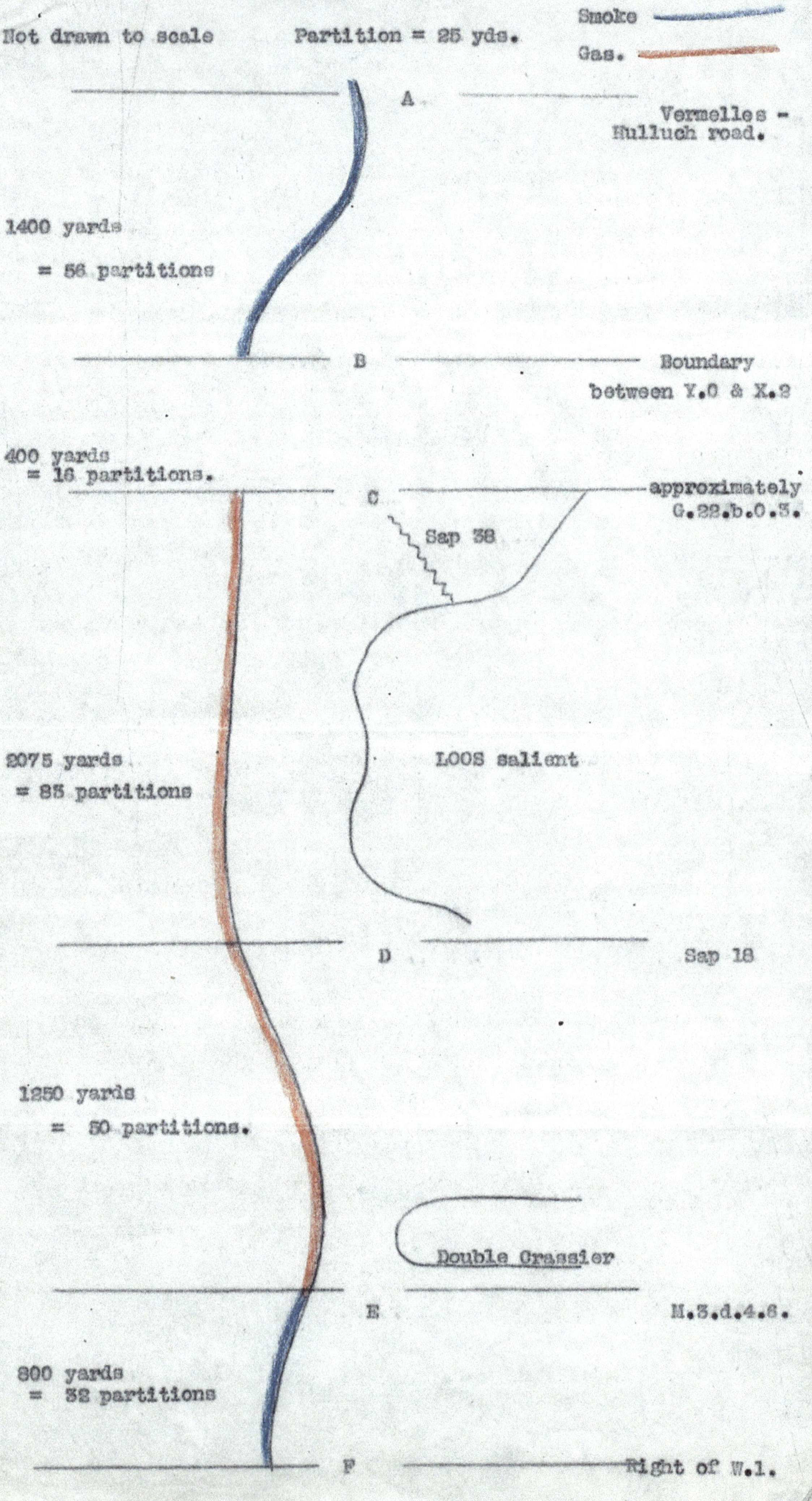

SECRET

Notes to explain Plan "A."

		Cylinders.	Candles.
A - B.	56 partitions - smoke.	168	952
B -C.	Nothing.		
	(B - B1 has been absorbed into B - C and C - D).	-	-
C - D.	83 partitions - gas.	1245	415
D - E.	50 partitions - gas.	750	250
E - F.	32 partitions - smoke.	96	544
		2259	2161
	Total arriving	2260	3500
	Spare	1	1339

The spare candles will be allotted as follows:-

1st Division	..	48
15th Division	..	35
47th Division	..	56

These are for use in making up any deficiencies in above numbers.

SECRET

IVth Corps No. H.R.S. 508/2

HEADQUARTERS 4th CORPS
7 SEP 1915
GENERAL STAFF

~~187th (Special) Co. R.E.~~
~~1st Division.~~
15th Division.
~~47th Division.~~

With reference to my H.R.S. 506/9 of 3rd September, and H.R.S. 506 of 1st September, paragraph 7.

1. There is no definite information as yet as regards the number of cylinders that will be available, but we must be prepared for the largest possible amount.

2. It is now proposed to make the front of the 1st Division a 'gas' front and to extend this front down to "C". That is to say, a front of 1,800 yards or 72 partitions. These partitions should all be prepared to hold 18 cylinders similarly to those on the fronts C--D and D--E.

3. At the rate of 15 cylinders per partition this will mean taking up 1080 cylinders, and arrangements should be made accordingly.

4. The allotment of cylinders to 15th and 47th Divisions will remain as before, i.e., 15th Division = 1245, 47th Division = 846.

5. The allotment of Sections of the 187th (Special) Company R.E. will be as follows:-

1st Division. - 5 Sections	= 5 Offrs	150 men.
15th Division. - 6 "	= 6 "	180 "
47th Division. - 6 "	= 6 "	180 "

6. The allotment of candles to 1st Division will be decreased to 400, and the reserve at MINX increased to 1800. The allotment to 15th and 47th Divisions remains as before.

7th September, 1915.

C. Alcan[illegible]
Brigadier General,
General Staff, IVth Corps.

P L A N "A"

Not to scale. Partition = 25 yds.

Smoke

Gas

SECRET

HEADQUARTERS 4th CORPS
7 SEP 1915
GENERAL STAFF

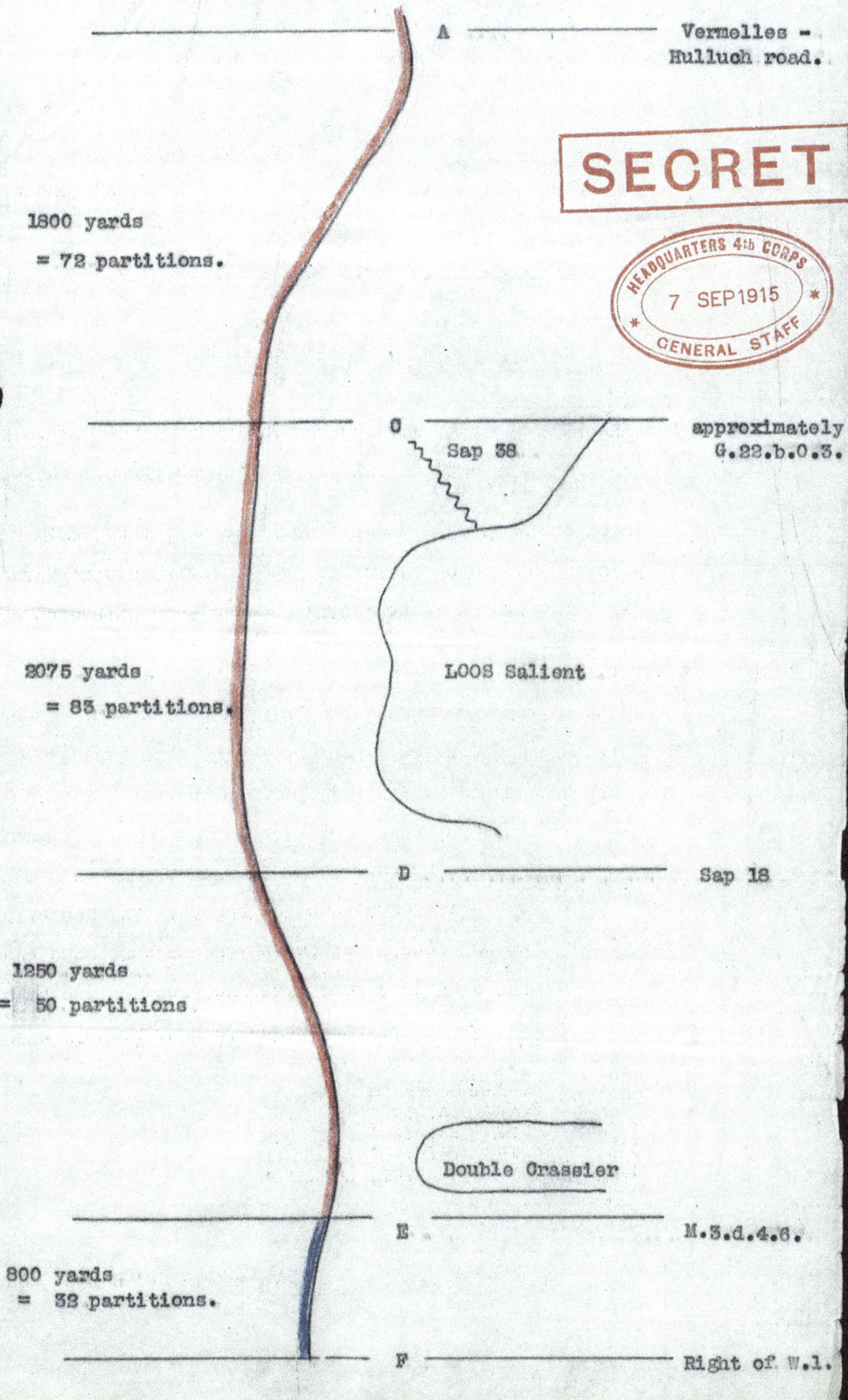

SECRET

IVth Corps No. H.R.S.______

NOTES TO EXPLAIN "PLAN 'A'".

			Cylinders	Candles.
A -- C	72 partitions	- Gas.	1080	360
C -- D	83 "	- Gas.	1245	415
D -- E	50 "	- Gas.	750	250
E -- F	32 "	- Smoke.	96	544
			3171	1569
		Total arriving(not known)		3500
		Spare		1931

Spare candles will be allotted as follows:-

1st Division	40
15th Division	35
47th Division	56

These are for use in making up deficiencies in the above numbers.

Reserve at MINX 1800

15 DW
412

SECRET

IVth Corps No. H.R.S. 508

HEADQUARTERS 4th CORPS
13 SEP 1915
GENERAL STAFF

~~1st Division.~~
15th Division.
~~47th Division.~~

Where Russian saps are being constructed forward from our lines, every precaution must be taken subsequent to the discharge of gas to ensure that they are safe before work is resumed.

X

R A K Montgomery

13th September, 1915.

Brigadier General,
General Staff, IVth Corps.

A

9 copies to 44th IB
46th —

SECRET.—(Not to be carried forward in the Assault).

TIME TABLE OF GAS.

Attacks South of the LA BASSEE CANAL.

(Minutes).	
0	Start the gas and run 6 cylinders one after the other at full blast until all are exhausted.
0-12‡—0-20	Start the smoke. The smoke is to run concurrently with the gas if the gas is not exhausted by 0-12.
0-20	Start the gas again and run 6 cylinders one after the other at full blast until all are exhausted.
0-32—0-40	Start the smoke again. The smoke is to run concurrently with the gas, if the gas is not exhausted by 0-32.
0-38	Turn all gas off punctually. Thicken up smoke with triple candles. Prepare for assault.
0-40	**ASSAULT.**

‡ On the 3-cylinder and no-cylinder fronts the smoke will be started at 0-6.

Note:—From 0 to 0-40, front system of hostile trenches will be kept under continuous shrapnel fire. Defences further in rear under bombardment of H.E. shell of all calibres.

At 0-40 artillery fire will lift as required.

1st Army Printing Section, R.E. 465

SECRET

IVth Corps No. H.R.S. 518

HEADQUARTERS 4th CORPS 16 SEP 1915 GENERAL STAFF

~~1st Division.~~
15th Division.
~~47th Division.~~
~~187th Company R.E.~~

1. The programme of the discharge of gas and smoke on the 'gas' fronts is amended to read

10 minutes	gas, followed by		(5 cylinders)
4 "	smoke	"	(4 candles - 2 at a time)
6 "	gas	"	(3 cylinders)
4 "	smoke	"	(4 candles - 2 at a time)
14 "	gas	"	(7 cylinders)
2 "	smoke		(1 triple candle, and 2 candles)

2. The 'smoke' front programme will be amended to read

6 minutes	gas followed by		(3 cylinders)
32 "	smoke	"	(32 candles - 2 at a time)
2 "	smoke		(1 triple candle, ~~or~~ and 2 candles)

3. (a) 2,400 cylinders will arrive at MINX at 5:p.m. on 17th.

The above will be allotted as follows:-

1st Division	-	792
15th Division	-	913
47th Division	-	646

These will be sent up and distributed - 11 to each 'gas' partition, and 3 to each 'smoke' partition, commencing on the night of 18th/19th.

(b) The remaining/

(b) The remaining 49, and the 770, still due to the IVth Corps to complete full numbers, and which will probably arrive later, ~~and~~ will be distributed as follows:-

1st Division	-	288
15th Division	-	331
47th Division	-	200

Further information as to the day of arrival will be notified to Divisions as soon as received.

4. The allotment of candles will now be

1st Division -	720 candles	plus 80 spare	=	800
	72 triple candles	" 1 "	=	73
15th Division	830 candles	" 70 "	=	900
	83 triple candles	" 1 "	=	84
47th Division	1588 candles	" 212 "	=	1800
	82 triple candles	" 1 "	=	83

5. The allotment of phosphor bombs and grenades will be

	2" Mortar bombs.	Stokes Mortar bombs	95 mm bombs	New Phosphor Hand Grenades	Threlfallite Hand grenades No. 2.	Free Phosphor
1st Div:	100	1000	500	500	1000	-
15th "	-	1000	500	500	1000	-
47th "	300	2000	2000	500	1500	400 lbs
Corps Res:	200	-	-	-	154	-

6. Candles, bombs, and grenades mentioned in paras 4 and 5 above, will be drawn from the Park.

7. As already arranged -

(a) Cylinders will be sent up by Divisions from MINX under arrangements made direct with O.C. 187th Co. R.E. Wagons to be at MINX at 6 p.m. each evening.

(b) O.C. 187th Company R.E. will be responsible that the necessary screws are taken out of the boxes before they leave MINX.

(c) Fatigue/

(c) Fatigue and carrying parties will be found as already arranged.

(d) O.C. 187th Company R.E. will be responsible for sending up the necessary poles and slings with the cylinders to the Divisional Dump.

(e) When done with, poles and slings will be collected by Divisions and returned to the 187th Company R.E.

(f) The personnel of the 187th Company R.E. will be withdrawn from the trenches as soon as possible after the discharge of gas and smoke is completed, and assemble at their billets in MAZINGARBE. They must be careful, however, not to delay the advance of the infantry supports and reserves moving forward.

A A Montgomery

16th September, 1915. Brigadier General,

General Staff, IVth Corps.

"A" Form. Army Form C. 2121.

MESSAGES AND SIGNALS. No. of Message

Prefix Code m.	Words	Charge	*This message is on a/c of:*	Recd. at m.
Office of Origin and Service Instructions	Sent		*Service.*	Date
	At m.			From
	To			
	By		(Signature of "Franking Officer.")	By

TO { 44 1 B
45 1 B
46 1 B.

SECRET

Sender's Number	Day of Month	In reply to Number	
* Special	18		AAA

From [illegible] onwards special
precaution [illegible]
taken to ensure that all
Infantry Vermorel Sprayers
[illegible] ready charged
and in good working order
in the front trenches if
possible near the [illegible].
aaa addressed 44 46
1 B repeated 45 1.B.

From
Place
Time 11.30 am.

[illegible] Major

The above may be forwarded as now corrected. (Z)

Censor. Signature of Addressor or person authorised to telegraph in his name.

* This line should be erased if not required.

11 Div

(15491) S. & Co. Ltd. W 14142/641. 90,000. 4/15. Forms C 2121/10.

"A" Form. Army Form C. 121.

MESSAGES AND SIGNALS.

No. of Message

Prefix Code m.	Words	Charge	This message is on a/c of:	Recd. at m.
Office of Origin and Service Instructions	Sent		Service.	Date
	At m.			From
	To			
	By		(Signature of "Franking Officer.")	By

TO — CRE — SECRET.

Sender's Number	Day of Month	In reply to Number	AAA
* Special	18.		

Please ensure that the top of all parapets are levelled and that the crest of parapet is not more than 1' 6" from the top of recesses AAA This is necessary to ensure that the discharge pipes may lie flat. AAA + Acknowledge.

+ Shown to CRE and handed to him

From

Place

Time 11.25 pm.

E. G. Hamilton Major GS 16 Div.

The above may be forwarded as now corrected. (Z)

Censor. Signature of Addressor or person authorised to telegraph in his name.

* This line should be erased if not required.

(15491) S. & Co. Ltd. W 14142/641. 90,000. 4/15. Forms C 2121/10.

"A" Form. Army Form C. 2121.

MESSAGES AND SIGNALS.

No. of Message

Prefix Code m.	Words / Charge	This message is on a/c of:	Recd. at m.
Office of Origin and Service Instructions	Sent	Service.	Date
	At m.		From
	To		By
	By	(Signature of "Franking Officer.")	

TO [illegible] SECRET
[illegible]
[illegible] R.E.

* Sender's Number	Day of Month	In reply to Number	AAA
[illegible]	18		

[illegible]

From			
Place			
Time 1.15 [illegible]			

The above may be forwarded as now corrected.

Censor.

(Z) [illegible]

Signature of Addressor or person authorised to telegraph in his name.

* This line should be erased if not required.

(15491) S. & Co. Ltd. W 14142/641. 90,000. 4/15. Forms C 2121/10.

SECRET

1st Army No. Q.432 (G). IVth Corps No. H.R.S. 518.

HEADQUARTERS 4th CORPS 18 SEP 1915 GENERAL STAFF

IVth Corps.

From a trial that has been made of the I.S.K. or Lachrymator hand grenades, it is found that the grenade bursts with a very small detonation and emits an invisible gas, which has a very powerful irritating effect on the eyes.

2. This would, especially in a confined space, temporarily incapacitate a man and it is thought that the grenades will be found of considerable value in trench and house fighting.

Adv. 1st Army.
17th Sept. 1915.

(Sd) R. Butler, Maj.-Gen.,
General Staff, First Army.

2.

~~1st Division.~~
15th Division.
~~47th Division.~~

Forwarded for your information.

[signature]

Brigadier-General,
General Staff, IVth Corps.

H.Q. IVth Corps.
18th September, 1915.

Not sent out
IBS

SECRET

IVth Corps No. H.R.S. 518/1

~~1st Division.~~
15th Division.
~~47th Division.~~
~~187th Company R.E.~~

HEADQUARTERS 4th CORPS
18 SEP 1915
GENERAL STAFF

LATEST GAS BULLETIN.

1. 2,409 cylinders are now at MINX:

147 more cylinders are due to arrive on 18th, 19th, or 20th, making a total of 2,556 available for issue on the nights 18th/19th, 19th/20th, 20th/21st.

2. Deducting 96 for the 32 'smoke' partitions in the 47th Division, this leaves 2,460 cylinders available for 205 'gas' partitions on the 1st, 15th, and 47th Division fronts.

3. No more cylinders will arrive.

The 2,556 cylinders therefore, will be distributed 12 to each 'gas' partition, and 3 to each 'smoke' partition.

4. The allotment of cylinders to Divisions is as follows:-

1st Division	- for 72 'gas' partitions	= 864 cylinders
15th "	83 'gas "	= 996 "
47th "	(50 'gas' " (32 'smoke' "	) = 696 "

5. The allotment of candles remains the same.

		Single Candles	Triple Candles
1st Division	-	800	73
15th "	-	900	84
47th "	-	1,800	83

6. A revised programme, which it is hoped will be final, is attached.

18th September, 1915.

[signature]

Brigadier General,
General Staff, IVth Corps.

Special.

SECRET.

46th Infantry Brigade.

Instructions for candlemen.

The 46th Infantry Brigade will detail 96 men to operate candles during the gas discharge, under the orders of O.C. 187th (Special) Company R.E.

The men will be taken from the troops in occupation of the front trenches on the last day of the bombardment, and will be told off in pairs to bays as under:-

116.	8.	26.	49.	78.
119.	10.	28.	52.	81.
122.	12.	29.	54.	84.
125.	14.	32.	58.	86.
127.	17.	34.	61.	end of Sap 10 (14A)
130.	19.	36.	64.	89.
133.	20.	41.	68.	95.
1.	21.	43.	70.	99.
4.	22.	44.B.	74.	
6.	23.	46.	76.	

48 bays or

96 men

The above bays have been marked up by the C.R.E.

2. The men will stand to their bays at 7 p.m. on the 24th instant, fully equipped but without packs.

The C.R.E. will arrange to issue to each pair of men by 7:30 p.m. 10 smoke candles, one triple smoke candle and four boxes of vesuvians.

He will also cause 21 smoke candles to be placed as a reserve in each of the two special bomb stores.

3. The gas-men will take over their duties at 8 p.m. on the 24th instant. The candlemen will be under their orders from that hour until the completion of the gas discharge, when they will at once come under the orders of their own Battalion commanders again.

Major G.S.

19th September, 1915. 15th Division.

SECRET

IVth Corps No. H.R.S. 528

HEADQUARTERS,
15th DIVISION
23 SEP. 1915
Reg. No. 578

~~1st Division.~~
15th Division.
~~47th Division.~~

Herewith four copies of First Army memorandum No. G.S. 177/5 (a), dated 22nd September, 1915, entitled "Notes in connection with the employment of Gas in the Attack".

These notes are not to be taken into the trenches, but are to be communicated to all ranks.

The scale of distribution is as follows:-

Div. H.Q.	..	1
Bde. H.Q. (one each)		3

Rack M4

Copies to all Bdes. under G 5

Brigadier-General,
General Staff, IVth Corps.

H.Q. IVth Corps.
22nd September, 1915.

4 ODS
Gordons
46

22

F 29 b 48

SECRET

HEADQUARTERS
15th. DIVISION
23 SEP. 1915
Reg. No. 578

First Army No. G.S.177/5 (a)

Note:- THIS PAPER IS NOT TO BE TAKEN INTO THE TRENCHES, BUT THE CONTENTS ARE TO BE COMMUNICATED TO ALL RANKS.

NOTES IN CONNECTION WITH THE EMPLOYMENT OF GAS IN THE ATTACK.

1. From the experience gained during the fighting round YPRES it is known that, if proper precautions are taken, (i.e. if gas helmets are worn and properly tucked in round the neck) men need have no fear of suffering any ill effects from gas fumes.

On the other hand, experience has shown that, if men are not prepared for a gas attack, and if they are not wearing their gas helmets or have not time to put them on properly, the effect of a sudden cloud of gas may be very great indeed, not only in the front trenches but also in the support and reserve trenches for some considerable distance in rear.

2. There is reason to believe that the Germans have not got an effective smoke helmet and, as we have not yet made use of gas in our attacks, it is likely that its use by us may come as a complete surprise to the enemy.

In these circumstances we must be prepared to take full advantage of the initial surprise, and, in view of the fact that the gas helmets now in the possession of our troops give (however dense the cloud of gas) complete immunity from all ill effects, there is every ground for hoping that, when it comes to close fighting in the gas area, our troops will have a very great advantage over those of the enemy who remain to resist our advance.

3. All men in the front trenches must have their smoke helmets on before the gas cylinders are opened.

The troops carrying out the attack are to wear a smoke helmet. This should be worn on the head and tucked in round the back of the neck in such a manner that it can be easily pulled down and adjusted on encountering gas.

The old pattern smoke helmet is quite proof against our own gas and, being lighter, should be worn by the troops carrying out the attack, and the tube helmet carried in the usual way by the man in addition in case of accident. It must be distinctly understood that every man must have a tube helmet with him.

4. Dug-outs and houses cannot be made gas tight. It is not likely, therefore, that the enemy will be able to stay in such places any more than in his front line trenches; and no time should be lost in the advance in waiting to make an immediate and close examination of these places.

The gas, being heavy, is likely to get lodged in low lying places such as trenches and dug outs. Although there is no reason why men with their helmets on should not go into those places, it must be remembered that they cannot be permanently occupied until cleared of gas. This must be done by the use of sprayers which must be brought forward. It is calculated that it will take one sprayer to clear each 15 yards of trench. Refils for the sprayers should be carried forward with the troops making the attack.

5. Machine guns should be well oiled before being taken forward into the gas area. This will obviate any chance of the guns jambing on account of gas corrosion.

8.30

6 357 3.2.

R Butler

Major General,
General Staff, First Army.

Adv. First Army.
22nd September, 1915.

8/

INSTRUCTIONS RE STORES.

MESSAGES AND SIGNALS.

No. of Message

Prefix	Code	m.	Words	Charge	This message is on a/c of:	Recd. at m.
Office of Origin and Service Instructions			Sent At m. To By		Service. (Signature of "Franking Officer.")	Date From By

TO — 46 I.B. SECRET.

Sender's Number	Day of Month	In reply to Number	AAA
Special	16.		

Herewith Summary of procedure for carrying stores on
18/19 Sept.
19/20 " and
20/21 ".

2. Working party table were left at your Headquarters this afternoon

3. As little as possible should be said by officers and men concerned in this work.

E. G. Henderson
Major GS
15 Division

From
Place
Time 10 30 pm.

The above may be forwarded as now corrected. (Z)
Censor. Signature of Addressor or person authorised to telegraph in his name.

MESSAGES AND SIGNALS.

No. of Message

Prefix	Code	m.	Words	Charge	This message is on a/c of:	Recd. at m.
Office of Origin and Service Instructions			Sent At m. To By		Service. (Signature of "Franking Officer.")	Date From By

TO

Sender's Number	Day of Month	In reply to Number	AAA

Dear Stewart

Herewith Summary.

2. Did I by any chance leave my time table showing wagons and cylinders at your house. If so would you kindly give bearer.

3. The stuff arrives at 5pm tomorrow.

Yours ever
E Henderson.

From
Place
Time

The above may be forwarded as now corrected. (Z)
Censor. Signature of Addressor or person authorised to telegraph in his name.

S E C R E T .

Extracts from Summary

Carrying of Stores on nights A.B.&.C.Sept 1915.

x x x

x x x

x x x

4. The detail of the bays has been slightly altered, one bay No.102, previously allotted to 46th Infantry Brigade being now allotted to 1st Division and an additional bay No.56 allotted to 44th Infantry Brigade.

The number of stores to be put in each bay will now be 1st night 7, 2nd night 4, and third night 4.

5. Unloading and carrying parties will march from billets through PHILOSOPHE and along the track usually taken by the regimental transport moving to QUALITY STREET (G.27.a.0.4.). On approaching the CORON of FOSSE 7 they will follow the wooden tram line to DUMP (G.26.b.8.1.) South corner of CORON of FOSSE 7.

x x x

x x x

x x x

9. All in the trenches or handling stores will carry smoke helmets ready for instant use, and Vermorel sprayers will be ready for the spraying not only of the trenches but of the dump by competent personnel, should any damage be done to the stores whether by shrapnel or by bullet.

44th and 46th Infantry Brigades will each provide two Vermorel sprayers with personnel nightly at DUMP.

44th Infantry Brigade will detail a medical officer to attend at DUMP on 1st and 3rd nights, 46th Infantry Brigade on 2nd night.

10. Carrying parties will have a call on any neighbouring troops for assistance in case of necessity.

Parties on reaching their destinations will deposit the stores which will then be put in position by personnel

(2 men

(2 men per bay) detailed by the C.R.E.

187th Coy R.E. has also detailed an officer and 4 other ranks to supervise generally.

11. Carrying parties after depositing stores will be conducted out of the trenches by their guides as follows:-

Parties filling bays from Sap 18 up to Boyau 12 will all move back into C.T. 26 and out by C.T. 1.A. as far as the Electric Power Station where they will emerge on to the open. Here each party of 14(or 8) will be formed up.

The remainder will file out by C.T.15 to PHILOSOPHE where again each party of 14 (or 8) will be formed up.

After being formed up the parties will march will poles and slings by shortest route to the 91st Field Coy Store at the Brewery near SAULCHOY FARM, MAZINGARBE, where these articles will be handed over to an N.C.O. detailed by 187th Coy R.E. Parties can then return to billets.

12. No one engaged on the above operation should smoke when East of the LES BREBIS to PHILOSOPHE Railway.

x x x

14. C.R.E. will detail one Pioneer or Sapper to attend to the bays from the time the stores are in place until the specialists of the 187th Coy R.E. take over at 8 p.m. on the last day of the bombardment.

Troops in the trenches will assist above in repairs to bays as may be required.

N.C.Os and men detailed by O.C. 187th Coy R.E. will patrol the trenches during this period and assist generally.

15. Special instructions will follow regarding candlemen to be detailed (2 per bay) from the troops in occupation of the front line of trenches on the last day of the bombardment.

Issued for instructional purposes only.

S E C R E T.

Carrying of Stores on Nights A.B.and C. September 1915.

SUMMARY.

1. Stores arrive Rail-head packed in wooded cases.

187th Coy. R.E. unload and remove all screws except one, which is loosened.

2. Stores (with one pole and a pair of slings for each also a spare pole and pair of slings per wagon) will be loaded by 187th Coy. R.E. into Wagons of Divisional Ammunition Column. A N.C.O. and 5 men of 187th Coy. R.E. will accompany the stores travelling in spare wagon of first group each day. They will assist and instruct in the slinging of stores and in procedure to be adopted should stores be damaged; also assist in case of any accident to the stores at the dump.

3. Wagons proceed to Dump. Divisional Mounted Troops have been detailed to mark points on route; also to hold up all traffic (from time to time only) between X roads L.17.d.2.0. and X roads L.23.b.7.6. to allow a clear road for wagons with stores. Troops will give way when meeting wagons loaded with these stores.

4. Major "X", 9th Black Watch, assisted by Captains "Y" and "Z", with 5 cyclists, will be in sole charge of operations at the dump, viz., unloading, slinging of stores, telling off carrying parties, detailing their guides, notifying routes to destinations in trenches, and despatch of parties.

The number of stores to be put in each selected bay will be 1st night 7, 2nd night 4, and third night 4.

Detailed table of unloading and carrying parties has been issued separately, together with a plan showing the bays prepared for the reception of stores.

Unloading parties and officers in charge of carrying parties, should, as far as possible, be the same every night. The guides will be the same each night.

Major "X", 9th Black Watch, will meet officers in charge of carrying parties and of guides (para: 7) tomorrow 17th instant, at 2 p.m. at 44th Infantry Brigade Headquarters, when details of work to be done will be explained. Time and place of subsequent meetings will be notified later.

5. Unloading and carrying parties will march from billets through PHILOSOPHE and along the track usually taken by the regimental transport moving to QUALITY STREET (G.27.a.0.4.), On approaching the CORON of FOSSE 7 they will follow the wooden tram line to DUMP (G.26.b.8.1.) South corner of CORON of FOSSE 7.

Each man will carry a slung rifle and 50 rounds S.A.A. in web bandolier. Shoulder pads (improvised out of sandbags) will be found useful.

6. Empty packing cases will be re-packed in wagons and returned the same evening to Rail-head. (Separate instructions as to this have been given to Divisional Ammunition Column).

7. Guides will be told off to each pair of selected bays, and <u>must</u> know the routes to them and out of the trenches - see map and paragraph 9 below.

Each Brigade will detail an officer in charge of guides.

8. Stores will arrive in trenches as follows:-

1st night	from 8:30 p.m. to 1 a.m.
2nd night	from 8:30 p.m. to 12:30 a.m.
3rd night	from 8:30 p.m. to 12 midnight.

All other traffic in the trenches will stop during the above hours. Wounded men even will not be moved but will be attended to on the spot and medical arrangements made accordingl

9. All in the trenches or handling stores will carry smoke

helmets ready for instant use, and Vermorel sprayers will be ready for the spraying not only of the trenches but of the DUMP by competent personnel, should any damage be done to the stores whether by shrapnel or by bullet.

44th and 46th Infantry Brigades will each provide 2 vermorel sprayers with personnel nightly at DUMP.

44th Infantry Brigade will detail a medical officer to attend at DUMP on 1st and 3rd nights, 46th Infantry brigade on the 2nd night.

10. Carrying parties will have a call on any neighbouring troops for assistance in case of necessity.

Parties on reaching their destinations will deposit the stores which will then be put in position by personnel (2 men per bay) detailed by the C.R.E._

187th Company R.E. has also detailed an officer and 4other ranks to supervise generally on each Brigade front.

As each officer's party completes itstask, a report will be sent to QUALITY STREET for the information of Major "X".

11. Carrying parties after depositing stores will be conducted out of the trenches by their guides as follows:-

Parties filling bays from Sap 18 up to BOYAU 12 will all move back into C.T. 26 and out by C.T. 1.A. as far as the Electric Power Station where they will emerge on to the open. Here each party of 15 (or 9) will be formed up.

The remainder will file out by C.T.15 to PHILOSOPHE where each party of 15 (or 9) will be formed up.

After being formed up the parties will march with poles and slings by shortest route to the 91st Field Coy store at the Brewery near SAULCHOY FARM, MAZINGARBE, where these articles will be handed over to a N.C.O. detailed by 187th Coy. R.E. Parties can then return to billets.

12. No one engaged on the above operation should smoke when East of the LES BREBIS to PHILOSOPHE Railway.

13 IT IS OF PARAMOUNT IMPORTANCE THAT THE STRICTEST SILENCE SHOULD BE OBSERVED AT ALL TIMES.

14. C.R.E. will detail one Pioneer or Sapper to attend to each group of 8 selected bays from the time the stores are in place until the specialists of the 187th Coy R.E. take over at 8 p.m. on the last day of the bombardment.

Troops in the trenches will assist above in repairs to bays as may be required.

N.C.Os and men detailed by O.C. 187th Coy R.E. will patrol the trenches during this period and assist generally.

15. Special instructions will follow regarding candlemen to be detailed (2 per bay) from the troops in occupation of the front line of trenches on the last day of the bombardment.

" A." Major,
General Staff, 15th Division.

SECRET.

Carrying of Stores on Nights A.B.&.C. September 1915.

SUMMARY.

1. Stores arrive Rail-head packed in wooden cases.

187 Coy unload and remove all screws except one which is loosened.

2. Stores (with one pole and a pair of slings for each) loaded by 187 Coy into wagons of Divl. Ammn. Col. An officer and 5 men of 187 Coy accompany stores in spare wagon of first group each day. They will instruct in the slinging of stores and also assist in case of any accident to the stores at the dump.

3. Wagons proceed to dump. Divl. Mtd. Troops have been detailed to mark route; also to hold up all traffic(from time to time only) between X roads L.17.d.2.0. and X roads L.23.b.7.6. to allow a clear road for wagons with stores. All troops will give way when meeting wagons loaded with these stores.

4. Major J.Stewart, 9th Black Watch, assisted by Captains Ravenhill and Troughton, with 5 cyclists, will be in sole charge of operations at the dump, viz., unloading, slinging of stores, telling off carrying parties, detailing their guides, notifying routes to destinations in trenches, and then away.

The detail of the carrying parties has been slightly altered, one bay, No. 102, previously allotted to 46th I.B. being now allotted to 1st Div. and an additional bay No. 56, allotted to 44th I.B.

A fresh detail of unloading and carrying parties also a plan is issued herewith.

Unloading parties, officers in charge of carrying parties and guides should as far as possible be the same every night.

Major Stewart, 9th Black Watch, would like to see officers in charge of carrying parties each day at a time (about 2 p.m.) and place to be arranged by him with Brigadiers, when details of work to be done can be explained.

5. Unloading and carrying parties will march from billets through PHILOSOPHE and along the track usually taken by the regimental transport moving to QUALITY STREET (G.27.a.0.4.), On approaching the CORON of FOSSE 7 (G26.b.8.1.) they will follow the wooden tram line to DUMP (G.27.c.4.8.). South corner of Coron Fosse 7.

Each man will carry a slung rifle and 50 rounds S.A.A. in web bandolier. Shoulder pads (made out of sandbags) will be found useful.

6. Empty packing cases will be re-packed in wagons and returned at once to Rail-head. (seperate instructions to Divl. Ammn. Col.)

7. Guides will be told off to each pair of bays and know the routes to them and out of the trenches.-see map and para 9 below. An officer will be detailed in charge of guides.

8. Stores will arrive at dump as follows:-

1st ~~and 2nd~~ nights.	8-30 p.m. to 1 a.m.
2nd night	8.30 12.30 a
3rd night.	8-30 p.m. to ~~11 p.m.~~ 12 MN.

All other traffic in the trenches will stop during the above hours. Wounded men even will not be moved but will be attended to on the spot and medical arrangements made accordingly.

All in the trenches or handling stores ~~should~~ must carry smoke helmets ready for instant use, and Vermorel sprayers ~~should~~ must be ready for the spraying not only of the trenches but of the Dump by competent personnel, should any damage be done to the stores whether by shrapnel or by bullet.

44 & 46 I.B. will each provide 4 Vermorel Sprayers with personnel at Dump

Carrying parties will have a call on any neighbouring troops for assistance in case of necessity.

Parties on reaching their destinations will deposit the stores which will then be put in position by personnel (2 men per bay) detailed by the C.R.E.

187 Coy has also detailed an officer and N.C.O's. and men to supervise generally.

As each ~~pair of bays is completed~~ officers party completes, a report will be sent by telephone to QUALITY STREET for the information of Major Stewart.

44 I.B. 1 Med Officer 1st & 3rd nights
46 " 1 " — 2nd nights

9. Carrying parties after depositing stores will be conducted out of the trenches by their guides as follows:-

Parties filling bays from Sap 18 up to Boyau 12 will all move back into C.T. 26 and out by C.T. IA. as far as the Electric Power Station where they will emerge onto the open Here each party of 14 (or 8) will be formed up.

The remainder will file out by C.T. 15 to PHILOSOPHE where again each party of 14 (or 8) will be formed up.

After being formed up the parties will march with poles and slings by shortest route to the 91st Field Coy store at the Brewery near SAULCHOY FARM, MAZINGARBE, where these articles will be handed over to an N.C.O. detailed by 187 Coy. Parties can then return to billets.

10. No one engaged on the above operation should smoke when East of the LES BRÉBIS to PHILOSOPHE railway.

11. It is of paramount importance that the strictest silence should as far as possible be observed at all times.

12. Special instructions regarding 96 special men (Candlemen) to be detailed for duty from the 3rd day onward ~~are attached~~ will follow.

13. No reference to this job on telephone except if urgent. Orderlies to be used as much as possible.

SECRET

Instruction for Candlemen - 46. I.B.

1. The 46. I.B. will tell off ~~94~~ 96 men to operate Candles during the gas attack, under the orders of the O.C. 187th Co.

The men will be told off in pairs for the foll. bays:-

116	8	26	49	78
119	10	28	52	81
122	12	29	54	84
125	14	32	58	86
127	17	34	61	End of Sap 10 (14A)
130	19	36	64	89
133	20	41	68	95
1	21	43	70	99
4	22	44B	74	~~100~~
6	23	46	76	

⊗ date will be notified later ~~14~~ 9.15

2. The men will commence their duties at 9 a.m. ⊗ ~~on the 11th inst.~~, fully equipped but without packs.

3. One man of each pair will attend to his duties in his bay, viz - to keep it clear of debris; the other will parade (at 9 a.m. ~~14~~ 9.15) at the 91st Fd Co. Store, Villa ARNAUD, MAZINGARBE, and draw 6 candles and 4 boxes of Vesuvians for use during the discharge of gas

4. The gas men will parade at the same place (Villa St ARNAUD) and gasmen and candle men (one of each pair) march together to their stations.

5. On completion of the gas discharge the Candlemen will at once come under the orders of their own battalion commanders again.

[signature] Major RE
15 Divn.

~~11~~ 14. 9. 15

Prefix	Code	m.	Words	Charge	This message is on a/c of:	Recd. at m.
Office of Origin and Service Instructions			Sent At m. To By		Service. (Signature of "Franking Officer.")	Date From By

TO 44 IB
46 IB

Sender's Number	Day of Month	In reply to Number	AAA
Special.	20		

The placing of special Stores in the trenches having been completed no further working parties will be required. ~~AAA~~ The residue of [illegible] carried [illegible] [illegible] transport [illegible] Co RE Stores at the Brewery [illegible] and please make sure that these wagons have [illegible] their duties [illegible] [illegible] Ration Head [illegible].

From 15 Dw.
Place
Time 11 · 30 pm.

The above may be forwarded as now corrected. (Z) [illegible signature] Major RE

Censor. Signature of Addressor or person authorised to telegraph in his name.

* This line should be erased if not required.

15 Division

(15491) S. & Co. Ltd. W 14142/641. 90,000. 4/15. Forms C 2121/10.

Prefix	Code	m.	Words	Charge	This message is on a/c of:	Recd. at m.
Office of Origin and Service Instructions			Sent At m. To By		Service. (Signature of "Franking Officer.")	Date From By

TO 15 Dw Art.

Sender's Number	Day of Month	In reply to Number	AAA
Special	20.		

Wagon teams for A B C etc not required any further the work having been completed last night.

From 15 Dw.
Place
Time 11. 40 am

The above may be forwarded as now corrected. (Z) [illegible signature]

Censor. Signature of Addressor or person authorised to telegraph in his name.

9

FIGHTING STRENGTHS.

FIGHTING STRENGTH RETURN OF THE 15th DIVISION at MIDNIGHT, FRIDAY, 3rd SEPTEMBER, 1915.

	A. Fighting strength in accordance with 1st Army Instructions No.908 A. of 3.4.15.		B. Included in Col. A. but not actually with units.		C. Drafts recd. since last return.		D. Explanation of any discrepancy between "Fighting Strength" shewn on this return and that on last return.
	Offrs.	O.R.	Offrs.	O.R.	Offrs.	O.R.	
H.Q., 15th Divn.	14	92	-	-	-	-	
15th Signal Coy.	6	213	4	109	-	2	O.R. 1 rejoined.
15th Div.Cavalry.	6	129	1	7	-	-	
15th Div.Cyclists.	8	180	1	11	-	1	Addition of O.R.8 caused by error in last week's return.
11th M.M.G. Battery.	4	54	-	1	-	-	
H.Q.15th Div.Art.	4	18	-	-	-	-	
70th Bde. R.F.A.	23	705	-	7	-	11	O.R. 6 evacuated. 3 rejoined.
71st Bde. R.F.A.	23	712	-	7	-	-	O.R. evacuated 2.
72nd Bde. R.F.A.	23	681	1	15	-	-	O.R. evacuated 5.
73rd Bde. R.F.A.	18	519	-	15	-	-	O.R. evacuated 2.
15th Div.Amm.Clm.	13	537	3	20	-	-	O.R. evacuated 2. transferred 2.
H.Q., C.R.E.	2	10	-	2	-	-	
73rd Fld.Coy. R.E.	6	216	-	9	-	8	O.R. rejoined 1. transferred 2.
74th Fld.Coy. R.E.	6	221	-	-	-	15	
91st Fld.Coy. R.E.	6	217	-	8	-	7	O.R. evacuated 1.
H.Q. 44th Inf.Bde.	5	37	1	7	-	-	
9th Black Watch	28	997	2	41	-	-	Offrs.1 died of wounds. O.R. 5 cas. 3 evac. 2 rejoined.
8th Seaforth Hrs.	28	966	-	11	-	-	O.R. evacuated 5.
10th Gordon Hrs.	27	1028	4	75	1	49	Offrs. 1 wounded. O.R. evacuated 1. rejoined 1.
7th Cameron Hrs.	29	999	1	11	-	-	O.R. 3 evacuated.

H.Q. 45th Inf.Bde.	5	56		-	-	-	
13th Royal Scots.	28	961	1	21	-	-	O.R. evacuated 1. transferred 1.
7th R.Scots Fus.	29	1015	1	29	-	-	O.R. evacuated 7. casualties 5.
6th Cameron Hrs.	31	965	1	18	-	-	Offrs. cas. 2. O.R. cas. 2. evac. 8. rejoined 8.
11th A. & S. Hrs.	29	1009	-	9	-	46	O.R. transferred 14. cas. 1. evac. 5. rejoined 1.
46th Inf.Bde. H.Q.	5	64	-	-	-	-	O.R. evac. 1. transferred 3. rejoined. 2. draft at Base 4.
7th K.O.S.B.	30	1005	2	48	-	27	
8th K.O.S.B.	28	952	-	18	-	-	O.R. rejoined 2. evacuated 1.
10th Sco. Rifles.	29	1008	-	34	-	30	O.R. 15 rejoined. evacuated 2.
12th H.L.I.	26	1016	-	27	-	-	~~O.R.~~
9th Gordon Hrs.(P).	29	1003	4	-	-	28	
15th Div. Train.	24	423	-	27	-	-	O.R. rejoined 1.
45th Fld. Ambce.	10	229	-	-	-	-	O.R. evacuated 5. joined 1. rejoined 1. Capt.Watson to England.
46th Fld. Ambce.	9	228	-	-	-	-	
47th Fld. Ambce.	10	230	-	-	-	-	O.R. 2 off strength.
32nd San. Sec.	1	27	-	14	-	-	
Fld.Amb.Wkshp.Unit	1	20	-	~~45~~	-	-	
27th Mob. Vet. Sec.	1	26	-	-	-	-	
	595	18768	27	~~646~~ 661	1	224	

4. 9. 15.

Major General,

Commanding 15th Division.

FIGHTING STRENGTH RETURN OF THE 15th DIVISION AT MIDNIGHT, FRIDAY, 3rd SEPTEMBER, 1915.

	A. Fighting strength in accordance with 1st Army Instructions No. 908 A. of 3. 4. 15		B. Included in Col. A. but not actually with units.		C. Drafts recd. since last return.		D. Explanation of any discrepancy between "Fighting Strength" shewn on this return and that on last return.
	Offrs.	O.R.	Offrs.	O.R.	Offrs.	O.R.	
H.Q., 15th Divn.	15	94	-	-	-	-	
15th Signal Coy.	6	215	4	111	-	2	
15th Div.Cavalry.	6	129	1	7	-	-	
15th Div.Cyclists.	8	184	1	11	-	-	O.R. 4 rejoined.
11th M.M.G. Battery.	4	54	-	1	-	-	
H.Q. 15th Div.Art.	4	19	-	-	-	-	O.R. 1 joined.
70th Bde. R.F.A.	24	704	1	4	1	2	O.R. 5 joined. 4 evacuated.
71st Bde. R.F.A.	23	703	-	6	-	1	O.R. 1 joined. 1 transferred. 2 killed. 7 evacuated.
72nd Bde. R.F.A.	23	693	-	6	-	11	O.R. 1 joined. 2 rejoined.
73rd Bde. R.F.A.	17	521	-	23	-	2	Officers. 1 evacuated. O.R. 2 joined.
15th Div.Amm.Clm.	13	538	1	20	-	3	Officers. 1 to 70th Bde. O.R. 2 evacuated.
H.Q., C.R.E.	2	10	-	2	-	-	
73rd Fld.Coy. R.E.	6	216	-	6	-	-	
74th Fld.Coy. R.E.	6	219	-	3	-	-	O.R. 2 rejoined. 4 evacuated.
91st Fld.Coy. R.E.	6	216	-	6	-	-	O.R. 2 evacuated.
H.Q. 44th Inf.Bde.	5	37	1	6	-	-	
9th Black Watch.	28	1029	2	30	-	50	O.R. 12 evacuated. 6 to Salvage Coy.
8th Seaforth Hrs.	28	1003	-	13	-	48	O.R. 20 evacuated. 9 rejoined.
10th Gordon Hrs.	27	1023	1	14	-	-	O.R. 5 evacuated.
7th Cameron Hrs.	24	987	3	29	-	-	Officers. 3 casualties. 1 to England. O.R. 7 evac. 5 killed.

H.Q. 45th Inf.Bde.	5	53	-	-	-	-	O.R. 4 rejoined.
13th Royal Scots	28	947	-	13	-	-	O.R. 14 evacuated.
7th R.Scots Fus.	29	971	1	9	-	-	O.R. 31 evacuated. 13 transferred. 10 Tunnelling Coy.
6th Cameron Hrs.	31	960	1	17	-	-	O.R. 8 evacuated. 3 rejoined.
11th A. & S. Hrs.	29	1003	-	9	-	-	O.R. 6 evacuated.
H.Q. 46th Inf.Bde.	5	64	-	-	-	-	
7th K.O.S.B.	30	1026	2	44	-	21	
8th K.O.S.B.	28	938	-	14	-	23	O.R. 1 casualty. 36 evacuated.
10th Sco. Rifles.	29	996	-	26	-	-	O.R. 1 casualty. 11 evacuated.
12th H.L.I.	26	1011	-	31	-	-	O.R. 10 evacuated. 5 rejoined.
9th Gordon Hrs. (P)	29	995	1	-	-	-	O.R. 13 evacuated. 5 rejoined.
15th Div. Train.	25	426	-	25	1	-	Officers. 1 joined. O.R. 1 transferred. 4 rejoined.
45th Fld. Ambce.	10	227	-	-	-	4	O.R. 6 evacuated.
46th Fld. Ambce.	10	231	-	-	-	-	Officers. 1 joined. O.R. 2 evacuated. 5 rejoined.
47th Fld. Ambce.	10	228	-	-	-	-	O.R. 2 evacuated.
32nd San. Sec.	1	27	-	12	-	-	
Fld.Amb.Wkshp.Unit	1	20	-	-	-	-	
27th Mob. Vet. Sec.	1	25	-	-	-	-	O.R. 1 evacuated.
	602	18742	20	498	2	167	

Major General,

11. 9. 15.

Commanding 15th Division.

G

FIGHTING STRENGTH RETURN OF THE 15th DIVISION AT MIDNIGHT, FRIDAY, 17th SEPTEMBER, 1915.

	A. Fighting strength in accordance with 1st Army Instructions No. 908 A. of 3. 4. 15		B. Included in Col. A. but not actually with units.		C. Drafts recd. since last return.		D. Explanation of any discrepancy between "Fighting Strength" shewn on this return and that on last return.
	Offrs.	O.R.	Offrs.	O.R.	Offrs.	O.R.	
H.Q., 15th Divn.	15	94	-	-	-	-	
15th Signal Coy.	6	215	4	111	-	-	
15th Div.Cavalry.	6	129	1	7	-	-	
15th Div.Cyclists.	8	189	-	11	-	-	Rejoined 5.
11th M.M.G.Batty.	4	54	-	6	-	-	
H.Q.,15th Div.Art.	4	20	-	-	-	1	O.R. 1 joined.
70th Bde. R.F.A.	24	704	1	6	-	-	
71st Bde. R.F.A.	23	702	-	-	-	4	O.R. 5 evacuated.
72nd Bde. R.F.A.	23	717	-	7	-	26	O.R. 2 evacuated.
73rd Bde. R.F.A.	18	522	-	20	1	8	O.R. 1 casualty. 6 evacuated.
15th Div.Amm.Clm.	11	531	-	21	1	1	Offrs. 3 transferred. O.R. 1 evacuated. 7 transferred.
H.Q., C.R.E.	2	10	-	2	-	-	
73rd Fld.Coy. R.E.	6	217	-	6	-	3	O.R. 1 evacuated. 1 transferred.
74th Fld.Coy. R.E.	6	223	-	3	-	1	O.R. 4 rejoined. 1 evacuated.
91st Fld.Coy. R.E.	6	217	-	7	-	1	
H.Q. 44th Inf.Bde.	5	37	-	5	-	-	
9th Black Watch	27	1024	1	24	-	-	Offrs. 1 evacuated. O.R. 4 transferred. 1 Died of wounds.
8th Seaforth Hrs.	28	1008	-	12	-	-	O.R. 5 evacuated. 10 rejoined.
10th Gordon Hrs.	27	1019	1	15	-	-	O.R. 3 casualties. 1 evacuated.
7th Cameron Hrs.	26	979	2	30	-	-	Offrs. 1 rejoined. O.R. 6 evacuated 1 discharged.

H.Q. 45th Inf.Bde.	5	53	-	-	-	-	
13th Royal Scots.	28	953	-	18	-	40	O.R. 6 killed. 30 wounded. 10 evacuated.
7th R.Scots Fus.	28	1008	-	19	-	30	Offrs. 1 to England. O.R. 1 commissioned. 8 rejoined.
6th Cameron Hrs.	31	966	1	21	-	-	O.R. 6 rejoined.
11th A. & S. Hrs.	29	996	-	9	-	-	O.R. 7 casualties.
H.Q. 46th Inf.Bde.	5	64	-	-	-	-	
7th K.O.S.B.	30	998	4	38	-	-	O.R. 1 killed. 5 wounded. 22 evacuated.
8th K.O.S.B.	28	935	-	16	-	-	O.R. 5 evac. 5 rejoined. 3 overstated strength of draft in last return.
10th Sco. Rifles.	29	993	1	19	-	-	O.R. 1 killed 2 evacuated.
12th H.L.I.	27	1021	-	31	-	21	Offrs 1 joined. O.R. 1 rejoined. 10 evac. 2 to Salvage Coy.
9th Gordon Hrs.(pP)	28	1002	1	-	-	-	Offrs. 1 evac. O.R. 5 evacuated. 12 rejoined.
15th Div. Train.	25	434	-	26	-	7	O.R. 3 rejoined.
45th Fld. Ambce.	10	236	-	-	1	6	O.R. 2 evac. 5 rejoined.
46th Fld. Ambce.	10	230	-	-	-	-	O.R. 1 evacuated.
47th Fld. Ambce.	10	230	-	-	-	3	O.R. 1 evacuated. 3 joined.
32nd San. Sec.	1	27	-	12	-	-	
Fld.Amb.Wkshp.Unit	1	20	-	-	-	-	
27th Mob. Vet. Sec.	1	27	-	-	-	-	O.R. 1 rejoined.
	601	18804	17	502	3	152	

Major General,

18. 9. 15. Commanding 15th Division.

FIGHTING STRENGTH RETURN OF THE 15th DIVISION AT MIDNIGHT, FRIDAY, 24th SEPTEMBER, 1915.

	A. Fighting strength in accordance with 1st Army Instructions No.908. A. of 3. 4. 15.		B. Included in Col.A. but not actually with units.		C. Drafts recd. since last return.		D. Explanation of any discrepancy between "Fighting Strength" shewn on this return and that on last retrun.
	Offrs.	O.R.	Offrs.	O.R.	Offrs.	O.R.	
H.Q., 15th Divn.	14	94	-	-	-	-	Offrs. 1 to G.H.Q.
15th Signal Coy.	6	216	4	112	-	1	1 joined.
15th Div.Cavalry.	6	129	1	5	-	-	
15th Div.Cyclists.	8	187	-	10	-	-	O.R. evacuated 4. rejoined 2.
11th M.M.G.Batty.	4	54	-	1	-	-	
H.Q. 15th Div.Art.	4	19	-	-	-	-	O.R. 1 to 72nd Bde.
70th Bde. R.F.A.	24	705	-	6	-	1	O.R. 1 joined. 2 evacuated. 2 rejoined.
71st Bde. R.F.A.	23	701	-	1	-	-	O.R. 1 evacuated.
72nd Bde. R.F.A.	24	713	-	7	1	4	Offrs. 1 joined. O.R. 4 joined. 1 transferred 7 evac.
73rd Bde. R.F.A.	18	517	-	23	-	-	O.R. Casualties 3. 5 evacuated. 3 rejoined.
15th Div.Amm.Clm.	11	516	-	12	-	-	O.R. 15 posted to 28th D.A.C.
H.Q. C.R.E.	2	9	-	2	-	-	O.R. 1 evacuated.
73rd Fld.Coy.R.E.	6	217	-	2	-	-	O.R. 4 rejoined.
74th Fld.Coy.R.E.	6	223	-	5	-	-	O.R. 1 evacuated.
91st Fld.Coy.R.E.	6	217	-	7	-	1	
H.Q. 44th Inf.Bde.	5	37	-	-	-	-	
9th Black Watch	27	1023	-	25	-	-	O.R. 1 evacuated.
8th Seaforth Hrs,	27	1005	-	16	-	-	Offrs. 1 evacuated.
10th Gordon Hrs.	26	956	2	19	-	-	Offrs. 1 cas. O.R. 43 cas. 2 evac. 18 transferred Tunnelling Coys.
7th Cameron Hrs.	26	970	-	40	-	-	Offrs. 2 evac. O.R. 7 evacuated. 2 to take up commission.

H.Q. 45th Inf.Bde.	5	53	-	-	-	-	
13th Royal Scots	28	952	1	15	-	-	O.R. 3 evacuated 2 rejoined.
7th R.Scots Fus.	28	1008	-	22	-	-	O?R. 17 evacuated. 2 rejoined.
6th Cameron Hrs.	31	961	-	14	-	-	O.R. 7 evac. rejoined 3. cas. 1. To take commn. 1.
11th A. & S. Hrs.	28	988	-	9	-	-	Offrs. 1 to T.M.Batty. O.R. 8 evac.
46th Inf.Bde. H.Q.	5	64	-	-	-	-	
7th K.O.S.B.	30	990	4	38	-	-	O.R. 1 transferred IV Corps. 9 evacuated. 1 rejoind
8th K.O.S.B.	28	921	-	15	-	-	O.R. 1 evac. 4 rejoined. 17 transferred to 180 Coy. R.E.
10th Sco. Rifles	29	993	3	28	-	-	
12th H.L.I.	27	1002	-	19	-	-	O.R. 13 evac. 6 rejoined. 12 transferred to 180 Coy. R.E.
9th Gordon Hrs. (P).	28	1000	1	-	-	-	O.R. 4 evacuated. 2 rejoined.
15th Div. Train.	25	434	-	26	-	-	
45th Fld. Ambce.	10	237	-	-	-	-	O.R. 2 rejoined.1 evacuated.
46th Fld. Ambce.	10	230	-	-	-	-	
47th Fld. Ambce.	10	229	-	-	-	-	O.R. 2 evacuated. 1 rejoined.
32nd San. Sec.	1	27	-	12	-	-	
Fld.Amb.Wkshp.Unit.	1	20	-	-	-	-	
27th Mob. Vet. Sec.	1	27	-	-	-	-	
Totals	~~568~~ 591	18644	13	490	1	7	

(10) E. Taylor

for Major G

24. 9. 15.

Commanding 15th Divi

FIGHTING STRENGTH OF 15th DIVISION ON 30th SEPTEMBER, 1915.

	Officers	Other ranks.	
Headquarters, 15th Division.	15	79	
15th Signal Company	6	216	
15th Divisional Cavalry	6	129	
15th Divisional Cyclist Company	8	178	
11th Motor Machine Gun Battery	2	53	
Headquarters, 15th Divnl. Artillery	4	19	
70th Bde. R.F.A.	24	692	
71st Bde. R.F.A.	23	683	
72nd Bde. R.F.A.	23	707	
73rd Bde. R.F.A.	18	517	
15th Divnl. Ammunition Column	11	525	
Headquarters, R.E.	2	9	
73rd Field Company, R.E.	2	237	
74th Field Company, R.E.	6	216	
91st Field Company, R.E.	5	206	
Headquarters, 44th Infantry Brigade.	4	37	
9th Black Watch	8	379	
8th Seaforth Highlanders	8	383	
10th Gordon Highlanders	21	626	55+1910
7th Cameron Highlanders	18	522	
Headquarters, 45th Infantry Brigade.	5	67	
13th Royal Scots	13	704	
7th Royal Scots Fusiliers	10	624	52+
6th Cameron Highlanders	14	676	2727
11th Argyll & Sutherland Hrs.	15	723	
Headquarters, 46th Infantry Brigade.	5	64	
7th King's Own Scottish Børderers	11	328	
8th King's Own Scottish Borderers	16	551	46+ 1860
10th Scottish Rifles	9	463	
12th Highland Light Infantry	10	518	
15th Divisional Train	26	430	
9th Gordon Highlanders (Pioneers)	19	790	
45th Field Ambulance	9	226	
46th Field Ambulance	9	227	
47th Field Ambulance	10	228	
32nd Sanitary Section	1	27	
15th Field Ambce. Workshop Unit	1	20	
27th Mobile Veterinary Section	1	27	
	398	13106	

Includes drafts arrived since 28th instant =
Officers 11. Other ranks 886.

Return for 24 September 1915 568 18644.

7th Bn K.O.Sco. Bord.

Table. 1.

	Officers	O.R.
Nos as per last Fighting Strength Return dated 24th Sept. 1915	30	990
Nos now on Fighting Strength	11./.	328 x
Difference	19	662

x Includes one private joining on transfer from 2nd Bn K.O.Sco. Bord. 27/7/15.

Table 2.

Difference accounted for as follows :--

	Officers	O.R.
Killed	6	12
Wounded	7	221
Missing	4	404
Other reasons	2 (died of wounds)	25 (8 sufferi[ng] from gas 17 transferre[d] to 180th Coy R.E.
	19	662

NOTE :-- Total of Table 2 must equal Total in last line of Table 1.

./. 4 of these officers are in hospital.

8th Bn K.O.Sco. Bord.

TABLE 1

	Officers	O.R.
Nos as per last Fighting Strength Return dated 24-9-15	28	921
Nos now on Fighting Strength excluding draft received 29/9/15	15	541
Difference	13	380

TABLE 2.

Difference accounted for as follows :--

	Officers.	O.R.
Killed	3	23
Wounded	6	124
Wounded and missing	1	34
Missing	3	194
Gassed		4
Other reasons (accidentally injured)		1
TOTAL	13	380

NOTE Total of Table 2 must equal Total in last line of Table 1.

10th Bn Sco. Rif.

Table 1

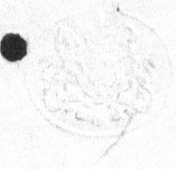

	Officers	O.R.
Nos as per last Fighting Strength dated midnight Friday 24th 1915.	29	993
Nos now on Fighting Strength 29.9.15. excluding draft.	7	355
Difference	21	638

Table 2.

Difference accounted for as follows :--

	Officers	O.R.
Killed	12	68
Wounded	5	318
Missing	4	239
Other Reasons (Gas)		13
Total	21	638

12th Bn High. L.I.

Table 1.

	Officers	O.R.
Nos as per last Fighting Strength Return dated 24th September 1915.	27	1002
Nos now on Fighting Strength including draft of one officer and 74 O.R.	9	518
Difference	18	484

Table 2.

	Officers	O.R.
Killed	7	59
Wounded	11	184
In hospital	1	
Missing	Nil	315
Total	19	558
Other reasons Draft received.	1	74
Total.	18.	484

NOTE Total OF Table 2 must equal Total in last line of Table 1.

10

C A S U A L T I E S .

15th Division 3/A.

A.A.G. 1st Army.

Fourth Corps.

The following is the return of total casualties suffered by the 15th Division for the period 25th, 26th, 27th September, called for by you 29/9/15.

KILLED.		Wounded and suffering from Gas Poisoning.		MISSING.	
Officers	Other Ranks.	Officers.	Other Ranks.	Officers.	Other Ranks.
79.	575.	109.	3268.	29.	2546.

Major General,

1. 10. 15. Commanding 15th Division.

MESSAGES AND SIGNALS. No. of Message

Prefix | Code | m. | Words | Charge
Office of Origin and Service Instructions: G
Sent At m. To By
This message is on a/c of: Service. (Signature of "Franking Officer.")
Recd. at m. Date From By

TO: A.G. G.H.Q. / Advanced 1st Army / Advanced IV Corps.

* Sender's Number	Day of Month	In reply to Number	AAA
S 16	25		

approximate casualties additional to those already reported AAA 5 officers 150 O.R. each 9th Black-atch, 8th Seaforths, 10th Gordons 7th Camerons AAA. 7th R.S.Fus 4 officers 200 O.R. AAA 6th Camerons 3 officers 50 O.R. AAA 7th K.O.S.B 3 officers including C.O. 100 O.R. AAA 10th Sco Rif 5 officers including C.O. 250 O.R. AAA 12th H.L.I. 4 officers 100 O.R. AAA 73rd Field Coy R.E 3 lieutenants 90 O.R. AAA 91st Field Coy R.E 2 lieutenants 60 O.R. AAA These are total R.E casualties to date and cancel R.E casualties reported my S.6 of today AAA. Added A.G. G.H.Q. repeated advanced 1st Army and advanced 4th Corps.

2nd Report

From: 15th Div.
Place
Time: 5.30 pm.

The above may be forwarded as now corrected. (Z) Censor. Capt. Signature of Addressor or person authorised to telegraph in his name.

* This line should be erased if not required.

(15491) S. & Co. Ltd. W 14142/641. 90,000. 4/15. Forms C 2121/10.

Prefix | Code | m. | Words | Charge
Office of Origin and Service Instructions: G.
Sent At m. To By
This message is on a/c of: Service. (Signature of "Franking Officer.")
Recd. at m. Date From By

TO: A.G. G.H.Q. / Advanced 1st Army / Advanced IV Corps

* Sender's Number	Day of Month	In reply to Number	AAA
S 36	26.		

approximate casualties 26th September AAA.

9th Black Watch	Officers 5	O.R. 450	AAA.
8th Seaforth Hrs	Officers 5	O.R. 450	AAA
[illegible] Gordon Hrs	Officers 5	O.R. 250	AAA
7th Cameron Hrs.	Officers 5	O.R. 400	AAA.
13th Royal Scots	Officers 15	O.R. 450	AAA.
7th R.S. Fusrs.	Officers 11	O.R. 250	AAA.
6th Cameron Hrs	Officers 12	O.R. 400	AAA
11th A & S Hrs.	Officers 15	O.R. 450	AAA.
7th K.O.S.B.	Officers 8	O.R. 500	AAA
8th K.O.S.B.	Officers 5	O.R. 300	AAA
10th Sco Rifles	Officers 5	O.R. 300	AAA
12th H.L.I.	Officers 4	O.R. 400	AAA.
9th Gordons (Pioneers)	Officers 10	O.R. 350	AAA

The includes casualties [illegible] and 15 [illegible] AAA [illegible] GHQ repeated advanced 1st Army, + advanced 4 Corps

From: 15 Div
Place
Time: 11.50 p.m.

The above may be forwarded as now corrected. (Z) Censor. Signature of Addressor or person authorised to telegraph in his name.

* This line should be erased if not required.

(15491) S. & Co. Ltd. W 14142/641. 90,000. 4/15. Forms C 2121/10.

MESSAGES AND SIGNALS.

No. of Message

Prefix Code m. | Words | Charge

Office of Origin and Service Instructions: G.

Sent At m. To By

This message is on a/c of: Service.

(Signature of "Franking Officer.")

Recd. at m. Date From By

TO: A.A.G IVth 1st Army Corps

Sender's Number	Day of Month	In reply to Number	AAA
S 34	26	AX 148	

Amendments to this office S30 of today aaa should read Sec Lieut S. MACDONALD Sec Lieut B.H. WATT Captain N. MACLEOD AAA Added 1st Army repeated IV Corps

From 15th Div.

Place

Time 8 pm.

The above may be forwarded as now corrected.

(Z) KS Capt.

Censor. Signature of Addressor or person authorised to telegraph in his name.

* This line should be erased if not required.

MESSAGES AND SIGNALS.

No. of Message

Prefix Code m. | Words | Charge

Office of Origin and Service Instructions: G.

Sent At m. To By

This message is on a/c of: Service.

(Signature of "Franking Officer.")

Recd. at m. Date From By

TO: A.A.G IVth 1st Army Corps

Sender's Number	Day of Month	In reply to Number	AAA
S 30	26		

Reference this office S28 of today AAA additional casualties 25th September AAA 1st Camerons killed Sec. Lieuts R.A. STUART E.G. TAYLOR S. McDONALD B. WATT AAA wounded and missing Major J. BARRON AAA wounded Captain N. McLEOD Captain L.R. DOUGLAS-HAMILTON Captain G.A.C. DAY Sec. Lieuts D.A. STUART A. McNIVEN AAA missing Captain W.H. KIRKLAND Captain E.K. CAMERON Sec. Lieut. S.E. CHAPMAN AAA no roll of other ranks possible yet AAA Added 1st Army repeated IVth Corps

From 15 Div

Place

Time 2.52 am

The above may be forwarded as now corrected.

(Z) KKan

Censor. Signature of Addressor or person authorised to telegraph in his name.

* This line should be erased if not required.

MESSAGES AND SIGNALS.

No. of Message

Prefix Code m. Words Charge

Office of Origin and Service Instructions: G.

Sent At m. To By

This message is on a/c of: Service.

(Signature of "Franking Officer.")

Recd. at m. Date From By

TO: AAG II 1st Army Corps

Sender's Number	Day of Month	In reply to Number	AAA
S 28	26		

Casualties 25th September AAA Information received the following reported up to 9.30 am today AAA 15 Div Cyclist Coy OR 1 killed 2 wounded AAA Div Artillery C/70 OR 2 wounded AAA D/73 OR 1 wounded B/73 OR 1 wounded C/73 OR 2 wounded AAA 73rd Field Coy RE killed Lieut. J.H.P. INGLIS 2/Lt M.E. NOLAN OR 10 AAA wounded and missing CAPT. E.B. CARDEW OR 15 AAA wounded 2/Lts C.F.M.N. RYAN F.H. JOHNSON OR 14 AAA missing OR 14 AAA 74th Field Coy RE OR 2 wounded AAA 180 Coy RE OR 8 wounded AAA 13th Royal Scots Lt. Col. H. MACLEAR DSO wounded at duty AAA 7 R.S. Fus wounded Major W.L. CAMPBELL Capt G.H.M. MAIR Capt. T.W. NESBITT at duty AAA Capt. E.G.J. MOYNA at duty AAA Lieut N.J.V.L. PRINSEP Lieut E.R. MACQUEEN AAA 11th A.&S. Hrs killed Capt. W.M. MACMILLAN

From

Place

Time

The above may be forwarded as now corrected. (Z)

Censor. Signature of Addressor or person authorised to telegraph in his name.

* This line should be erased if not required.

(15491) S. & Co. Ltd. W 14142/641. 20,000. 4/15. Forms C2121/10.

MESSAGES AND SIGNALS.

No. of Message

Prefix Code m. Words Charge

Office of Origin and Service Instructions

Sent At m. To By

This message is on a/c of: Service.

(Signature of "Franking Officer.")

Recd. at m. Date From By

TO

Sender's Number	Day of Month	In reply to Number	AAA

Lt. A.C. FROST AAA Lt W.D. DEAS wounded at duty AAA OR 3 wounded AAA 12th H.L.I. Capt. G.M. HARLEY killed AAA There are many more which will be reported as soon as [illegible] obtainable AAA Addsd AAG 1st Army repeated 4th Corps

From 15 Divn

Place

Time 11.35. am.

The above may be forwarded as now corrected. (Z) W [illegible] Capt.

Censor. Signature of Addressor or person authorised to telegraph in his name.

* This line should be erased if not required.

(15491) S. & Co. Ltd. W 14142/641. 20,000. 4/15. Forms C2121/10.

MESSAGES AND SIGNALS.

No. of Message

Prefix ____ Code ____ m. | Words | Charge | This message is on a/c of: | Recd. at ____ m.

Office of Origin | Service Instructions. | Sent At ____ m. To ____ By ____ | Service. | Date ____ From ____ By ____

G

(Signature of "Franking Officer.")

TO: A A G 1st Army / IV Corps

Sender's Number	Day of Month	In reply to Number	AAA
S55	28		

Casualties 27th September AAA R.F.A A/70th Bde. Major M.R.F. COURAGE wounded AAA HQ 70th Bde. O.R. one wounded AAA A/71st Bde O.R. three wounded AAA D/71st Bde O.R. one wounded AAA C/73rd Bde O.R. one wounded AAA 180 Coy R.E. O.R. 2 missing believed killed AAA 187 Coy R.E. O.R. 1 wounded 2 gas poisoned AAA 6th Cameron Hrs died of wounds Capt. J. H. McCANN AAA reported in this office S48 as wounded and missing AAA 11th A & S Hrs died of wounds Lieut W. D. DEAS AAA reported in this office S28 as wounded at duty AAA 45th Fld Amb. O.R. 3 wounded AAA 47th Fld Amb O.R. one wounded AAA added 1st Army repeated IV Corps.

From: 15th Div.
Place:
Time: 4.20 pm.

The above may be forwarded as now corrected. (Z) [signature] Capt.

Censor. Signature of Addressor or person authorised to telegraph in his name

*This line should be erased if not required.

MESSAGES AND SIGNALS.

No. of Message

Prefix ____ Code ____ m. | Words | Charge | This message is on a/c of: | Recd. at ____ m.

Office of Origin | Service Instructions. | Sent At ____ m. To ____ By ____ | Service. | Date ____ From ____ By ____

G

(Signature of "Franking Officer.")

TO: A A G 1st Army / IV Corps

Sender's Number	Day of Month	In reply to Number	AAA
S56	28		

My wire S48 of today AAA 7th K.O.S.B. Lieut J. W. JARVIS wounded not killed AAA Added 1st Army repeated IV Corps.

From: 15th Div.
Place:
Time: 6.40 pm

The above may be forwarded as now corrected. (Z) [signature] Capt.

Censor. Signature of Addressor or person authorised to telegraph in his name

*This line should be erased if not required

Prefix | Code | m. | Words | Charge | This message is on a/c of: Service. | Recd. at m. | Date | From | By

Office of Origin and Service Instructions: G

Sent At m. To By (Signature of "Franking Officer.")

TO: A.A.G. 1st Army
II Corps

Sender's Number	Day of Month	In reply to Number	
* S48	28		AAA

Casualties 26th September AAA R.F.A
B/70th Bde Sec Lieut W.N. ARNOLD wounded
O.R. 1 killed 8 wounded AAA D/70th Bde
OR 1 wounded AAA 71st Bde B.A.C
OR 1 wounded 71st Bde O.R one killed
2 missing 9 wounded 2 gas poisoned
AAA A/72nd Bde Sec Lieut V.R. BARRON
wounded AAA C/72nd Bde O.R one wounded
AAA. C/73 Bde O.R one killed one wounded AAA
D/73 Bde O.R one killed two wounded AAA
11th M.M. Gun Batty Capt B. ARTHUR wounded
Lieut J.T. MACFARLANE wounded O.R 3 wounded
AAA 15th Div Cyclist Coy O.R ~~3 wounded 1 killed~~
4 wounded AAA R.E 74th Fld Coy O.R 3 killed
1 wounded 1 missing 10 gas poisoned AAA
180 Coy O.R. 1 killed 14 wounded AAA
184 Coy O.R 2 gas poisoned AAA

From
Place
Time

The above may be forwarded as now corrected. (Z)

Censor. Signature of Addressor or person authorised to telegraph in his name.

* This line should be erased if not required.

Prefix | Code | m. | Words | Charge | This message is on a/c of: Service. | Recd. at m. | Date | From | By

Office of Origin and Service Instructions

Sent At m. To By (Signature of "Franking Officer.")

TO: (2)

Sender's Number	Day of Month	In reply to Number	
* S48 cont'd			AAA

91st Fld Coy LIEUT F.C. MacNAUGHT wounded
and missing O.R. 9 killed 29 wounded
2 wounded believed killed 11 missing AAA
9th Black Watch killed Major M.W. HENDERSON
Capt J.M. BELL Capt D.H.N. GRAHAME Lieut
[redacted] J. CRIGHTON Lieut J.C. HENDERSON-HAMILTON
Lieut A. SHARP Sec Lieut J. MILLAR died of
wounds CAPT and Adjt R.E. HARVEY wounded
Capt A.K. McLEOD Lieut R. ANDREW Lieut
A.C. DENNISTOUN Lieut E.R. WILSON Sec Lieuts
D.T. GLENNY J. CAMPBELL R. STIRLING
G. SCOTT-PEARSE W.T. LESLIE F.R. WILSON
Capt F.A. BEARN R.A.M.C (M.O) at duty wounded
and missing Lieut J.H. CAMERON AAA
O.R killed wounded and missing 672 AAA
8th Seaforth Highrs killed Major A.J.N.
TREMEARNE Capt A.G. RAVENHILL Lieut A. MILLER

Place
Time

The above may be forwarded as now corrected. (Z)

Censor. Signature of Addressor or person authorised to telegraph in his name.

* This line should be erased if not required.

12

MESSAGES AND SIGNALS. No. of Message

Prefix Code m. | Words | Charge | This message is on a/c of: Service. | Recd. at m.
Office of Origin and Service Instructions | Sent At m. To By | (Signature of "Franking Officer.") | Date From By

TO (3)

Sender's Number	Day of Month	In reply to Number	AAA
S48 cont^d			

Sec Lieut G.M. CALDER wounded Lt Col
N.A. THOMSON Major U.P. SWINBURNE Capt
H.F. MUNRO Capt R.M. POWELL Lieut D.B
MACAULAY Sec Lieut^s A.W. TURNBULL J.R.S
PAYNE Lieut D.M. DUNLOP Sec Lieut J.M.L.
NICHOLSON Sec Lieut W. HEATH missing
Lieut^s J.V. HARFORD J. E KENNEDY Sec Lieut
F.L. M^c CRAE W.C TREMEARNE G. MACGREGOR
AAA O.R. killed wounded and missing 740
AAA 10th Gordon Hrs Wounded Lieut R.L.
WATSON Sec Lieut^s G.W. SYME Sec Lieut G.J.S
LUMSDEN (at duty) Sec Lieut L.G. ROBERTSON
(at duty) wounded and missing Major C.J.
MAITLAND-MAKGILL-CRICHTON Lieut R.C.
CHRISTISON AAA O.R. not yet available AAA
7th Cameron Highrs O.R. killed 30 wounded
217 missing 313 AAA.

From
Place
Time

The above may be forwarded as now corrected. (Z)
Censor. Signature of Addressor or person authorised to telegraph in his name.

MESSAGES AND SIGNALS. No. of Message

Prefix Code m. | Words | Charge | This message is on a/c of: Service. | Recd. at m.
Office of Origin and Service Instructions | Sent At m. To By | (Signature of "Franking Officer.") | Date From By

TO (4)

Sender's Number	Day of Month	In reply to Number	AAA
S48 cont^d			

13th Royal Scots. killed Major G.D. MACPHERSON
Capt I.C. PENNEY B.D. BRUCE G.S. ROBERTSON
Lieut C.B. MUNRO Sec Lieut D.D. BROWN AAA
wounded Capt J.H. GLOVER Capt and Adjt
K.G. BUCHANAN Lieut H.J. UNDERWOOD Sec Lieut
H.M. SCOTT Sec Lieut G.V.F. DAVIES Sec Lieut
H.G. CROWDEN Sec Lieut K.G. McL BRAMALL
wounded at duty Lieut R.J.M. CHRISTIE wounded
and missing Lieut R.A. McFARLANE AAA O.R.
killed 37 wounded 224 missing 105
gas poisoned 4 AAA 6th Cameron Highrs
killed Lieut Col A.F. DOUGLAS-HAMILTON Capt
and Adjt H.W. MILNE (7th Division) Capt H.
AUTROBIS Capt E.E.G. MACDOUGALL Lieut D.C.D.
MACMASTER Lieut R.D. CAMERON Sec Lieut K.
BIGGAR wounded Capt A.J. CAMPBELL-
COLQUHOUN Sec Lieut J.M. MACKINTOSH Sec Lieut

From
Place
Time

The above may be forwarded as now corrected. (Z)
Censor. Signature of Addressor or person authorised to telegraph in his name.

"A" Form. Army Form C. 2121.

MESSAGES AND SIGNALS.

No. of Message

Prefix	Code	m.	Words	Charge	This message is on a/c of:	Recd. at m.
Office of Origin and Service Instructions			Sent		Service.	Date
			At m.			From
			To			
			By		(Signature of "Franking Officer")	By

TO 5

Sender's Number	Day of Month	In reply to Number	AAA
* S48 contd.			

J. P. THOMSON. Sec Lieut P. McDIARMID Lieut
A. F. P. CHRISTISON wounded and missing Sec Lieut
G. F. CAMERON Lieut S. H. MACDONALD Capt J. H
McCANN gas poisoned Sec Lieut H. LEITCH AAA
OR killed 30 wounded 270 missing
70 AAA 11th A & S Highlrs killed Capt
N. McLELLAN Lieut G. JACKSON Sec Lieut
W. M. DICKSON wounded Major W. MACALISTER
-HALL Capt J. W. M. ALSTON Lieut R. R. LANGTRY
Lieut O. E. O. JACKSON Sec Lieut A. H. St CLAIR
Lieut A. A. RICHARDSON AAA OR killed wounded
and missing 350 AAA 7th R. S. Fusrs killed
Capt F. G. BURR Sec Lieut F. D. HAY Sec Lieut G. S.
SHARER Sec Lieut J. E. WATSON wounded
Capt A. W. BAKER Lieut J. C. GRANVILLE Sec Lieut
W. J. CUTHBERT missing Capt F. P. SKIPWORTH
AAA O. R. killed 63 wounded 240 missing 83 AAA

From			
Place			
Time			

The above may be forwarded as now corrected. (Z)

"A" Form. Army Form C. 2121.

MESSAGES AND SIGNALS.

No. of Message

Prefix	Code	m.	Words	Charge	This message is on a/c of:	Recd. at m.
Office of Origin and Service Instructions			Sent		Service.	Date
			At m.			From
			To			
			By		(Signature of "Franking Officer")	By

TO 6

Sender's Number	Day of Month	In reply to Number	AAA
* S48 contd.			

7th K. O. S. Bs killed Capt F. R. HUTT Capt P
NEWTON Capt and Adjt R. L. LETHBRIDGE
Lieut J. W. JARVIS Lieut J. M. SELLAR Lieut
J. SCOTT Sec Lieut M. W. BUIRS Sec Lieut F. M. C.
TOD. Sec Lieut J. L. S. ALLAN AAA died of wounds
Sec Lieut W. HADDON [illegible]
Sec Lieut M. C. G. B. YOUNG AAA wounded
Lt Col. G de W. VERNER Capt M. F. B. DENNIS
Lieut A. K. GILMOUR Lieut J. FREW Sec
Lieut A. Y. M. TUCK Sec Lieut W. G. KERR AAA
wounded and missing Major T. A. GLENNY
Capt T. BLACKBURN AAA [illegible] other
ranks not available AAA 8 KOSB killed
Capt H. H. SMITH Sec Lieut W. G. HERBERT
-SON Sec Lieut P. C. DRUMMOND AAA
wounded Major H. M. FORSTER Capt
A. P. HART Capt S S LANG Capt W. W. HOME

From			
Place			
Time			

The above may be forwarded as now corrected. (Z)

4

MESSAGES AND SIGNALS. No. of Message

Prefix — Code — m. | Words | Charge | This message is on a/c of: | Recd. at — m.

Office of Origin and Service Instructions | Sent At — m. To By | Service. (Signature of "Franking Officer") | Date From By

TO 7

Sender's Number	Day of Month	In reply to Number	AAA

* Sec Lieut H.G. MITCHELL Sec Lieut C.K.
THURSBY PELHAM Lieut V.N.F. SURTEES.
AAA wounded & missing Sec Lieut S.G.
MCLELAND AAA missing Capt H.T. CRUICK
SHANK Lieut P.M. ROSS Sec Lieut J.R.
ARDILL AAA Other ranks not available
AAA 10 Co Rifles Killed Major J.H. SCOTT
Capt. W.H. ROBERTSON DURHAM Capt. F.T.
TRONTON Lieut A.O.C. MULL Lieut O.G.
YOUNG Sec Lieut G.A.W. FLYNN Sec
Lieut D.A.B. LINDSAY Sec Lieut T. PAISLEY
Capt & Adjut J.F. DUNCAN AAA wounded
believed dead Lieut R.G.C. ROBB Lieut
W. ANDERSON AAA wounded Lt Col A.V.
USSHER Major F.L. GRANT Lieut W.G. PATON
Lieut A. STENHOUSE 2/Lt. L.C. PATON Sec
Lieut J.C. LOVELL AAA wounded & missing.

From
Place
Time

The above may be forwarded as now corrected. (Z)

Censor. Signature of Addressor or person authorised to telegraph in his name.

* This line should be erased if not required.

5

MESSAGES AND SIGNALS. No. of Message

Prefix — Code — m. | Words | Charge | This message is on a/c of: | Recd. at — m.

Office of Origin and Service Instructions | Sent At — m. To By | Service. (Signature of "Franking Officer") | Date From By

TO 6.

Sender's Number	Day of Month	In reply to Number	AAA

* Capt. A.S. PRINGLE Sec Lieut J.J. CARSWELL AAA
missing Capt. E.H. BAILLIE Sec Lieut D. McCALLUM
AAA Other ranks not available AAA 12 H.L.I.
Killed Capt. G.M. HARLEY Capt J. GEMMELL
Lieut K.G. CAMPBELL Lieut F.J. NICOLL
Lieut M. SHAW Sec Lieut H.M. PORTEOUS Sec
Lieut G. ADAMSON Sec Lieut D. BROWN AAA
wounded Capt. R.S. DIXON Capt W.D. SHAW Capt. A.L.
YOUNG Lieut H. McE LINTON Lieut & Adjut A.E.
McLELLAN Lieut & QrMr J. CARPENTER Sec Lieut
H.C. JONAS Sec Lieut L. LUCAS Sec Lieut O.G.
CAMPBELL AAA wounded & missing Sec Lieut
N.H. McNEIL AAA no other ranks available
AAA 9/Gordons Pioneers Killed Lieut J.G. ALLAN
Sec Lieut K.R.B. KERSHAW Sec Lieut C.A.
MacGREGOR Sec Lieut J.M. USHER AAA
wounded Capt. T. MacWHIRTER Sec Lieut G.D.

From
Place
Time

The above may be forwarded as now corrected. (Z)

Censor. Signature of Addressor or person authorised to telegraph in his name.

* This line should be erased if not required.

MESSAGES AND SIGNALS.

No. of Message

Prefix	Code	m.	Words	Charge
Office of Origin and Service Instructions			Sent At m. To By	

This message is on a/c of: Service. (Signature of "Franking Officer")

Recd. at m. Date From By

TO 9

Sender's Number	Day of Month	In reply to Number	AAA

PITCAIRN Sec Lieut W. T. MURRAY Capt F.G.
MACGREGOR. AAA Wounded and missing
believed dead - Sec Lieut W. F. E. BISSET AAA
Other ranks killed 21 wounded 179 wounded
and missing 16 missing 47 ~~[illegible]~~ gas
poisoned 4 missing believed killed 1 AAA
45 Field Ambulance OR 1 wounded AAA 46 Field
Ambulance Lieut J. R. TURNER suffering gas
poisoning OR 2 gas poisoned AAA 47 Field
Ambulance OR 1 wounded AAA Brigade
Machine Gun Officer 44th Brigade Capt C. S. TUKE
missing believed killed AAA Addressed A.
1st Army repeated 4th Corps

From 15 Division
Place
Time 2 a.m.

The above may be forwarded as now corrected. (Z) [illegible]

Censor. Signature of Addressor or person authorised to telegraph in his name.

MESSAGES AND SIGNALS.

Prefix	Code	m.	Words	Charge
Office of Origin and Service Instructions: G			Sent At m. To By	

This message is on a/c of: Service. (Signature of "Franking Officer.")

Recd. at m. Date From By

TO A.A.G. 1st Army
IV Corps

Sender's Number	Day of Month	In reply to Number	AAA
A 168	29		

Casualties 25th September AAA RFA
13/72 Bde OR one wounded AAA
187 Coy RE OR one wounded AAA
45th Fld Amb OR one wounded five
missing AAA 46th Fld Amb OR one
gas poisoned AAA 91st Fld Coy RE
one wounded AAA Addsd 1st Army
repeated IV Corps

From 15th Div.
Place
Time 10.10 am

The above may be forwarded as now corrected. (Z) [illegible]

Censor. Signature of Addressor or person authorised to telegraph in his name

MESSAGES AND SIGNALS.

Prefix	Code	m.	Words	Charge	This message is on a/c of:	Recd. at m.
Office of Origin and Service Instructions: G			Sent At m. To By		Service. (Signature of "Franking Officer")	Date From By

TO: A.A.G. 1st Army / 17 Corps

* Sender's Number	Day of Month	In reply to Number	AAA
S58	29		

Additional casualties 26 September AAA 7th Cameron Hrs Lieut. W.G.S. STUART wounded at duty AAA 7th R.S. Fusrs. Killed Sec Lieut R.T. STEWART AAA Wounded Capt A.W. FERGUSON Lieut P.R.N. CARLETON Lieut J. GARDNER AAA Amendments to casualties reported AAA the offices were S28 dated 26/9/15 Capt E.G.J. MOYNA killed not wounded at duty Lieut W.D. DEAS killed not wounded at duty AAA the offices were S48 dated 28/9/15 ^Seaforth Capt J.H. McCANN killed not wounded and missing Lieut S.H. MacDONALD missing not wounded and missing Sec Lieut G.F. CAMERON missing not wounded and missing AAA 11th A & S Hrs Sec Lieut A.A. RICHARDSON wounded and missing not wounded only AAA additional casualties 26th September Sec Lieut

From
Place
Time

The above may be forwarded as now corrected. (Z)

Censor. Signature of Addressor or person authorised to telegraph in his name.

* This line should be erased if not required.

Prefix	Code	m.	Words	Charge	This message is on a/c of:	Recd. at m.
Office of Origin and Service Instructions			Sent At m. To By		Service. (Signature of "Franking Officer")	Date From By

TO: (2)

* Sender's Number	Day of Month	In reply to Number	AAA
S58			

D.C.H. WATSON wounded AAA Added A.A.G. 1st Army repeated 17th Corps

From 15th Div
Place
Time

The above may be forwarded as now corrected. (Z) Capt

Censor. Signature of Addressor or person authorised to telegraph in his name.

* This line should be erased if not required.

Prefix | Code | m. | Words | Charge

Office of Origin and Service Instructions: G

Sent At m. To By

This message is on a/c of: Service.

(Signature of "Franking Officer")

Recd. at m. Date From By

TO A A G 1st Army IV Corps

Sender's Number	Day of Month	In reply to Number	AAA
A 210	1		

Amendments to casualties 26th September the office S48 of 28th Sept AAA 8th Seaforth Hrs killed Lieut R.C.MILLAR not Lieut A.MILLER AAA Lieut J.V.HARFORD missing should be Lieut J.V.STANFORD killed AAA 7th Cameron Hrs OR Killed 64 not 30 Wounded 255 not 217 missing 215 not 373 AAA ~~Added 1st Army repeated IV Corps~~. 9th Gordons Pioneers 2/Lieut W.F.E.BISSET killed not wounded & missing AAA added 1st Army repeated IV Corps.

From 15th Div

Place

Time 9.40 am.

The above may be forwarded as now corrected. (Z) Censor.

Capt

Signature of Addressor or person authorised to telegraph in his name.

Prefix | Code | m. | Words | Charge

Office of Origin and Service Instructions: G

Sent At m. To By

This message is on a/c of: Service.

(Signature of "Franking Officer.")

Recd. at m. Date From By

TO A.A.G 1st Army IVth Corps

Sender's Number	Day of Month	In reply to Number	AAA
A 234	2		

Casualties 1 October AAA 187 Coy R.E. other ranks two wounded AAA this office S48 of 28th September Lieut S.H.MACDONALD 6th Cameron Hrs reported wounded and missing now reported wounded AAA Lieut R.R.LANGTRY reported wounded now reported died of wounds AAA added 1st Army repeated IVth Corps.

HEADQUARTERS, 15th DIVISION 2-OCT.1915 Reg. No.

From 15th Division

Place

Time 9.55 am.

The above may be forwarded as now corrected. (Z) Censor.

Capt

Signature of Addressor or person authorised to telegraph in his name.

* This line should be erased if not required.

MESSAGES AND SIGNALS.

No. of Message

Prefix	Code	m.	Words	Charge	This message is on a/c of:	Recd. at m.
Office of Origin and Service Instructions: G			Sent At m. To By		Service. (Signature of "Franking Officer.")	Date From By

TO: A.A.G 1st Army / IV Corps

Sender's Number	Day of Month	In reply to Number	AAA
* A 259	3		

This office wire S48 of 28th September AAA 7th K.O.S.Bs Lieut J.M SELLAR and Sec. Lieut F.M.C TOD killed now reported missing believed killed AAA 8th K.O.S.Bs Lieut V.N.F. SURTEES wounded now reported wounded at duty AAA 10th Sco. Rifles Lieut A. STENHOUSE wounded now reported killed AAA [redacted] Lieut R.G.C ROBB wounded believed dead now reported missing AAA Lieut W. ANDERSON wounded believed dead now reported killed AAA Sec. Lieut J.J. CARSWELL wounded & missing now reported killed AAA Added 1st Army repeated IV Corps

From: 15th Division
Place:
Time: 6.50 pm

The above may be forwarded as now corrected. (Z)

Censor. — Signature of Addressor or person authorised to telegraph in his name: Capt

* This line should be erased if not required.

MESSAGES AND SIGNALS.

No. of Message

Prefix	Code	m.	Words	Charge	This message is on a/c of:	Recd. at m.
Office of Origin and Service Instructions: G			Sent At m. To By		Service. (Signature of "Franking Officer.")	Date From By

TO: A.A.G 1st Army / IV Corps

Sender's Number	Day of Month	In reply to Number	AAA
* A 248	3		

Casualties 2nd October AAA RFA D/71st Bde OR 1 wounded AAA C/71st Bde OR 3 wounded AAA D/71 Bde OR 1 wounded AAA 9th Black Watch OR 1 wounded AAA A S C 15th Div Train Capt. J H LUXMORE wounded AAA Reference this office S48 of 28th Sept. Lieut G F CAMERON now reported wounded not wounded and missing AAA [redacted]
Casualties 2nd October. 184 Coy. R.E. O.R. 3 wounded. AAA Added 1st Army repeated IV Corps.

From: 15th Division
Place:
Time:

The above may be forwarded as now corrected. (Z)

Censor. — Signature of Addressor or person authorised to telegraph in his name: Capt

* This line should be erased if not required.

11

INSTRUCTIONS FOR ATTACK ON 26th SEPTEMBER.

SECRET

1Vth Corps No. H.R.S. 525

HEADQUARTERS, 15th DIVISION
21 SEP. 1915
Reg. No. 500

HEADQUARTERS 4th CORPS
21 SEP 1915
GENERAL STAFF

1st Division.
15th Division.
47th Division.
~~4th Corps Artillery.~~
~~No.1 Group H.A.R.~~)
~~Xlth Corps.~~) For information.
~~"Q" 4th Corps.~~)

---

1. On the night of the 24th/25th the 21st and 24th Divisions will move up to the line NOEUX-LES-MINES - BEUVRY, the heads of the columns arriving on this line by the morning of the 25th. The divisions will bivouac along the roads of advance.

2. The 21st Division will march through 1Vth Corps area, the head of the column leaving LOZINGHEM at 6 p.m., and will bivouac along the road NOEUX LES MINES - FOUR A CHAUX (square K.15.d.) - PLACE A BRUAY (villages of HOUCHIN and HALLICOURT exclusive).

D.A.C. to LA BUISSIERE - BETHUNE road.

Refilling Point - HESDIGNEUL or HALLICOURT.

3. In view of this move all details of the 1Vth Corps must be clear of MARLES LES MINES by 6 p.m.

4. All artillery ammunition required for expenditure on the 24th and 25th will be brought up on the night of 23rd/24th. Authority is hereby given to draw up ammunition from the Park for this purpose if necessary.

A. Holland(?)

Brigadier General.

21st September, 1915.

General Staff, 1Vth Corps.

2

A Ku(?)

21/9

1AS

ALM(?)

SECRET

HEADQUARTERS 4th CORPS
21 SEP 1915
GENERAL STAFF

lVth Corps No. H.R.S. 518.

~~1st Division.~~
15th Division.
~~47th Division.~~
~~4th Corps Artillery.~~
~~1st Group H.A.R.~~
~~187th Coy., R.E.~~

---

1. 1st., 15th.,and 47th Divisions, 4th Corps Artillery, No.1 Group H.A.R., and 187 Coy. R.E. will each send an officer to Corps Advanced Headquarters at 5 p.m. on 24th September to check their watches by Corps time.

2. The Corps time will again be checked by telephone at 3 a.m. on 25th.

3. The 187th Company R.E. will be responsible that the programme from 0 to 0.40 is carried out by Corps time and infantry officers in the front trenches will check their watches with those of the 187th Company, R.E.

Each officer and man of the 187th Company R.E. in the trenches on the 25th will have a watch which will have been set to Corps time.

R.A.K. Montgomery

H.Q.lVth Corps.
21st September, 1915.

Brigadier General.
General Staff lVth Corps.

Rack
G 458

Demonstration
44E Bde Fm Tr.
Fire open by 40 = Bde

SECRET

IVth Corps No. H.R.S. 530/1

HEADQUARTERS 4th CORPS 24 SEP 1915 GENERAL STAFF

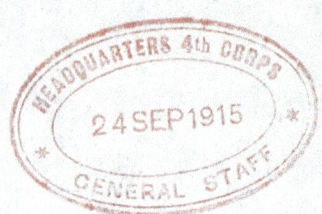

~~Adv 1st Division.~~
Adv 15th Division.
~~Adv 47th Division.~~
~~IVth Corps Art.~~

~~187th Co. R.E.~~
~~"Q".~~
~~A.P.M.~~
~~No. 1 Group, H.A.R.~~ } for information.
~~Adv 1st Corps.~~ }

1. The weather forecast at 9.45 p.m. indicates that a west or south-west wind may be anticipated to-morrow the 25th September.

2. Operation Order No. 36 of 20th September holds good.

3. The hour of zero will be notified later during the night.

All troops will hold themselves in readiness for the attack with gas and smoke to take place when ordered.

4. Acknowledge receipt by wire.

A A Montgomery

Brigadier-General,
General Staff, IVth Corps.

H.Q. IVth Corps.
24th September, 1915.

Rec'd 0.40 am 25/9

Ack'd G.39
Et

SECRET IVth Corps No. H.R.S. 530

HEADQUARTERS 4th CORPS
25 SEP 1915
GENERAL STAFF

~~Adv. 1st Division.~~
Adv.15th Division.
~~Adv.47th Division.~~
IVth Corps Artillery.
Adv. 1st Army.)
Adv. 1st Corps.)
Adv.11th Corps.)
3rd Cavalry Division.) for information.
Cavalry Corps.)
1st Group H.A.R.)
~~XXIst French Corps.~~)

1. The 15th Division, with 62nd Brigade attached, will attack the redoubt on Hill 70, H.31, tomorrow. The attack, which will be preceded by an hour's intense bombardment by all available guns of IVth Corps Artillery and 1st H.A.R., will take place at 9 a.m.

2. The 1st Division will attack HULLUCH at 11 a.m.; this attack will also be preceded by an hour's intense bombardment of all available guns of IVth Corps Artillery and 1st H.A.R. commencing at 10 a.m.

3. The 21st and 24th Divisions are attacking the enemy's position between CITE ST.AUGUSTE and HULLUCH ~~after the redoubt on Hill 70 and HULLUCH have been captured~~. at 11.0 am

4. Barrages will be established by IVth Corps Artillery on the enemy's trenches South and East of HILL 70 during and after the attack of the 15th Division.

5. The 1st H.A.R., in addition to the intense bombardment preceding the attacks of the 1st and 15th Divisions will bombard the trenches to be attacked by the 21st and 24th Divisions.

6. The 7th Division is attacking the enemy's position at and North of HULLUCH at 11 a.m.

7./

7. The 47th Division will maintain their present position but be prepared, if necessary, to support the 15th Division with such troops as they may have in reserve.

8. The 2nd Brigade will rejoin the 1st Division tomorrow morning under arrangements to be made between the 1st and 15th Divisions.

9. The French Xth Army will attack South of LENS at 8.20 a.m. preceded by a bombardment commencing at 6 a.m.

10. Corps Advanced Headquarters will remain at VAUDRICOURT until further orders.

11.55pm
25/9/15

C A Montgomery

Brigadier General,
General Staff, IVth Corps.

SECRET

IVth Corps No. H.R.S. 530/2

HEADQUARTERS 4th CORPS
24 SEP 1915
GENERAL STAFF

~~Adv. 1st Division.~~
Adv. 15th Division.
~~Adv. 47th Division.~~
~~IVth Corps Artillery.~~
~~"Q" IVth Corps.~~
~~A.P.M. IVth Corps.~~
~~187th Company R.E.~~
~~1st Group H.A.R.~~ } for information.
~~Adv. 1st Crps.~~ }

Zero is at 5-50 (five-fifty.).

All accessories to be used everywhere possible.

Acknowledge by wire.

25th September, 1915.

R Stewart Maj
GS
for Brigadier General,
General Staff, IVth Corps.

SECRET

IVth Corps No. H.R.S. 530/1

~~Adv. 1st Division.~~
Adv. 15th Division.
~~Adv. 47th Division.~~
~~IVth Corps Art.~~
~~6th Cavalry Bde. (through Adv. 15th Div)~~
~~Advanced First Army.~~)
~~Advanced 1st Corps.~~)
~~Advanced 11th Corps.~~)
~~Guards Division.~~) ~~for information.~~
~~3rd Cavalry Division.~~)
No. 1 Group, H.A.R.)

1. The 47th Division is holding from the west end of the DOUBLE CRASSIER to the south end of the LOOS CRASSIER.

2. The 1st Division is holding from about H.18.c.5.2 to H.18.b.9.2.

3. The 6th Cavalry Brigade has relieved the 15th Division in LOOS.

4. The Guards Division is being moved up to relieve the 21st and 24th Divisions between LOOS and the right of the 1st Division.

5. The 47th Division will continue to hold and consolidate their position, which should, if possible, include the CHALK PIT in M.6.a and the LOOS CRASSIER.

6. The 6th Cavalry Brigade will continue to hold LOOS and will maintain close touch with the 47th Division on its right, and the Guards Division on its left.

7. The 1st Division will maintain and consolidate its present position, keeping touch with the Guards Division on its right and the 1st Corps on its left.

8. The

8. The 15th Division (less Divisional Artillery) will be withdrawn and concentrate during the night at MAZINGARBE.

9. The 15th Divisional Artillery will remain in position under the orders of the Corps Artillery Commander.

10. Every endeavour should be made by divisions to collect any detached parties, so that the divisions may be prepared for a further advance.

11. Acknowledge receipt by wire.

9. 55pm.

Brigadier-General,
General Staff, IVth Corps.

Adv.H.Q. IVth Corps.
26th September, 1915.

"C" Form (Duplicate). Army Form C. 2123.

MESSAGES AND SIGNALS.

No. of Message

Charges to Pay. £ s. d.

Office Stamp.

Service Instructions. 2 aaa

Handed in at 1 S IX ECO Office 1.5a m. Received 1.55 m.

TO Adv 15th Divn

Sender's Number	Day of Month	In reply to Number	AAA
G188	27		

The	3rd	Cav	Divn	has
been	placed	under	orders	of
4th	Corps	aaa	3rd	Cav
Divn	will	hold	LOOS	connecting
up	with	right	of	guard
Divn	at	G.29.D.	5.8 aaa	Genl
Griggs	will	take	over	command
of	troops	in	Loos	from
Genl	Campbell	aaa	The	28th
Divn	on	arrival	will	relieve
the	1st	Divn	aaa	as
soon	after	relief	as	possible
the	1st	Divn	will	move
round	and	take	over	the
front	held	tonight	by	the
3rd	Cav	Divn	between	the
left	of	the	47th	Divn

FROM

PLACE & TIME

(6900) W.9668—1672. 50,000 Pads—12/14. F. T. & Co., Ltd.—Forms/C.2123.

"C" Form (Duplicate). Army Form C. 2123.

MESSAGES AND SIGNALS.

No. of Message

Charges to Pay. £ s. d.

Office Stamp.

Service Instructions.

Handed in at Office 1.5 m. Received 1.53 m.

TO Adv 15th Div G

Sender's Number	Day of Month	In reply to Number	AAA

and	the	right	of	the
guards	Divn	aaa	the	15th
Divn	less	Divnl	Artillery	will
move	tomorrow	to	HAILLICOURT	
DROUVIN	and	HOUCHIN	where	it
will	be	in	ghq	reserve
aaa	Acknowledge		aaa	Addsd
Advd	1st	advd	15th	adv
47th	Divns	4th	Corps	Artillery
3rd	Cav	Divn	repeated	advd
1st	Army	1st	HQR	advd
1st	Corps	advd	11th	Corps

Received 2.20 am

ackd by G 150

FROM Advd 4th Corps

PLACE & TIME 12.45am

(6900) W.9668—1672. 50,000 Pads—12/14. F. T. & Co., Ltd.—Forms/C.2123.

12

MAPS AND TRACINGS.

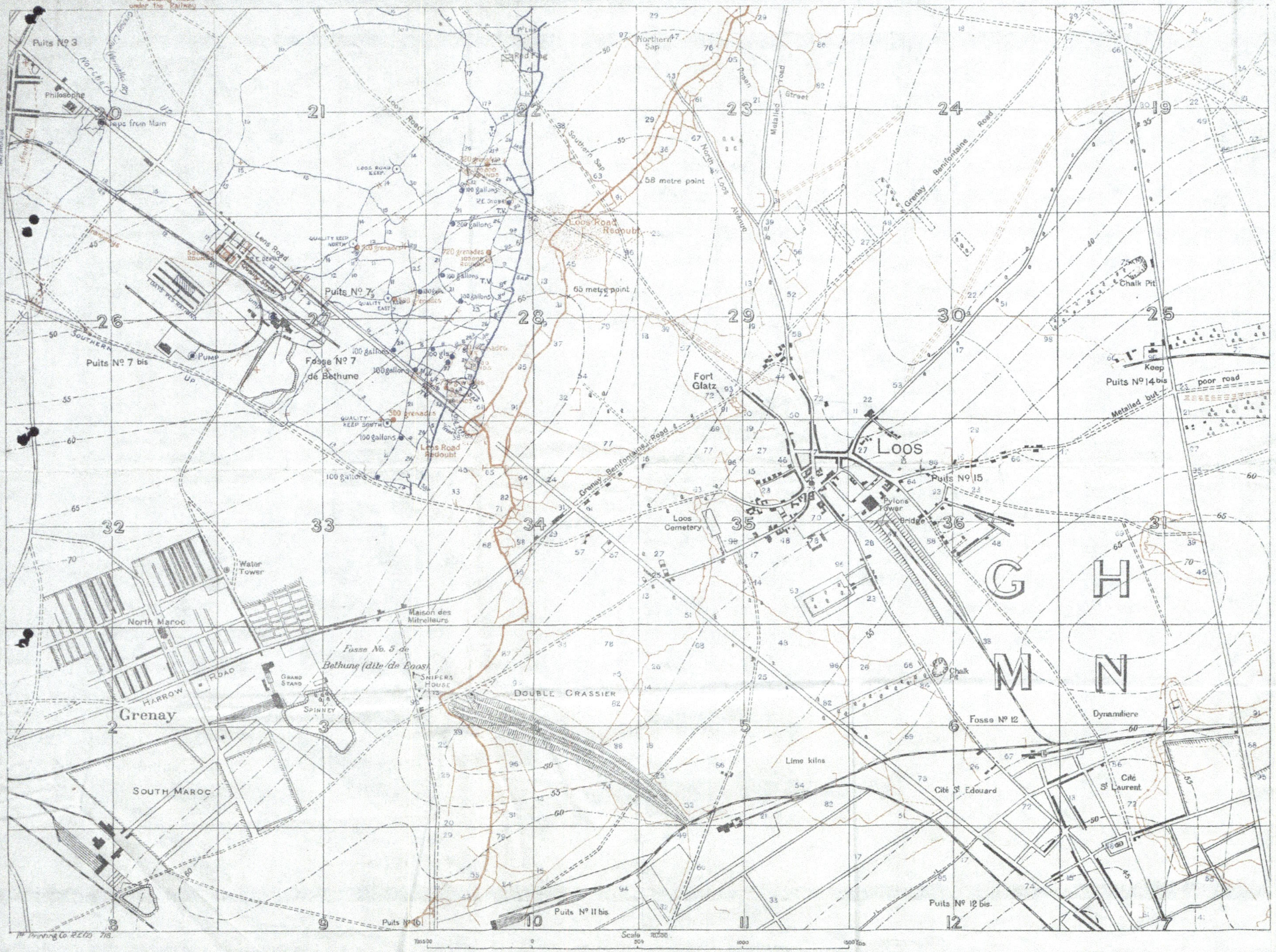

Puits Nº 3
Philosophe
To cutting made under the Railway
Lens Road
Loos Road
Puits Nº 7
Fosse Nº 7 de Bethune
Puits Nº 7 bis
Pump
Loos Road Redoubt
Lens Road Redoubt
Northern Sap
Southern Sap
58 metre point
65 metre point
North Loos Avenue
Metalled Road
Grenay Benifontaine Road
Fort Glatz
Loos
Loos Cemetery
Puits Nº 15
Pylons Tower
Bridge
Chalk Pit
Keep
Puits Nº 14 bis
poor road
Metalled but
G
H
M
N
Water Tower
North Maroc
Maison des Mitrailleurs
Fosse No. 5 de Bethune (dite de Loos)
Snipers House
Double Crassier
Grenay
Harrow Road
Grand Stand
Spinney
South Maroc
Lime kilns
Fosse Nº 12
Dynamitiere
Cité St Edouard
Cité St Laurent
Puits Nº 16
Puits Nº 11 bis
Puits Nº 12 bis
Scale

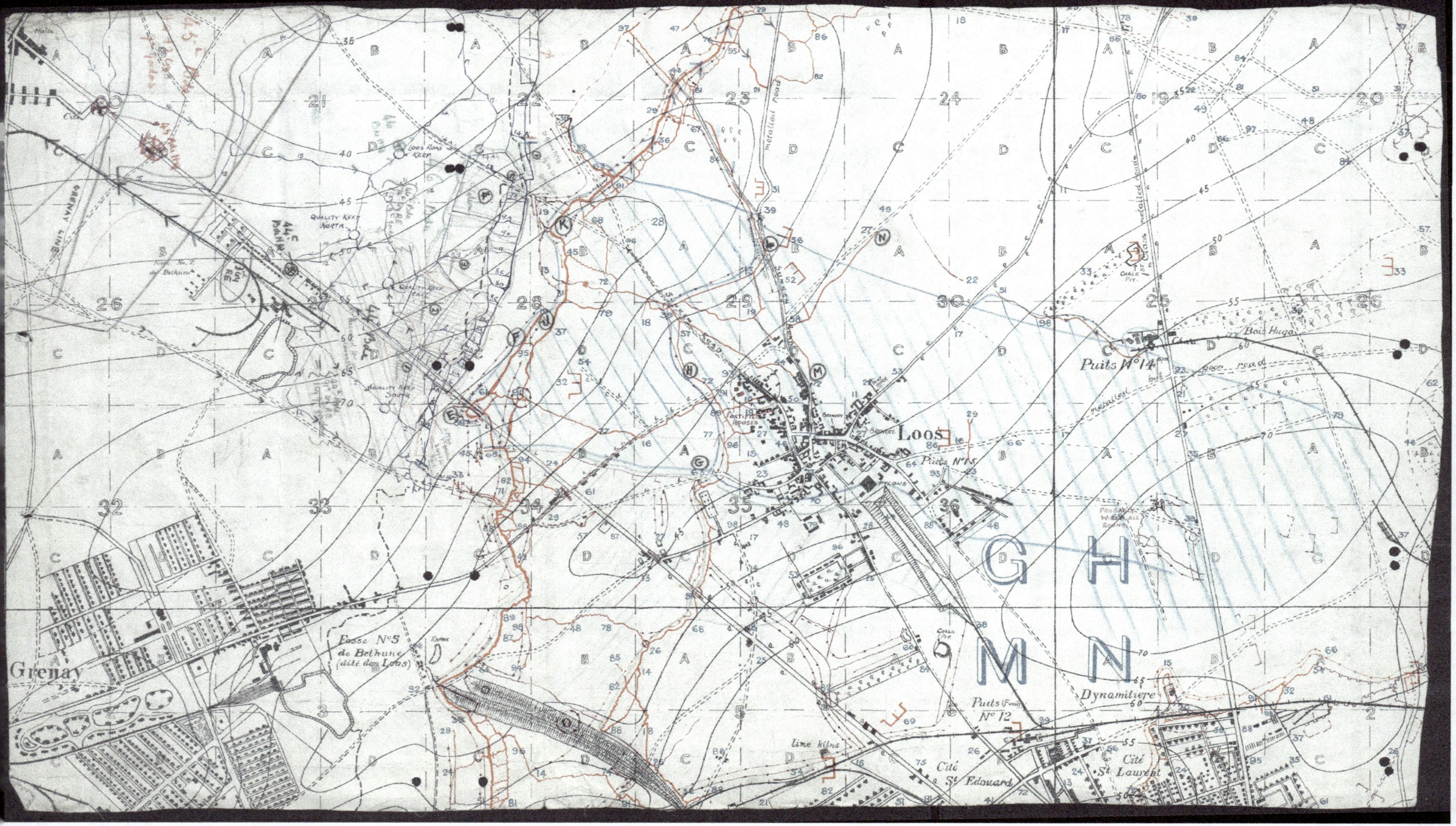

Loos
Puits No 14
Puits No 15
Puits (Fosse) No 12
Bois Hugo
Dynamitiere
Cité St Laurent
Cité St Edouard
Fosse No 5 de Bethune (dite de Loos)
Grenay
Grenay Line
metalled road
Quality Keep North
Quality Keep South
Loos Road Keep
Fortified Houses
line kilns
Chalk Pit
G
H
M
N

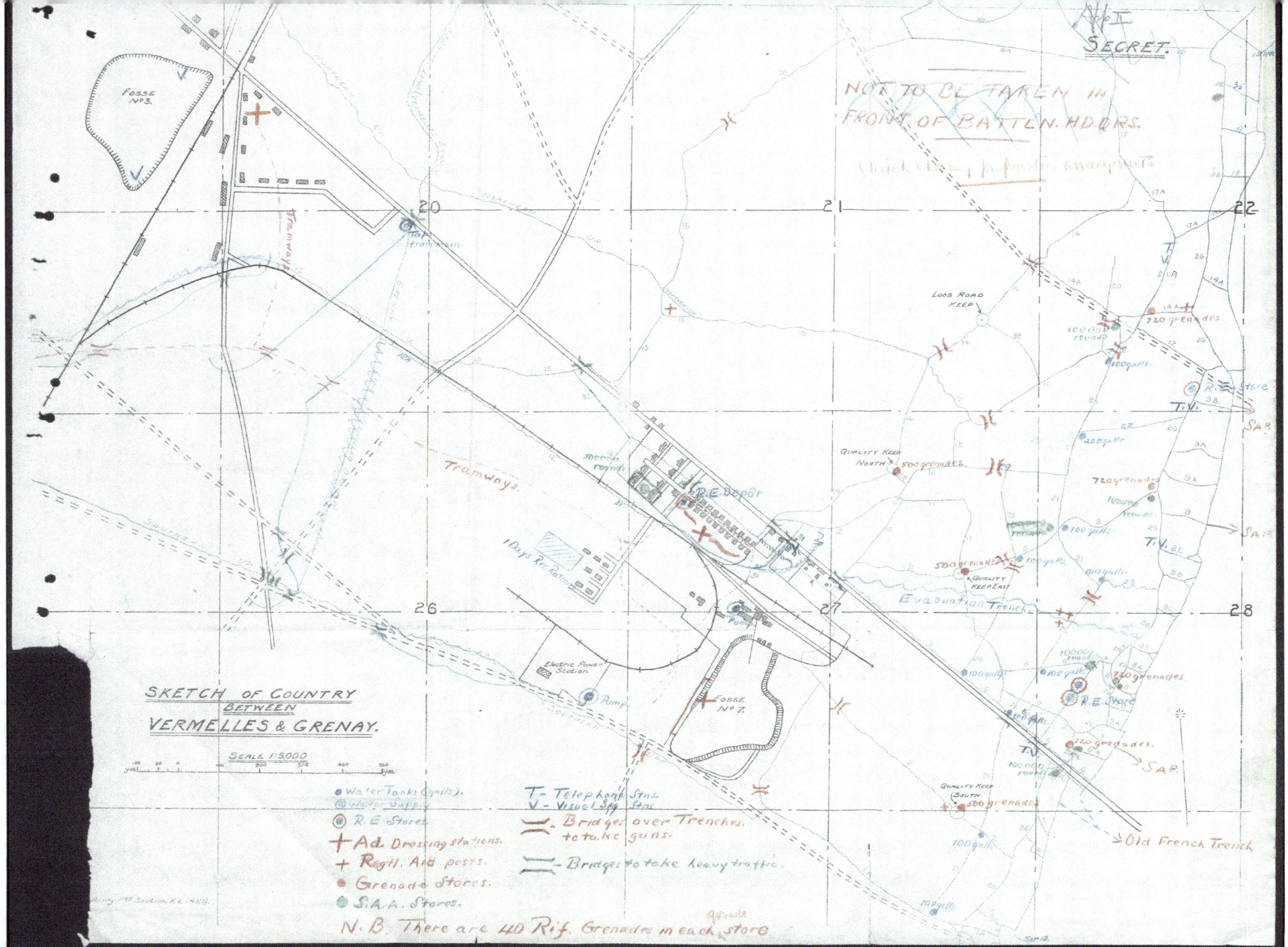
SECRET.
NOT TO BE TAKEN IN FRONT OF BATTLN. HD.QRS.
SKETCH OF COUNTRY BETWEEN VERMELLES & GRENAY.
SCALE 1:5000
Fosse No3.
Fosse No7.
Tramways
Tramways.
Tap from main.
Loos Road Keep
Quality Keep North
Quality Keep East
Quality Keep South
R.E. Depôt
R.E. Store
Evacuation Trench
Electric Power Station.
Pump
1 Days Res. Rations
720 grenades
500 grenades
100 galls.
SAP.
Old French Trench
Water Tanks (galls).
R.E. Stores.
Ad. Dressing stations.
Regtl. Aid posts.
Grenade Stores.
S.A.A. Stores.
T - Telephone Stns.
V - Visual Sig. Stns.
Bridges over Trenches, to take guns.
Bridges to take heavy traffic.
N.B. There are 40 Rif. Grenades in each grenade store

Sketch of Country between

VERMELLES AND GRENAY

Showing Preparatory Arrangements.

● Water Tanks (gallons).	+ Advanced Dressing Stations.
◉ Water Supply.	+ Regimental Aid Posts.
◉ R.E. Stores.	● S.A.A. Stores.
T. Telephone Stations.	● Grenade Stores.
V. Visual Signalling Stations.	Bridges over trenches to take guns.
	„ to take heavy traffic.

N.B.—There are 40 Rifle Grenades in each Grenade Store.

Puits No 3
Philosophe
Loos Road
Lens Road
Puits No 7
Fosse No 7 de Bethune
Puits No 7 bis
London Road
Finchley Road
North Maroc
Water Tower
Grenay
Harrow Road
South Maroc
Grand Stand
Spinney
Maison des Mitrailleurs
Snipers House
Double Crassier
Loos Road Redoubt
Lens Road Redoubt
58 metre point
55 metre point
Northern Sap
Southern Sap
North Loos Avenue
Metalled road
Fort Glatz
Grenay Benifontaine Road
Loos Cemetery
Loos
Pylons Tower
Puits No 15
Chalk Pit
Keep
Puits No 14 bis
Metalled but poor road
Fosse No 12
Dynamitiere
Lime kilns
Cité St Edouard
Cité St Laurent
Puits No 11 bis
Puits No 12 bis
G
H
M
N

HEADQUARTERS,
15th DIVISION
21 SEP. 1915
Reg. No. 502

XV Division

Map showing distribution of troops on night 24/25 Sep. attached

G.W. Howard Major
Bde Major
46 I.B

21 IX/15

HEADQUARTERS
No. M/145
21 SEP. 1915
46th INFANTRY BRIGADE

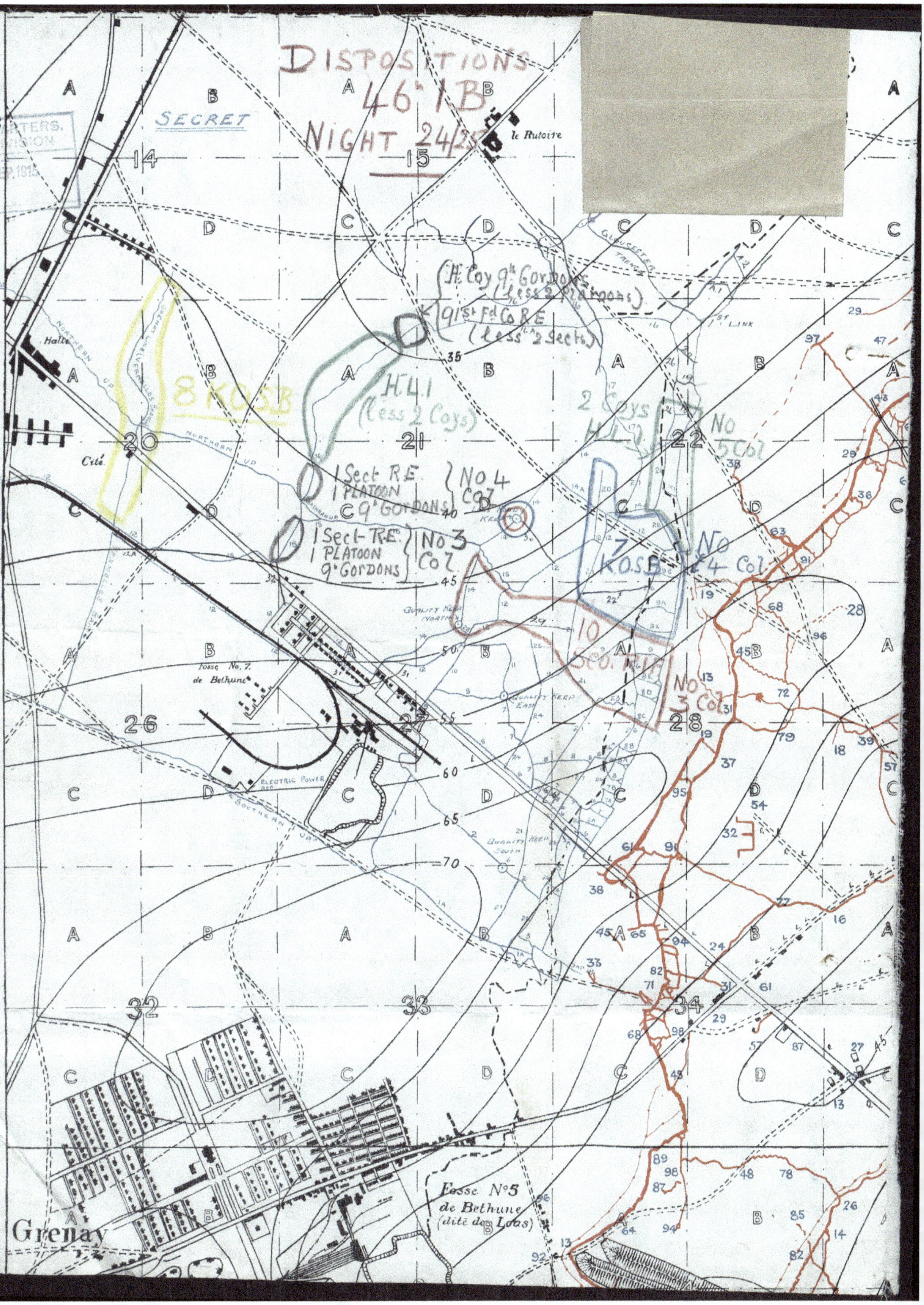
DISPOSITIONS
46th I.B.
NIGHT 24/25
SECRET
HEADQUARTERS, 15th DIVISION
6 - SEP. 1915
le Rutoire
A Coy 9th Gordons (less 2 platoons)
91st Fd Co R.E (less 2 Sects)
8 KOSB
H.L.I (less 2 Coys)
2 Coys H.L.I
No 5 Col
1 Sect R.E 1 PLATOON 9th GORDONS
No 4 Col
1 Sect R.E. 1 PLATOON 9th GORDONS
No 3 Col
7 K.O.S.B
No 4 Col
10 Sco. Rif
No 3 Col
Halte
Cité
Fosse No. 7 de Bethune
Electric Power
Fosse No 5 de Bethune (dite de Loos)
Grenay

"A" Form. Army Form C. 2121.

MESSAGES AND SIGNALS. No. of Message

Prefix Code m.	Words Charge	This message is on a/c of:	Recd. at m.
Office of Origin and Service Instructions	Sent At m. To By	Service. (Signature of "Franking Officer.")	Date From By

TO 15th Div.

Sender's Number	Day of Month	In reply to Number	AAA
* BM 639	24.9.15		

Herewith a plan of the position of the battalion of the 44th Inf Bde on the night of Sept 24th 1915

J. R. Haines Major B.M.
44th Inf Bde

The Seaforths are shown in BLUE
" Black Watch " " " RED
all other units in RED

From
Place
Time

The above may be forwarded as now corrected. (Z)

Censor. Signature of Addressor or person authorised to telegraph in his name

* This line should be erased if not required.

(5191) S. & Co. Ltd. W 14142/641. 90,000. 4/15. Forms C 2121/10.

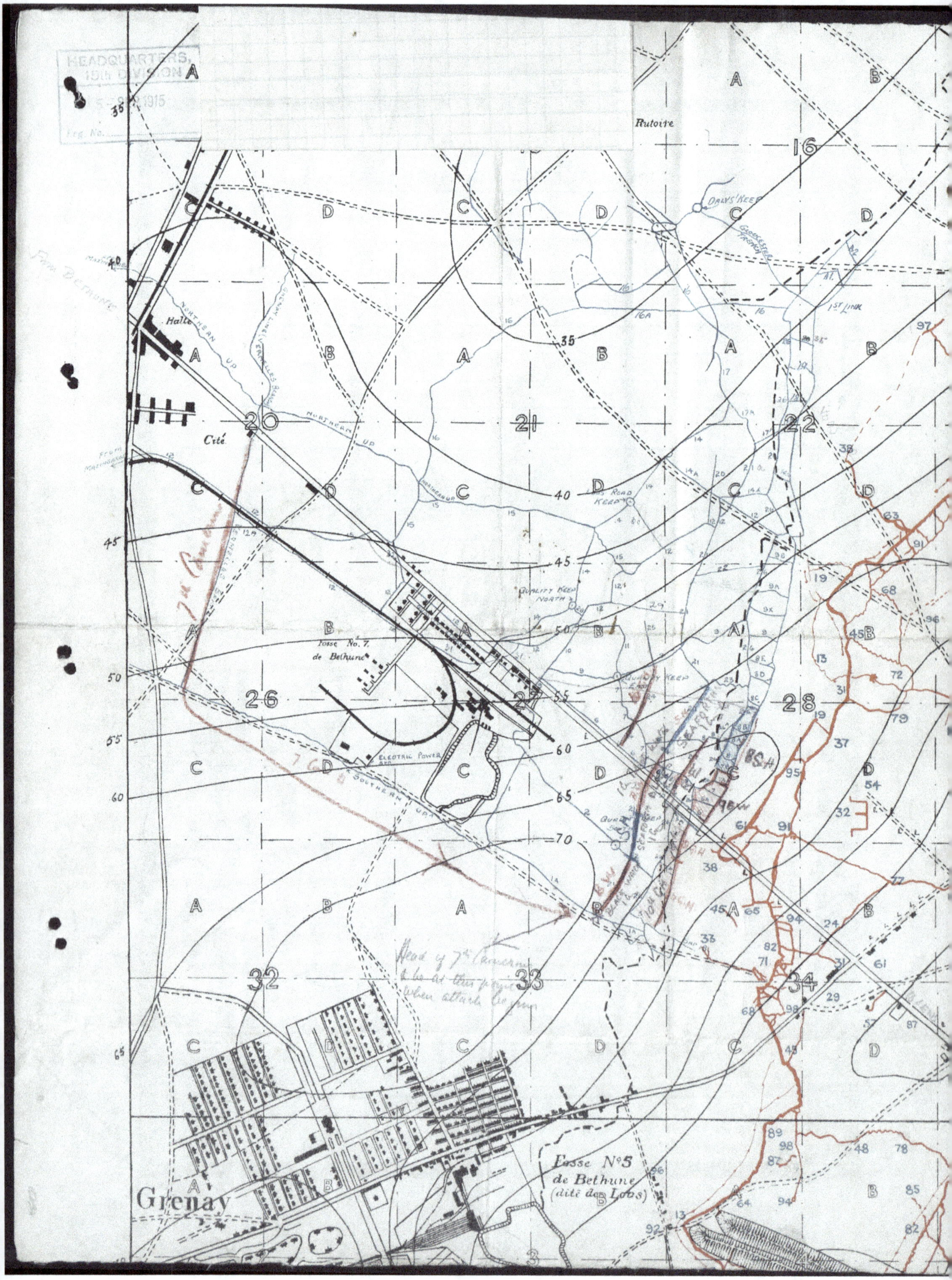

HEADQUARTERS, 15th DIVISION
Rutoire
Daly's Keep
1st Link
From Bethune
Halte
Cité
Northern Up
Fosse No. 7 de Bethune
Quality Keep North
Electric Power Stn.
Southern Up
7th Cameron
Head of 7th Camerons to be at this point when attack begins
Fosse No 5 de Bethune (dite des Loos)
Grenay

[illegible] Sept 24

APP. II
SECRET
Puits Nº 3
Philosophe
NOT TO BE TAKEN IN FRONT OF BATT. H.Q.
Loos Road
TAPS FROM MAIN
TRAMWAY
Lens Road
Quality Street
Puits Nº 7
EVACUATION TRENCH
Puits Nº 7 bis
Fosse Nº 7 de Bethune
Electric Power Station
Lens Road Redoubt
OLD FRENCH TRENCH
SKETCH of COUNTRY BETWEEN VERMELLES & GRENAY
REFERENCE.
WATER TANKS. (GALLS)
WATER SUPPLY
R.E. STORES.
GRENADE STORES
S.A.A. STORE
Water Tower
North Maroc
Maison des Mitrailleurs
G.S.G.S. 3094.
Scale 1:5,000
Yards 100
Kilomètre 1

SECRET

AUCHY LENS

1st EDITION JUNE 11th 1915.

NOTE.—The contours shown on the 1 : 40,000 and the 1 : 20,000 and the French maps are incorrect. The long high ridge shown on these maps running out to Haisnes does not exist.

The form lines shown in black on this map represent the general shape of the country, but must not be regarded as accurate contours.

The numbers shown on this map are the co-ordinates on the system explained at the foot of G.S.G.S. squared maps 1 : 20,000 and 1 : 40,000 scales.

In referring to the numbers the square must invariably be fully identified as well as the co-ordinates, e.g., H. 14. c 23.

The same system may be applied to points for which numbers have not been printed.

The following table shows the co-ordinates of the arbitrary numbers on the La Bassée map (G.S.G.S. 2040 A) where the two maps overlap.

Arbitrary Numbers.	Co-ordinate References.
E 1	A 21 B. 63
2	A 21 B. 75
3	A 21 B. 77
4	A 21 B. 92
5	A 21 B. 99
6	A 22 A. 06
7	A 22 A. 18
8	A 22 A. 22
9	A 22 A. 34
10	A 22 A. 37
11	A 22 A. 39
12	A 22 A. 59
13	A 22 A. 72
14	A 22 A. 80
15	A 22 A. 64

Loos
Lens
Grenay
Puits No 14
Bois Hugo
Dynamitière
Brickfields
Cité St Edouard
Cité St Laurent
Cité St Emile
Cité St Pierre
Cité St Elisabeth
Cité St Théodore
Cité de la Plaine
Fosse No 5 de Béthune
Fosse Calonne
Halte
Puits No 12
Puits No 11
Fme Des Mines De Lens
Cité St Auguste
46th Bde
Conventional Signs

Secret

Identification Trace for use with Artillery Maps.

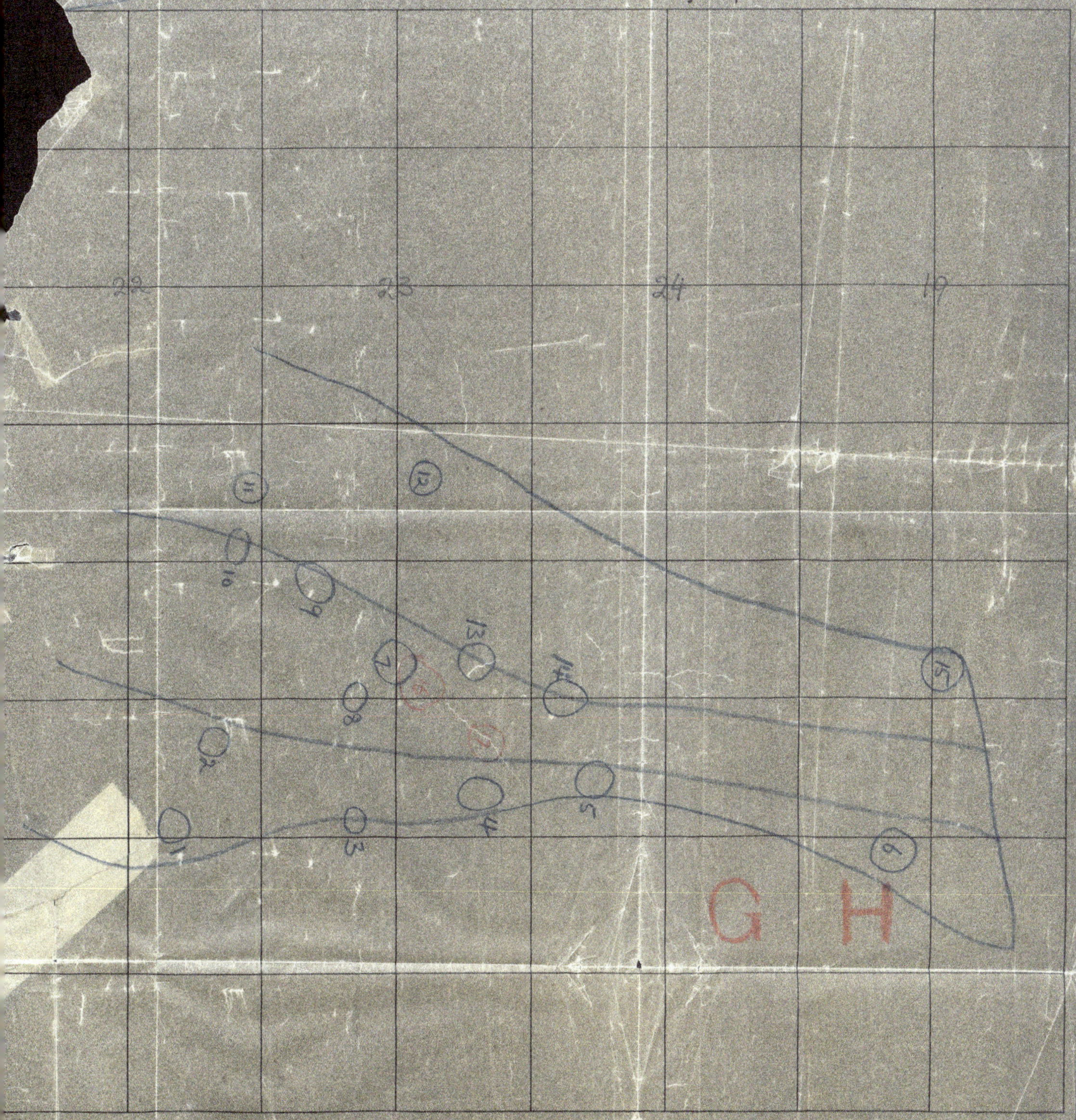

NOTE.—(1). These traces are intended to facilitate the communication of information as to the position of targets, which have been located on a squared map.

(2). The squares on this trace are 1,000 yards in length on the 1/20,000 scale, and 2,000 yards in length on the 1/40,000 scale.

(3). The squares on the trace are fitted to the squares of the map showing the targets, which are then drawn on the trace. Sufficient letters and numbers must also be added to enable the recipient to place the trace in the correct position on his own map. A little detail may also be traced, but this is not essential. The name and scale of the map to which the trace refers must be always given. The trace can be used for either the 1/20,000 or 1/40,000 scale.

G.S.G.S. 3023

Tracing taken from Sheet AUCHY-LENS

of the 1/10000 map of France

Signature [illegible] Maj

Date 12/9/15

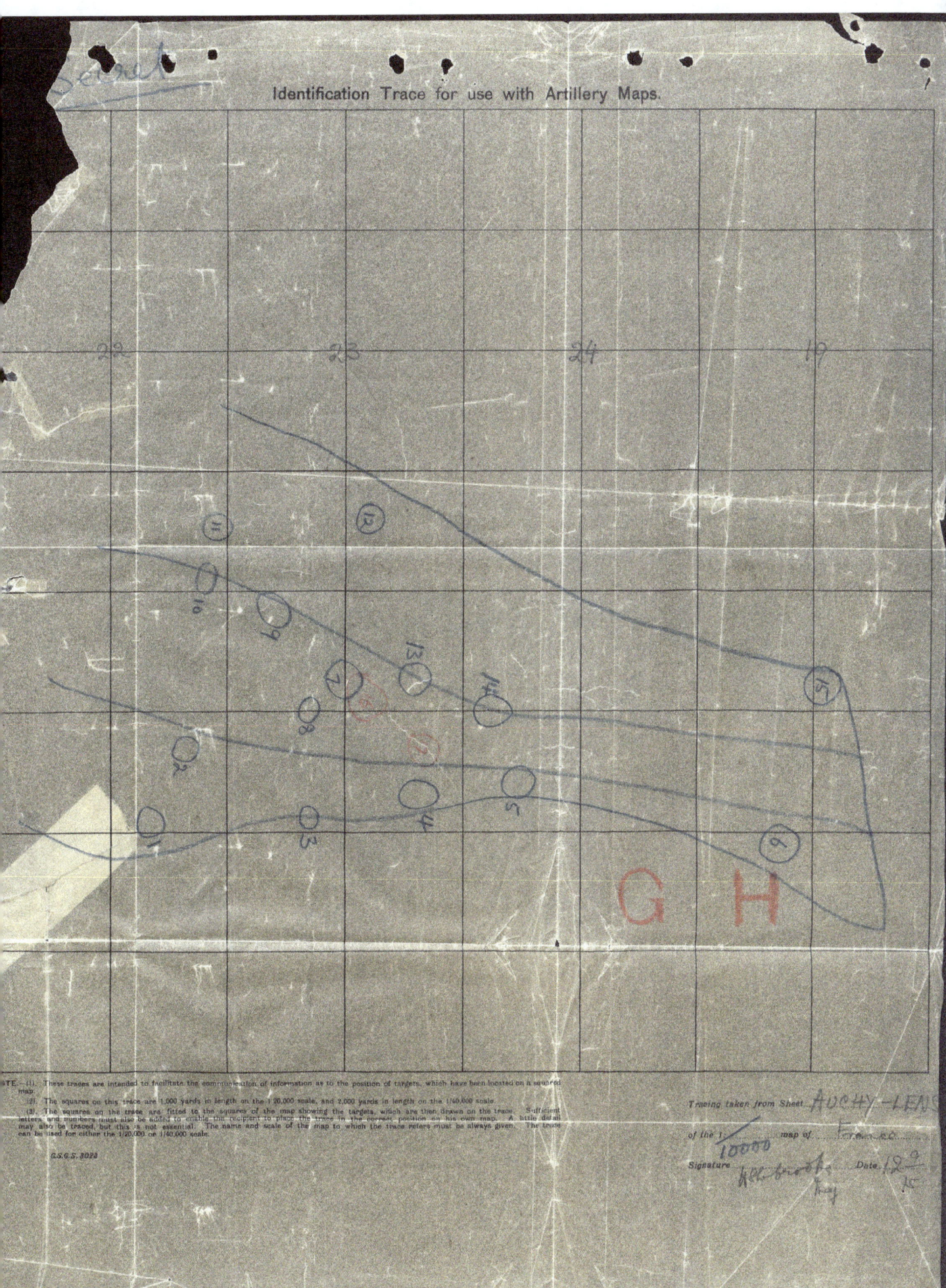

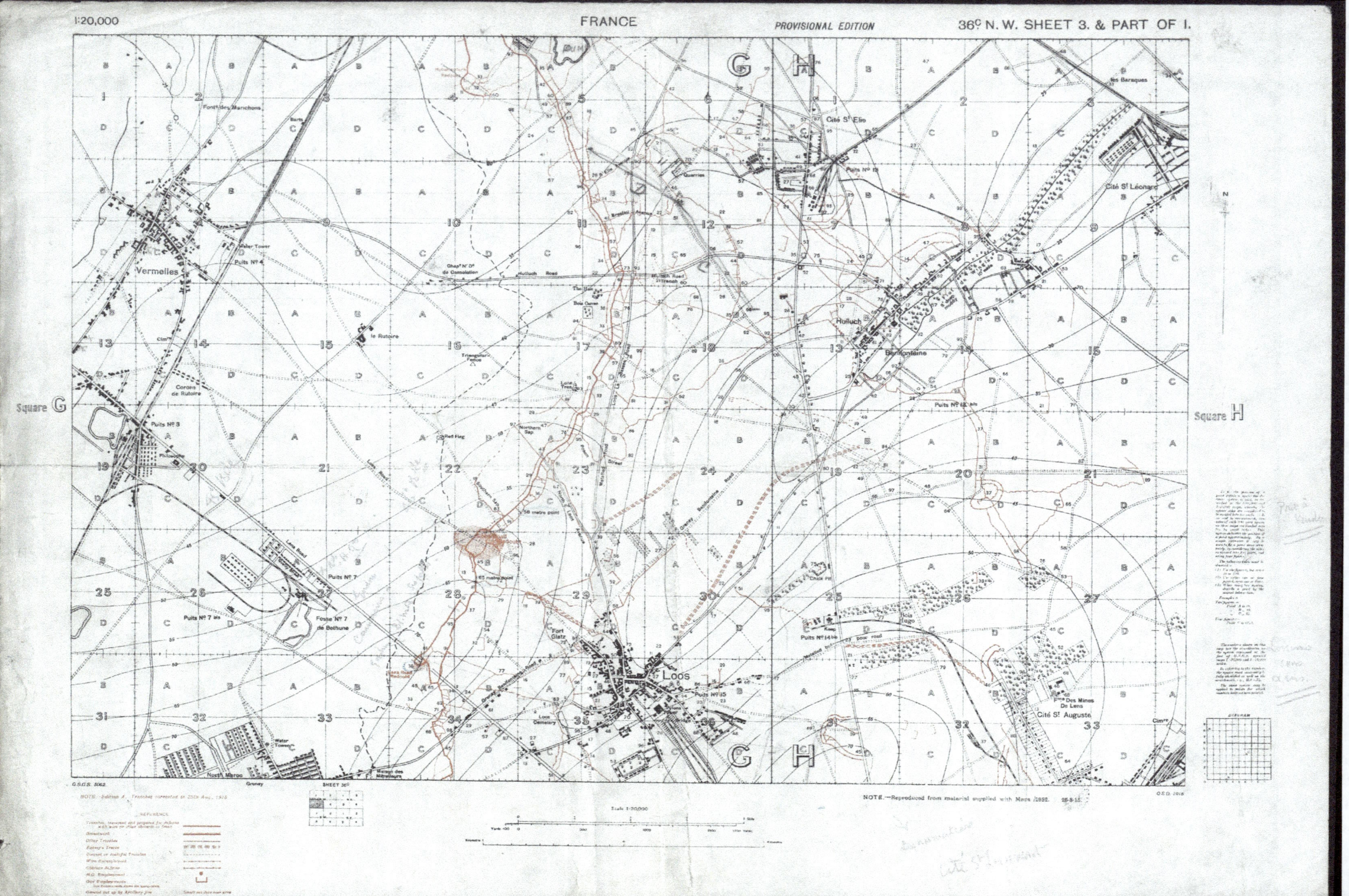

1:20,000
FRANCE
PROVISIONAL EDITION
36c N.W. SHEET 3. & PART OF I.
Square G
Square H
Vermelles
Water Tower
Puits No 4
Fontaine les Marichons
le Rutoire
Corons de Rutoire
Puits No 3
Chapl N.D. de Consolation
Hulluch Road
Triangular Fence
Red Flag
Northern Sap
Lone Tree
Bois Carré
Lens Road
Puits No 7
Fosse No 7 de Bethune
Puits No 7 bis
58 metre point
65 metre point
Fort Glatz
Loos
Loos Cemetery
Puits No 15
North Maroc
Water Towers
Maison des Mitrailleurs
Quarries
Cité St Elie
Puits No 13
Cité St Léonard
les Baraques
Hulluch
Benifontaine
Puits No 12 bis
Puits No 14 bis
Bois Hugo
Chalk Pit
Fosse Des Mines De Lens
Cité St Auguste
NOTE.—Reproduced from material supplied with Maps 1882.
SHEET 36c
Scale 1:20,000
REFERENCE

15.9.5.
Sept 1915 –

FRANCE

PROVISIONAL EDITION

Scale 1:10,000

Yards 100 0 500 1000 1500 1700 Yards

1 Mile

Kilometre 1 0 1 Kilometre

NOTE.—Reproduced from material suppli

3	4	24	16
4	14	29	32
14	9	15	24
7	8	13	[illegible]
7	7	7	8
6	7	7	18
40	49	96	129

1575 Sept 15.

P.P.C.L.I. 27th Division 1–31 August 15

www.ingramcontent.com/pod-product-compliance
Lightning Source LLC
Chambersburg PA
CBHW080918230426
43668CB00014B/2155
* 9 7 8 1 4 7 4 5 0 9 2 7 5 *